As Others Saw Them

As Others Saw Them

OBSERVATIONS OF EMINENT
LITERARY FIGURES
BY THEIR CONTEMPORARIES

by
Lyle Larsen

McFarland & Company, Inc., Publishers
Jefferson, North Carolina, and London

Library of Congress Cataloging in Publication Data

Larsen, Lyle, 1942–
  As others saw them.

  Includes index.
  1. Authors, English — Anecdotes, facetiae, etc.
2. Authors, American — Anecdotes, facetiae, satire, etc.
3. Authors, English — Biography — Dictionaries. 4. Authors,
American — Biography — Dictionaries. 5. Authors,
English — Quotations. 6. Authors, American — Quotations.
I. Title.
PR108.L37   1985   828'.02   84-43205

ISBN 0-89950-161-3

For acknowledgment of permissions to reprint and for
copyright notices, see pages ix and x, which
shall be considered extensions of this copyright page.

Printed in the United States of America

McFarland & Company, Inc., Publishers
Box 611, Jefferson, North Carolina 28640

For my mother, Bernyce Stiles

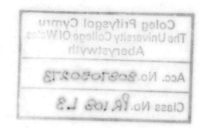

TABLE OF CONTENTS

ACKNOWLEDGMENTS

I wish to thank the following publishers and copyright holders for permission to use extracts from copyright works:

Autobiographies by William Butler Yeats. Copyright 1916, 1936 by Macmillan Publishing Co., Inc.; renewed 1944, 1964 by Bertha Georgie Yeats. Reprinted by permission of Macmillan Publishing Company; Macmillan London, Ltd.; and Michael Yeats.

Experiment in Autobiography by H.G. Wells. Copyright 1934 by Herbert George (H.G.) Wells; renewed © 1962 by George Philip Wells and Francis Richard Wells. Reprinted by permission of Faber and Faber Publishers and Little, Brown and Company.

An Unfinished Woman by Lillian Hellman. Copyright © 1969 by Lillian Hellman. Reprinted by permission of Little, Brown and Company, The Lantz Office, and the Estate of Lillian Hellman.

At Random: Reminiscences of Bennett Cerf by Bennett Cerf. Copyright © 1977 by Random House, Inc. Reprinted by permission of Random House, Inc.

Autobiography of Bertrand Russell. Copyright © 1967. Reprinted by permission of George Allen & Unwin, Ltd.

Portraits from Memory by Bertrand Russell. Copyright © 1956. Reprinted by permission of George Allen & Unwin, Ltd.

The Autobiography of Alice B. Toklas by Gertrude Stein. Copyright 1933; renewed 1961 by Alice B. Toklas. Reprinted by permission of Random House, Inc. and the estate of Gertrude Stein.

PREFACE

This book is not another collection of literary anecdotes. Of criticism it takes little notice. Rather it is a miscellany of personal observations and accounts of well-known literary figures taken from the biographies, autobiographies, memoirs, recollections, reminiscences, journals, diaries, letters and table-talk of their contemporaries — most of whom were well-known literary figures themselves. What did the people who knew Edgar Allan Poe think of him, for example? How did Mark Twain view his friend Bret Harte, and what did Alexander Pope recall of Jonathan Swift? The emphasis here is on intimate biography — observations made at first-hand.

In compiling a book like this, one is faced with certain limitations. The greatest is the limitation of space. Ideally, I would like to have included authors of many nationalities, but since that would have produced a volume two or three times this size, the work is confined to British and American writers. Excluded are living authors, and also excluded are accounts entirely in verse.

It will be seen that the number of pages devoted to a particular author is not always proportionate to that author's fame or greatness. Much more space is given to De Quincey, for instance, than to Milton or Shakespeare. In this I am obviously hindered by the material available. A wealth of material exists for some writers, and nothing for others. In determining the length of entries, therefore, I have often been guided more by the quality of the biographical accounts than by considerations of the subjects' importance to literature.

Finally, there is the matter of my own individual judgment. I hope this will not be considered too great a limitation, but such a compilation must inevitably be selective and selectivity reflects personal taste. I have chosen, out of a vast amount of material, those authors and accounts that, to my mind, seemed the most illuminating.

Lyle Larsen, Santa Monica, California

JOSEPH ADDISON

Samuel Johnson

Mr. Addison was, to be sure, a great man. His learning was not very deep, but his morality, his humour, and his elegance of writing set him very high. — *Boswell's London Journal*, 6 July 1763.

Abbé Philippeaux of Blois

Mr. Addison stayed above a year at Blois. He would get up so early as between two and three in the height of the summer, and lay abed till between eleven and twelve in the depth of winter. He was untalkative whilst here and often thoughtful, and sometimes so lost in thought that I have come into his room and stayed five minutes there before he has known anything of it.

He had his masters generally at supper with him, kept very little company besides, and had no amour whilst here that I know of — and I should have known it if he had had any. — Spence's *Observations, Anecdotes, and Characters of Books and Men* (1966).

Alexander Pope

Addison was perfect good company with intimates, and had something more charming in his conversation than I ever knew in any other man. But with any mixture of strangers, and sometimes with only one or with any man he was too jealous of, he seemed to preserve his dignity much, with a stiff sort of silence. He was very kind to me at first but my bitter enemy afterwards.

His prose character was the chief point of his excellence, but he did not think so. *Cato*, his *Campaign*, and some other little things in poetry were what he thought he was to be immortalized by. He did not so much value himself on his *Spectators* and *Guardians*, etc., though he wrote prose with so great ease, fluency and happiness. Many of his *Spectators* he wrote very fast, and often sent them to the press as soon as they were written. It seems to have been best for him not to have had too much time to correct. Mr. Addison could not give out a common order in writing, from his endeavouring always to word it too finely. He had too beautiful an imagination to make a man of business.

Addison passed each day alike, and much in the manner that Dryden did. Dryden employed his mornings in writing, dined *en famille*, and then went to Will's — only he came home earlier a'nights. Addison usually studied all the morning, then met his party at Button's, dined there, and stayed five or six hours — and sometimes far into the night. I was of the company for about a year, but found it too much for me. It hurt my health, and so I quitted it.

Addison and Steele were a couple of H——s. I am sorry to say so, and there are not twelve people in the world that I would say it to at all. Steele had the greatest veneration for Addison, and used to show it in all companies in a particular manner. Addison now and then used to play a little upon him, but he always took it well. — Spence's *Observations, Anecdotes, and Characters of Books and Men* (1966).

SHERWOOD ANDERSON

Sylvia Beach

One day I noticed an interesting-looking man lingering on the doorstep [of the bookshop Shakespeare and Company], his eye caught by a book in the window. The book was *Winesburg, Ohio*, which had recently been published in the United States. Presently he came in and introduced himself as the author. He said he hadn't seen another copy of his book in Paris....

Sherwood Anderson was full of something that had happened to him, a step he had taken, a decision he had made that was of the greatest importance in his life. I listened with suspense to the story of how he had suddenly abandoned his home and a prosperous paint business, had simply walked away one morning, shaking off forever the fetters of respectability and the burden of security.

Anderson was a man of great charm, and I became very fond of him. I saw him as a mixture of poet and evangelist (without the preaching), with perhaps a touch of the actor. Anyhow, he was a most interesting man.

I knew Adrienne [Monnier] would like Sherwood Anderson and that he would like her, so I took him to her bookshop, and she was indeed struck by him.... Describing him to me afterward, she said he resembled an old woman, an Indian squaw, smoking her pipe at the fireside. Adrienne had seen squaws at Buffalo Bill's show in Paris — *Shakespeare and Company* (1959).

Ernest Hemingway

Sherwood Anderson was a slob. Un-truthful (not just inventing untruthful; all fiction is a form of lying) but untruthful in the way you *never* could be about a picture. Also he was wet and sort of mushy. He had very beautiful bastard Italian eyes and if you had been brought up in Italy (with very beautiful Italian eyes) you always knew when he was lying. From the first time I met him I thought he was a sort of retarded character. The sort that gets to be Minister of Culture in a new chicken-shit Republic where there are no standards except charm. You know we boys who are bad, I mean brought up roughly, never trust a man with a Southern accent nor a man with beautiful eyes. — From a letter to Bernard Berenson, 24 January 1953.

MATTHEW ARNOLD

Charlotte Brontë

Those who have only seen Mrs. Arnold once will necessarily, I think, judge of her unfavourably; her manner on introduction disappointed me sensibly, as lacking that genuineness and simplicity one seemed to have a right to expect in the chosen life-companion of Dr. [Thomas] Arnold.... It is observable that Matthew Arnold, the eldest son ... inherits his mother's defect. Striking and prepossessing in appearance, his manner displeases from seeming foppery. I own it caused me at first to regard him with regretful surprise; the shade of Dr. Arnold seemed to me to frown on his young representative. I was told, however, that 'Mr. Arnold improved upon acquaintance.' So it was: ere long a real modesty appeared under his assumed conceit, and some genuine intellectual aspirations, as well as high educational acquirements, displaced superficial affectations. I was given to understand that his theological opinions were very vague and unsettled, and indeed he betrayed as much in the course of conversation. Most unfortunate for him, doubtless, has been the untimely loss of his father. — From a letter to James Taylor, 15 January 1851.

Lytton Strachey

Certainly it is a curious and instructive case, that of Matthew Arnold: all the more so since no one could suppose that he was a stupid man. On the contrary, his intelligence was above the average, and he could write lucidly, and he got up his subjects with considerable care. Unfortunately, he mistook his vocation. He might, no doubt, if he had chosen, have done some excellent and lasting work upon the movements of glaciers or the fertilization of plants, or have been quite a satisfactory collector in an up-country district in India. But no; he *would* be a critic. — "A Victorian Critic" (1914).

Mrs. Humphry Ward

Matthew Arnold was very different in outward aspect [from the rest of his family]. The face, strong and rugged, the large mouth, the broad lined brow, and vigorous coal-black hair, bore no resemblance, except for that fugitive yet vigorous something which we call "family likeness," to either his father or mother — still less to the brother so near to him in age. But the Celtic trace is there, though derived, I have sometimes thought, rather from an Irish than a Cornish source. Doctor Arnold's mother ... was partly of Irish blood.... And I have seen in Ireland faces belonging to the "black Celt" type — faces full of power and humor, and softness, visibly molded out of the good common earth by the nimble spirit within, which have reminded me of my uncle. Nothing, indeed, at first sight could have been less romantic or dreamy than his outer aspect. "Ineffectualness" was not to be thought of in connection with him. He stood four-square — a courteous, competent man of affairs, an admirable inspector of schools, a delightful companion, a guest whom everybody wanted and no one could bind for long; one of the sanest, most independent, most cheerful and lovable of mortals. Yet his poems show what was the real inner life and genius of the man. — *A Writer's Recollections* (1918).

JOHN AUBREY

Anthony à Wood

Aug. 31, [1667] S., John Aubrey of Easton-Piers in the parish of Kington S. Michael in Wiltsh. was in Oxon. with Edward Forest, a book-seller living against Alls. Coll., to buy books. He then saw lying on the stall *Notitia Academiae Oxoniensis*; and asking who the author of that book was, he answer'd the report was that one Mr. Anthony Wood of Merton Coll. was the author, but was not. Whereupon Mr. Aubrey, a pretender to antiquities, having been contemporary to A. Wood's elder brother in Trin. Coll. and well acquainted with him, he thought that he might be as well acquainted with A.W. himself. Whereupon repairing to his lodgings, and telling him who he was, he got into his acquaintance, talk'd to him about his studies, and offer'd him what assistance he could make, in order to the completion of the work that he was in hand with. Mr. Aubrey was then in a sparkish garb, came to towne with his man and two horses, spent high and flung out A.W. at all reckings. But his estate of 700 li. per an. being afterwards sold, and he reserving nothing of it to himself, liv'd afterwards in a very sorry condition, and at length made shift to rub out by hanging on Edmund Wyld esq. living in Blomesbury neare London, on James Bertie earl of Abendon, whose first wife was related to him, and on Sir John Aubrey, his kinsman, living sometimes in Glamorganshire, and sometimes at Borstall neare Brill in Bucks. He was a shiftless person, roving and magotie-headed, and sometimes little better than crased. And being exceedingly credulous, would stuff him many letters sent to A.W. with fooleries, and misinformations, which somtimes would guid him into the paths of errour. — *The Life and Times of Anthony à Wood*.

FRANCIS BACON

Arthur Wilson

He was of *middling stature*, his countenance had indented with

Age before he was old; his *Presence* grave and comely; of a high-flying and lively *Wit*, striving in some things to be rather admired than understood, yet so quick and easie where he would express himself, and his *Memory* so strong and active, that he appeared the *Master* of a large and plenteous *store-house* of *Knowledge* being (as it were) *Nature's Midwife*, stripping her *Callow-brood*, and clothing them in new *Attire. — The History of Great Britain, Being The Life and Reign of King James the First* (1653).

AMBROSE BIERCE

Adolphe de Castro

On my birthday, November 10, 1886, [Henry Derby] Bigelow brought Ambrose Bierce to my office. I was then twenty years of age and Bierce was forty-four. He was strikingly handsome, well-built and lean, easily six feet tall, with an erect military carriage. His thick, wavy, unsubmissive yellow hair was combed upward, away from the forehead. His brows were long, bushy and turned upward. Beneath them were deep-set steel-blue eyes, small and flashing. He was ruddy-faced, clean-shaven except for a well-turned yellow mustache beneath a straight Nordic nose. His ears were finely shaped — a musician's ears — the oval face terminating in a strong, if slightly cleft chin....

There was one quality he possessed that was exceedingly fine. It was his love for the Greek conception of the term *cosmos* — symmetry, harmony, beauty. Bierce was inwardly glad that he was well-made. He was handsome. He disliked hair on the face, for instance, but had conceived the idea that a well-kept mustache, with the Arabic curl at both ends, enhanced the beauty of the facial expression. And although he disclaimed a desire to see himself as others saw him — that is, to have himself photographed, pretending he could not face the camera — he was nevertheless fairly addicted to this sort of thing, and the future will not be impoverished for want of Bierce pictures.

From the year 1886 to the year 1908, the Bierce portrait always showed beauty, symmetry, harmony and a clean-cut expression. Those who saw him only in his photographs cannot possibly conceive what he looked like in the flush of youth and at the height of manhood. He had everything to recommend him; and his almost perfect physical aspect was excelled a thousandfold by his intellectual caliber....

I have indicated that Bierce was averse to suffering disfigurement. Even when shaving, in which he was inexpert and thus often cut himself, he covered the gashes with white court plaster; and he was peevish until he could take off the disfiguring patches. This does not mean that he was a coward — I have never found any human being in all my life less afraid of fear than Ambrose Bierce. The emotion was entirely foreign to his nature.

Several of his pets were poisonous but he was not afraid of them, although he had a real dread of dogs. And here again we find that peculiar psychological manifestation in Bierce's character: it was not the dog he feared but the consequences of the dog's bite if the dog were mad — the fearful disfigurement caused by convulsions from rabies. Time and again he spoke of this dread to me....

As far as death itself was concerned, Ambrose Bierce was unconcerned when he died but he minded much how he died. Had he had the choice he would have preferred *hara-kiri* to being shot when the shot might disfigure his face. It was the peculiar psychology of the man. He would have walked, if doomed to do so, a thousand miles, to fall exhausted and content to die, but to be "shot to rags" was a horror. — *Portrait of Ambrose Bierce* (1929).

H.L. Mencken

So far in this life, indeed, I have encountered no more thoroughgoing cynic than Bierce was. His disbelief in man went even further than Mark Twain's; he was quite unable to imagine the heroic, in any ordinary sense. Nor, for that matter, the wise. Man to him, was the most stupid and ignoble of animals. But at the same time the most amusing. Out of the spectacle of life about him he got an unflagging and Gargantuan joy. The obscene farce of politics delighted him. He was an almost amourous connoisseur of theology and theologians. He howled with mirth whenever he thought of a professor, a doctor or a husband.

Another character that marked him, perhaps flowing out of this same cynicism, was his curious taste for the macabre. All of his stories show it. He delighted in hangings, autopsies, dissecting-rooms. Death to him was not something repulsive, but a sort of low comedy — the last act of a squalid and rib-rocking buffoonery. When, grown old and weary, he departed for Mexico, and there — if legend is to be believed — marched into the revolution then going on, and had himself shot, there was certainly nothing in the transaction to surprise his acquaintances. The whole thing was typically Biercian. He died happy, one may be sure, if his executioners made a botch of dispatching him — if there was a flash of the grotesque at the end. Once I enjoyed the curious experience of going to a funeral with him. His conversation to and from the crematory was superb — a long series of gruesome but highly amusing witticisms. He had tales to tell of crematories that had caught fire and singed the mourners, of dead bibuli whose mortal remains had exploded, of widows guarding the fires all night to make sure that their dead husbands did not escape. The gentleman whose carcass we were burning had been a literary critic. Bierce suggested that his ashes be molded into bullets and shot at publishers, that they be presented to the library of the New York Lodge of Elks, that they be mailed anonymously to Ella Wheeler Wilcox, then still alive. Later on, when he heard that they had been buried in Iowa, he exploded in colossal mirth. The last time I saw him he predicted that the Christians out there would dig them up and throw them over the State line. On his own writing desk, he once told me, he kept the ashes of his son. I suggested idly that the ceremental urn must be a formidable ornament. "Urn, hell!" he answered. "I keep them in a cigar-box!" — *Prejudices: Sixth Series* (1927).

WILLIAM BLAKE

Alexander Gilchrist

In person, there was much in Blake which answered to the remarkable man he was. Though low in stature, not quite five feet and a half, and broad shouldered, he was well made, and did not strike people as short. For he had an upright carriage and a good presence; he bore himself with dignity, as not unconscious of his natural claims. The head and face were strongly stamped with the power and character of the man. There was great volume of brain in that square, massive head, that piled-up brow, very full and rounded at the temples, where, according to phrenologists, ideality or imagination resides. His eyes were fine — 'wonderful eyes,' someone calls them; prominently set, but bright, spiritual, visionary; not restless nor wild, but with 'a look of clear heavenly exaltation.' The eyes of some of the old men in his *Job* recall his own to surviving friends. His nose was insignificant as to size, but had that peculiarity which gives to a face an expression of fiery energy, as of a high-mettled steed — 'a little *clenched* nostril; a nostril that opened as far as it could, but was tied down at one end.' His mouth was wide, the lips not full, but tremulous, and expressive of the great sensibility which characterized him. He was short-sighted, as the prominence of his eyes indicated; a prominence in keeping with his faculty for languages, according to the phrenologists again. He wore glasses only occasionally. — *Life of Blake* (1880).

Samuel Palmer

His knowledge was various and extensive, and his conversation so nervous and brilliant, that, if recorded at the time, it would now have thrown much light upon his character, and in no way lessened him in the estimation of those who know him only by his works....

He was energy itself, and shed around him a kindling influence; and atmosphere of life, full of the ideal. To walk with him in the country was to perceive the soul of beauty through the forms of matter; and the high, gloomy buildings between which, from his study window, a glimpse was caught of the Thames and the Surrey shore, assumed a kind of grandeur from the man dwelling near them. Those may laugh at this who never knew such an one as Blake; but of him it is the simple truth.

He was a man without a mask; his aim single, his path straightforwards, and his wants few; so he was free, noble and happy.

His voice and manner were quiet, yet all awake with intellect. Above the tricks of littleness, or the least taint of affectation, with a natural dignity which few would have dared to affront, he was gentle and affectionate, loving to be with little children, and to talk about them. 'That is heaven,' he said to a friend, leading him to the window, and pointing to a group of them at play.

Declining, like Socrates, whom in many respects he resembled, the common objects of ambition, and pitying the scuffle to obtain them, he thought that no one could be truly great who had not humbled himself 'even as a little child.' This was a subject he loved to dwell upon, and to illustrate.

His eye was the finest I ever saw: brilliant, but not roving, clear and intent, yet susceptible; it flashed with genius, or melted in tenderness. It could also be terrible. Cunning and falsehood quailed under it, but it was never busy with them. It pierced them, and turned away. Nor was the mouth less expressive; the lips flexible and quivering with feeling. I can yet recall it when, on one occasion, dwelling upon the exquisite beauty of the parable of the Prodigal, he began to repeat a part of it, but at the words, 'When he was yet a great way off, his father saw him,' could go no further; his voice faltered, and he was in tears....

He had great powers of argument, and on general subjects was a very patient and good-tempered disputant; but materialism was his abhorrence: and if some unhappy man called in question the world of spirits, he would answer him 'according to his folly,' by putting forth his own views in their most extravagant and startling aspect. This might amuse those who were in the secret, but it left his opponent angry and bewildered.

Such was Blake, as I remember him. — From a letter to Alexander Gilchrist, 23 August 1855; Gilchrist's *Life of Blake* (1880).

George Richmond

I used constantly to go to see Mr. and Mrs. Blake when they lived near Blackfriars Bridge, and never have I known an artist so spiritual, so devoted, so single-minded, or so full of vivid imagination as he. Before Blake began a picture he used to fall on his knees and pray that his work might be successful. The room was squalid and untidy. And once Mrs. Blake, in excuse for the general lack of soap and water, remarked to me: *'You see, Mr. Blake's skin don't dirt!'* — Quoted by A.M.W. Stirling in *The Richmond Papers* (1926).

Henry Crabb Robinson

[Dec. 1825.] Shall I call him artist or genius — or mystic — or madman? Probably he is all. He has a most interesting appearance. He is now old — pale, with a Socratic countenance and an expression of great sweetness, but bordering on weakness except when his features are animated by expression, and then he has an air of inspiration about him....

He dwells in Fountain Court in the Strand. I found him in a small room which seems to be both a working-room and a bed-room. Nothing could exceed the squalid air both of the apartment and his dress; but in spite of dirt — I might say filth — an air of natural gentility is diffused over him; and his wife, notwithstanding the same offensive character of her dress and appearance, has a good expression of countenance, so that I shall have a pleasure in calling on and conversing with these worthy people. But I fear I shall not make any progress in ascertaining his opinions and feelings, — that there being really no system or connection in his mind, all his future conversation will be but varieties of wildness and incongruity. — *The Diary of Henry Crabb Robinson*.

JAMES BOSWELL

Fanny Burney

He spoke the Scotch accent strongly, though by no means so as to affect, even slightly, his intelligibility to an English ear. He had an odd mock solemnity of tone and manner, that he had acquired imperceptibly from constantly thinking of and imitating Dr. Johnson; whose own solemnity, nevertheless, far from mock, was the result of pensive rumination. There was, also, something slouching in the gait and dress of Mr. Boswell, that wore an air, ridiculously enough, of purporting to personify the same model. His clothes were always too large for him; his hair, or wig, was constantly in a state of negligence; and he never for a moment sat still or upright upon a chair. Every look and movement displayed either intentional or involuntary imitation. Yet certainly it was not meant as caricature; for his heart, almost even to idolatry, was in his reverence of Dr. Johnson.... When he met with Dr. Johnson, he commonly forbore even answering anything that was said, or attending to anything that went forward, lest he should miss the smallest sound from that voice to which he paid such exclusive, though merited homage. But the moment that voice burst forth, the attention which it excited in Mr. Boswell amounted almost to pain. His eyes goggled with eagerness; he leant his ear almost on the shoulder of the Doctor; and he seemed not only to dread losing a word, but to be anxious not to miss a breathing; as if hoping from it, latently, or mystically, some information. Once at a party given by the Thrales, Boswell placed himself directly behind Johnson; in a few minutes, Dr. Johnson, whose eye did not follow him, and who had concluded him to be at the other end of the table, said something gaily and good-humouredly, by the appellation of Bozzy; and discovered, by the sound of the reply, that Bozzy had planted himself, as closely as he could, behind and between the elbows of the new usurper [Fanny herself] and his own; the Doctor turned angrily round upon him, and clapping his hand rather loudly upon his knee, said, in a tone of displeasure, "What do you do there, Sir? — go to the table, Sir!" ... But, ever restless when not at the side of Dr. Johnson, he presently recollected something that he wished to exhibit, and, hastily rising, was running away in its search; when the Doctor, calling after him, authoritatively said: "What are you thinking of, Sir? Why do you get up before the cloth is removed? — come back to your place, Sir!" — *Memoirs of Doctor Burney. By His Daughter* (1832).

The beautiful chapel of St George, repaired and finished by the best artists at an immense expense, which was now opened after a very long shutting up for its preparations, brought innumerable strangers to Windsor, and, among others, Mr Boswell.

This, I heard, in my way to the chapel, from Mr Turbulent, who overtook me, and mentioned having met Mr Boswell at the Bishop of Carlisle's the evening before. He proposed bringing him to call upon me; but this I declined, certain how little satisfaction would be given here by the entrance of a man so famous for compiling anecdotes. But yet I really wished to see him again, for old acquaintance' sake, and unavoidable amusement from his oddity and good humour, as well as respect for the object of his constant admiration, my revered Dr Johnson. I therefore told Mr Turbulent I should be extremely glad to speak with him after the service was over.

Accordingly, at the gate of the choir, Mr Turbulent brought him to me. We saluted with mutual glee: his comic-serious face and manner have lost nothing of their wonted singularity; nor yet have his mind and language, as you will soon confess.

'I am extremely glad to see you indeed,' he cried, 'but very sorry to see you here. My dear ma'am, why do you stay? — it won't do, ma'am! you must resign! — we can put up with it no longer. I told my good host the Bishop so last night; we are all grown quite outrageous!' [Boswell is referring to Miss Burney's unhappy situation of being Assistant Keeper of the Robes to Queen Charlotte.]

Whether I laughed the most, or stared the most, I am at a loss to say; but I hurried away from the cathedral, not to have such treasonable declarations overheard, for we were surrounded by a multitude.

He accompanied me, however, not losing one moment in continuing his exhortations:

'If you do not quit, ma'am, very soon, some violent measures, I assure you, will be taken. We shall address Dr Burney in a body; I am ready to make the harangue myself. We shall fall upon him all at once.'

I stopped him to inquire about Sir Joshua [Reynolds]; he said he saw him very often, and that his spirits were very good. I asked about Mr [Edmund] Burke's book [*Reflections on the Revolution in France*].

'Oh,' cried he, 'it will come out next week: 'tis the first book in the world, except my own, and that's coming out also very soon; only I want your help.'

'My help?'

'Yes, madam; you must give me some of your choice little notes of the Doctor's; we have seen him long enough upon stilts; I want to show him in a new light. Grave Sam, and great Sam, and solemn Sam, and learned Sam — all these he has appeared over and over. Now I want to entwine a wreath of the graces across his brow; I want to show him as gay Sam, agreeable Sam, pleasant Sam: so you must help me with some of his beautiful billets to yourself.'

I evaded this by declaring I had not any stores at hand. He proposed a thousand curious expedients to get at them, but I was invincible....

He then told me his *Life of Dr Johnson* was nearly printed, and took a proof sheet out of his pocket to show me; with crowds passing and repassing, knowing me well, and staring well at him: for we were now at the iron rails of the Queen's Lodge.

I stopped; I could not ask him in: I saw he expected it, and was reduced to apologize, and tell him I must attend the Queen immediately.

He uttered again stronger and stronger exhortations for my retreat, accompanied by expressions which I was obliged to check in their bud. But finding he had no chance for entering, he stopped me again at the gate, and said he would read me a part of his work.

There was no refusing this; and he began, with a letter of Dr Johnson to himself. He read it in strong imitation of the Doctor's manner, very well, and not caricature. But Mrs Schwellenberg was at her window, a crowd was gathering to stand round the rails, and the King and Queen and Royal Family now approached from the Terrace. I made a rather quick apology, and, with a step as quick as my now weakened limbs have left in my power, I hurried to my apartment.

You may suppose I had inquiries enough, from all around, of 'Who was the gentleman I was talking to at the rails?' And an injunction rather frank not to admit him beyond those limits.

However, I saw him again the next morning, in coming from early prayers, and he again renewed his remonstrances and his petition for my letters of Dr Johnson.

I cannot consent to print private letters, even of a man so justly celebrated, when addressed to myself; no, I shall hold sacred those revered and but too scarce testimonies of the high honour his kindness conferred upon me. One letter I have from him that is a masterpiece of elegance and kindness united. 'Twas his last. — *The Diary of Fanny Burney*, October 1790.

Thomas Green

From his open, communicative, good-humoured variety, which leads him to display events and feelings that other men, of more frequent, though slighter pretensions, would have studiously concealed, he depressed himself below his just level in public estimation. His information is extensive; his talents far from despicable, and he seems so exactly *adapted*, even by his very foibles, that we might almost suppose him purposely created to be the chronicler of Johnson. — *Extracts from the Diary of a Lover of Literature* (1810), 29 September 1796.

Thomas Holcroft

It was his custom during the sessions to dine daily with the Judges, invited or not. He obtruded himself everywhere. Lowe (mentioned by him in his life of Johnson) once gave me a humourous picture of him. Lowe had requested Johnson to write him a letter, which Johnson did, and Boswell came in while it was writing. His attention was immediately fixed; Lowe took the letter, retired, and was followed by Boswell.

'Nothing,' said Lowe, 'could surprise me more. Till that moment he had so entirely overlooked me, that I did not imagine he knew there was such a creature in existence; and he now accosted me with the most overstrained and insinuating compliments possible: —

'How do you do, Mr. Lowe? I hope you are very well, Mr. Lowe? Pardon my freedom, Mr. Lowe, but I think I saw my dear friend, Dr. Johnson, writing a letter for you.'

'Yes, sir.'

'I hope you will not think me rude, but if it would not be too great a favour, you would infinitely oblige me, if you would just let me have a sight of it. Every thing from that hand, you know, is so inestimable.'

'Sir, it is on my own private affairs, but —'

'I would not pry into a person's affairs, my dear Mr. Lowe, by any means. I am sure you would not accuse me of such a thing, only if it were no particular secret.'

'Sir, you are welcome to read the letter.'

'I thank you, my dear Mr. Lowe, you are very obliging, I take it exceedingly kind. (Having read) It is nothing, I believe, Mr. Lowe, that you would be ashamed of.'

'Certainly not.'

'Why then, my dear sir, if you would do me another favour, you would make the obligation eternal. If you would but step to Peele's coffee-house with me, and just suffer me to take a copy of it, I would do any thing in my power to oblige you.'

'I was overcome,' said Lowe, 'by this sudden familiarity and condescention, accompanied with bows and grimaces. I had no power to refuse; we went to the coffee-house, my letter was presently transcribed, and as soon as he had put his document in his pocket, Mr.

Boswell walked away, as erect and proud as he was half an hour before, and I ever afterward was unnoticed. Nay, I am not certain,' added he sarcastically, 'whether the Scotchman did not leave me, poor as he knew I was, to pay for my own dish of coffee.' — *The Memoirs of Thomas Holcroft*

Samuel Johnson

Boswell is a man who I believe never left a house without leaving a wish for his return. — Boswell's *Life of Samuel Johnson* (1791).

Sir, if I were to lose Boswell, it would be a limb amputated. — Boswell's *Life of Samuel Johnson* (1791).

Anna Seward

An ungrateful impudent man ... capable of insulting any person who cannot inflict the punishment of corporal correction. Defenceless against such a being is every woman, who has neither father nor brother to awe the assailant. — From a letter to Mrs. Stokes, 20 March 1794.

John Thomas Smith

James Boswell, the faithful biographer of Dr. Johnson, meeting him [Joseph Nollekens] in the pit of the Pantheon, loudly exlaimed, "Why, Nollekens, how dirty you go now! I recollect when you were the gayest dressed of any in the house." To whom Nollekens made, for once in his life, the retort-courteous of "That's more than I could ever say of you!" Boswell certainly looked very badly when dressed; for, as he seldom washed himself, his clean ruffles served as a striking contrast to his dirty flesh. — *Nollekens and his Times* (1828).

Himself

I have given a little sketch of Dr. Johnson: my readers may wish to know a little of his fellow traveller. Think then, of a gentleman of ancient blood, the pride of which was his predominant passion. He was then in his thirty-third year, and had been about four years happily married. His inclination was to be a soldier; but his father, a respectable Judge, had pressed him into the profession of the law. He had travelled a good deal, and seen many varieties of human life. He had thought more than any body supposed, and had a pretty good stock of general learning and knowledge. He had all Dr. Johnson's principles, with some degree of relaxation. He had rather too little, than too much prudence; and, his imagination being lively, he often said things of which the effect was very different from the intention. He resembled sometimes 'The best good man, with the worst natur'd muse.' He cannot deny himself the vanity of finishing with the encomium of Dr. Johnson, whose friendly partiality to the companion of his Tour represents him as one, 'whose acuteness would help my inquiry, and whose gaiety of conversation, and civility of manners, are sufficient to counteract the inconveniences of travel, in countries less hospitable than we have passed.'—*Journal of a Tour to the Hebrides with Samuel Johnson*, 18 August 1773.

My fellow-traveller and I talked of going to Sweden; and, while we were settling our plan, I expressed a pleasure in the prospect of seeing the king.—*JOHNSON*. 'I doubt, sir, if he would speak to us.'—Colonel M'Leod said, 'I am sure Mr. Boswell would speak to *him*.' But, seeing me a little disconcerted by his remark, he politely added, 'and with great propriety.'—Here let me offer a short defence of that propensity in my disposition, to which this gentleman alluded. It has procured me much happiness. I hope it does not deserve so hard a name as either forwardness or impudence. If I know myself, it is nothing more than an eagerness to share the society of men distinguished either by their rank or their talents, and a diligence to attain what I desire. If a man is praised for seeking knowledge, though mountains and seas are in his way, may he not be pardoned, whose ardour, in the pursuit of the same object, leads him to encounter difficulties as great, though of a different kind?—*Journal of a Tour to the Hebrides with Samuel Johnson*, 16 September 1773.

JOHN BUNYAN

George Cokayne

He appeared in Countenance to be of a stern and rough Temper; but in his Conversation mild and affable, not given to Loquacity, or much Discourse in Company, unless some urgent Occasion required it; observing never to boast of himself, or his Parts, but rather seem low in his own Eyes, and submit himself to the Judgment of others, abhorring

Lying and Swearing, being just in all that lay in his Power to his Word, not seeming to revenge Injuries, loving to reconcile Differences, and make Friendships, withal he had a sharp quick Eye, accomplished with an excellent discerning of Persons, being of good Judgment and quick Wit. As for his Person, he was tall of Stature, strong-boned, tho' not corpulent, somewhat of a ruddy Face, with sparkling Eyes, wearing his Hair on his upper Lip, after the old *British* Fashion; his Hair reddish, but in his latter Days, Time had sprinkled it with grey, his Nose well set, but not declining or bending, and his Mouth moderate large; his Forehead something high, and his Habbit always plain and modest; And thus here we impartially describe the internal and external Parts of a Person, whose Death hath been much regretted; a Person who had tried the Smiles and Frowns of Time; not puffed up in Prosperity, nor shaken in Adversity, always holding the golden mean. — "A Continuation of Mr. Bunyan's life; beginning where he left off" added to the 1692 edition of *Grace Abounding*.

LORD BYRON

Lady Blessington

The impression of the first few minutes disappointed me, as I had, both from the portraits and descriptions given, conceived a different idea of him. I had fancied him taller, with a more dignified and commanding air; and I looked in vain for the hero-looking sort of person with whom I had so long identified him in imagination. His appearance is, however, highly prepossessing; his head is finely shaped, and the forehead open, high, and noble; his eyes are grey and full of expression, but one is visibly larger than the other; the nose is large and well shaped, but, from being a little *too thick*, it looks better in profile than in front-face; his mouth is the most remarkable feature in his face: the upper lip of Grecian shortness, and the corners descending; the lips full and finely cut. In speaking, he shows his teeth very much, and they are white and even; but I observed that even in his smile — and he smiles frequently — there is something of a scornful expression in his mouth that is evidently natural, and not, as many suppose, affected. This particularly struck me. His chin is large and well shaped, and finishes well the oval of his face. He is extremely thin, indeed so much so that his figure has almost a boyish air; his face is peculiarly pale, but not the paleness of ill-health, as its character is that of fairness — the fairness of a dark-haired person — and his hair (which is getting rapidly grey) is of a very dark brown, and curls naturally; he uses a good deal of oil in it, which makes it look still darker. His countenance is full of expression, and changes with the subject of conversation; it gains on the beholder the more it is seen, and leaves an agreeable impression. I should say that melancholy was its prevailing character, as I noticed that when any observation elicited a smile — and they were many, as the conversation was gay and playful — it appeared to linger but for a moment on his lip, which instantly resumed its former expression of seriousness. His whole appearance is remarkably gentlemanlike, and he owes nothing of this to his toilet, as his coat appears to have been many years made, is much too large, and all ready-made, so ill do they fit him. There is a *gaucherie* in his movements, which evidently proceeds from the perpetual conscious-ness of his lameness, that appears to haunt him; for he tries to conceal his foot when seated, and when walking, has a nervous rapidity in his manner. He is very slightly lame, and the deformity of his foot is so little remarkable that I am not now aware which foot it is. His voice and accent are peculiarly agreeable, but effeminate — clear, harmonious, and so distinct, that though his general tone in speaking is rather low than high, not a word is lost. His manners are as unlike my precon-ceived notions of them as is his appearance. I had expected to find him a dignified, cold, reserved and haughty person, resembling those mysteri-ous personages he so loves to paint in his works, and with whom he has been so often identified by the good-natured world; but nothing can be more different; for were I to point out the prominent defect of Lord Byron, I should say it was flippancy, and a total want of that natural self-possession and dignity which ought to characterize a man of birth and education. — *Conversations of Lord Byron with the Countess of Blessington* (1834).

Leigh Hunt

Lord Byron's appearance at that time [1815–1816] was the finest I ever saw it. He was fatter than before his marriage, but only just enough so to complete the elegance of his person; and the turn of his head and countenance had a spirit and elevation in it which, though not unmixed with disquiet, gave him altogether a very noble look. His dress was black, with white trousers, and which he wore buttoned close over the body, completed the succinctness and gentlemanliness of his appear-ance. I remember one day, as he stood looking out of the window, he re-sembled, in a lively manner, the portrait of him by Phillips, by far the best and the most like him in features as well as expression....

In a room at the end of the garden to this house was a magnificent rocking-horse, which a friend had given my little boy; and Lord Byron, with a childish glee becoming a poet, would ride upon it. Ah! why did he ever ride his Pegasus to less advantage? Poets should never give up their privilege of surmounting sorrow with joy. — *Autobiography* (1859).

Charles Lamb

It was quite a mistake that I could dislike anything you should write against Lord Byron; for I have a thorough aversion to his character, and a very moderate admiration of his genius: he is great in so little a way. To be a Poet is to be the Man, not a petty portion of occasional low passion worked up in a permanent form of humanity. — From a letter to Joseph Cottle, 1819.

So we have lost another Poet. I never much relished his Lordship's mind, and shall be sorry if the Greeks have cause to miss him. He was to me offensive, and I never can make out his great *Power*, which his admirers talk of. Why, a line of Wordsworth's is a lever to lift the immortal spirit! Byron can only move the Spleen. He was at best a Satyrist, — in any other way, he was mean enough. I squeeze a tear to his memory. He did not like the world, and he has left it, as Alderman Curtis advised the Radicals, "If they don't like their Country, damn 'em, let 'em leave it," they possessing no rood of ground in England, and he 10,000 acres. Byron was better than many Curtises. — From a letter to Bernard Barton, 15 May 1824.

Thomas Medwin

During the few minutes that Lord Byron was finishing his letter, I took an opportunity of narrowly observing him, and drawing his portrait in my mind.... I saw a man about five feet eight, apparently forty years of age: as was said of Milton, he barely escaped being short and thick. His face was fine, and the lower part symmetrically moulded; for the lips and chin had that curved and definite outline which distinguishes Grecian beauty. His forehead was high, and his temple broad; and he had a paleness in his complexion, almost to wanness. His hair thin and fine, had almost become grey, and waved in natural and graceful curls over his head, that was assimilating itself fast to the "bald first Caesar's." He allowed it to grow longer behind than it is accustomed to be worn, and at that time had mustachios, which were not sufficiently dark to be becoming. In criticising his features it might, perhaps, be said that his eyes were placed too near his nose, and that one was rather smaller than the other; they were of a greyish brown, but of a peculiar clearness, and when animated possessed a fire which seemed to look through and penetrate the thoughts of others, while they marked the inspirations of his own. His teeth were small, regular, and white; these, I afterwards found, he took great pains to preserve.

I expected to discover that he had a club, perhaps a *cloven* foot; but it would have been difficult to distinguish one from the other, either in size or in form, though it is true they were not the most symmetrical.

On the whole his figure was manly, and his countenance handsome and prepossessing, and very expressive; and the familiar ease of his conversation soon made me perfectly at home in his society. — *Medwin's Conversations of Lord Byron* (1824).

Samuel Rogers

When we sat down to dinner, I asked Byron if he would take soup? "No; he never took soup." — Would he take some fish? "No; he never took fish." — Presently I asked him if he would eat some mutton? "No; he never ate mutton." — I then asked him if he would take a glass of wine? "No; he never tasted wine." — It was now necessary to inquire what he *did* eat and drink; and the answer was, "Nothing but hard biscuits and soda-water." Unfortunately, neither hard biscuits nor soda-water were at hand; and he dined upon potatoes bruised down at his plate and drenched with vinegar. — My guests stayed till very late, discussing the merits of Walter Scott and Joanna Baillie. — Some days after, meeting [John Cam] Hobhouse, I said to him "How long will Lord Byron persevere in his present diet?" He replied, "Just as long as you continue to notice it." — I did not then know, what I now know to be a fact, — that Byron, after leaving my house, had gone to a Club in St. James's Street, and eaten a hearty meat-supper....

After Byron had become the *rage*, I was frequently amused at the manoeuvres of certain noble ladies to get acquainted with him by means of me: for instance, I would receive a note from Lady —— requesting the pleasure of my company on a particular evening, with a postscript, "Pray, could you not contrive to bring Lord Byron with you?" — Once, at a great party given by Lady Jersey, Mrs. Sheridan ran up to me and said, "Do, as a favour, try if you can place Lord Byron beside me at supper."

Byron had prodigious facility of composition. He was fond of suppers; and he used often to sup at my house and eat heartily (for he had then given up the hard biscuit and soda-water diet): after going home, he would throw off sixty or eighty verses, which he would send to press next morning.

He one evening took me to the green-room of Drury Lane Theatre, where I was much entertained. When the play began, I went round to the front of the house, and desired the box-keeper to show me into Lord Byron's box. I had been there about a minute, thinking myself quite alone, when suddenly Byron and Miss Boyce (the actress) emerged from a dark corner.

In those days at least, Byron had no readiness of reply in conversation. If you happened to let fall any observation which offended him, he would say nothing at the time; but the offence would lie rankling in his mind; and perhaps a fortnight after, he would suddenly come out with some very cutting remarks upon you, giving them as his deliberate opinions, the results of his experience of your character....

My latest intercourse with Byron was in Italy. We travelled some time together; and, if there was any scenery particularly well worth seeing, he generally contrived that we should pass through it in the dark.

As we were crossing the Apennines, he told me that he had left an order in his will that Allegra, the child who soon after died, his daughter by Miss C., should never be taught the English language. — You know that Allegra was buried at Harrow: but probably you have not heard that the body was sent over to England in *two* packages, that no one might suspect what it was....

At this time we generally had a regular quarrel every night; and he would abuse me through thick and thin, raking up all the stories he had heard which he thought most likely to mortify me, — how I had behaved with great cruelty to Murphy, refusing to assist him in his distress, &c. &c. But next morning he would shake me kindly by both hands; and we were excellent friends again.

When I parted from him in Italy (never to meet him more), a good many persons were looking on, anxious to catch a glimpse of the "famous lord." — *Recollections of the Table-Talk of Samuel Rogers* (1856).

Lady William Russell

We were all fascinated by him — his conversation and his bearing. He was not natural, but I was struck with his remarkable shrewdness. I often met him in London, and also at Cheltenham, where he had gone for his health. This must have been about 1809. I was a girl at the time — I was much interested in him — all the women adored him — I adored him, and partly on that account, and partly because his manners were affected, the men hated him.

He had a magnificent head, a melodious voice, and a very

curious and "dangerous underlook" with his beautiful eyes; but his shoulders sloped, and altogether he had a mean figure, rather below the middle height. As he entered the room his feet made a clump, clump, on the floor, as if he wore very heavy shoes; they looked like peasants' shoes. He wore loose nankeen trousers, while everybody else was attired in knee-breeches — tights.

These nankeens were strapped over his feet; his coat was peculiar in cut, and while it was universally the fashion to wear a high cravat, he walked about with his throat bare. He always seized the first opportunity of sitting down. — Quoted by Frederick Locker-Lampson in *My Confidences* (1896).

Sir Walter Scott

In talents he was unequalled, and his faults were those rather of a bizarre temper arising from an eager and irritable nervous habit, than any depravity of disposition. He was devoid of selfishness, which I take to be the basest ingredient in the human composition. He was generous, humane, and noble-minded, when passion did not blind him. The worst I ever saw about him was that he rather liked indifferent company, than that of those with whom he must from character and talent have necessarily conversed more upon an equality. I believe much of his affected misanthropy, for I never thought it real, was founded upon instances of ingratitude and selfishness experienced at the hands of those from whom better could not have been expected. — From a letter to Lady Abercorn, 4 June 1824.

Edward John Trelawny

In external appearance Byron realised that ideal standard with which imagination adorns genius. He was in the prime of life, thirty-five; of middle height, five feet eight and a half inches; regular features, without a stain or furrow on his pallid skin, his shoulders broad, chest open, body and limbs finely proportioned. His small, highly-finished head and curly hair, had an airy and graceful appearance from the massiveness and length of his throat: you saw his genius in his eyes and lips. In short, Nature could do little more than she had done for him, both in outward form and in the inward spirit she had given to animate it. But all these rare gifts to his jaundiced imagination only served to make his one personal defect (lameness) the more apparent, as a flaw is magnified in a diamond when polished; and he brooded over that blemish as sensitive minds will brood until they magnify a wart into a wen....

Knowing and sympathising with Byron's sensitiveness, his associates avoided prying into the cause of his lameness; so did strangers, from good breeding or common humanity. It was generally thought his halting gait originated in some defect of the right foot or ankle — the right foot was the most distorted and it had been made worse in his boyhood by vain efforts to set it right. He told me that for several years he wore steel splints, which so wrenched the sinews and tendons of his leg, that they increased his lameness; the foot was twisted inwards, only the edge touched the ground, and that leg was shorter than the other. His shoes were peculiar — very high heeled, with the soles uncommonly thick on the inside and pared thin on the outside — the toes were stuffed with cotton-wool, and his trousers were very large below the knee and strapped down so as to cover his feet. The peculiarity of his gait was now accounted for; he entered a room with a sort of run, as if he could not stop, then planted his best leg well forward, throwing back his body to keep his balance. In early life whilst his frame was light and elastic, with the aid of a stick he might have tottered along for a mile or two; but after he had waxed heavier, he seldom attempted to walk more than a few hundred yards, without squatting down or leaning against the first wall, bank, rock, or tree at hand, never sitting on the ground, as it would have been difficult for him to get up again. In the company of strangers, occasionally, he would make desperate efforts to conceal his infirmity, but the hectic flush on his face, his swelling veins, and quivering nerves betrayed him, and he suffered for many days after such exertions. Disposed to fatten, incapable of taking exercise to check the tendency, what could he do? If he added to his weight, his feet would not have supported him; in this dilemma he was compelled to exist in a state of semi-starvation; he was less than eleven stone when at Genoa, and said he had been fourteen in Venice. The pangs of hunger which travellers and shipwrecked mariners have described were nothing to what he suffered; their privations were temporary, his were for life, and more unendurable, as he was in the midst of abundance. — *Recollections of the Last Days of Shelley and Byron* (1858).

THOMAS CARLYLE

Charles Darwin

His talk was very racy and interesting, just like his writings, but he sometimes went on too long on the same subject. I remember a funny dinner at my brother's, where amongst a few others were [Charles] Babbage and [Sir Charles] Lyell, both of whom like to talk. Carlyle, however, silenced everyone by haranguing during the whole dinner — on the advantages of silence. After dinner Babbage in his grimmest manner thanked Carlyle for his very interesting Lecture on Silence.

Carlyle sneered at almost everyone; one day in my house, he called Grote's History 'a fetid quagmire, with nothing spiritual about it.' I always thought until his Reminiscences appeared, that his sneers were partly jokes, but this now seems rather doubtful. His expression was that of a depressed, almost despondent, yet benevolent man; and it is notorious how heartily he laughed. I believe that his benevolence was real, though stained by not a little jealousy. No one can doubt about his extraordinary power of drawing vivid pictures of things and men, — far more vivid, as it appears to me, than any drawn by Macaulay. Whether his pictures of men were true ones is another question. — *Autobiography* (1974).

Ralph Waldo Emerson

Carlyle was a man from his youth, an author who did not need to hide from his readers, and as absolute a man of the world, unknown and exiled on that hill-farm, as if holding on his own terms what is best in London. He was tall and gaunt, with a cliff-like brow, self-possessed, and holding his extraordinary powers of conversation in easy command; clinging to his northern accent with evident relish; full of lively anecdote, and with a streaming humour, which floated everything he looked upon....

We talked of books. Plato he does not read, and he disparaged Socrates; and, when pressed, persisted in making Mirabeau a hero. Gibbon he called the splendid bridge from the old world to the new. His own reading had been multifarious. "Tristram Shandy" was one of his first books after "Robinson Crusoe," and Robertson's "America" an early favourite. Rousseau's "Confessions" had discovered to him that he was not a dunce; and it was now ten years since he had learned German, by the advice of a man who told him he would find in that language what he wanted. — *English Traits* (1856).

Frederick Locker-Lampson

Although we had many friends in common, I seldom had speech with Mr. Carlyle. *Vidi tantum*: I first met him at Mr. Thomas Erskine's (of Linlathen), and afterwards at Louisa Lady Ashburton's (Lochlui-chart). I saw him at his house; once or twice with Tennyson, who honoured his character and valued his opinion. He gave Eleanor [Loc-ker] his essays on 'Johnson' and on 'Burns.' I met Mrs. Carlyle two or three times, perhaps oftener; she must have been nearly fifty when I first saw her; as far as I recollect, she had a pair of bright eyes, but no other remains of beauty. I have seen her in a crimson gown, and I remember some babbler told me she was fond of smart clothes and smart people, as most intelligent people are. She was supposed not to utter when Carlyle was within hearing, but she gave me the impression that she might be keen and sarcastic. The following is all that I can now recollect of her conversation. Her husband had 'just returned from Paris,' where he had been maddened by the ticking of a clock in his bedroom; 'instead of banishing it to the passage, or tilting, and so stopping it, as anybody else would have done, he dashed it down and broke it — so like him!'

Carlyle was a master of vituperation, and if he had merely spoken a good deal of what he has left behind him in writing, it would not have appeared offensive; for often and often after a volley thereof, delivered with a strong Dumfriesshire accent, he would burst into a roar of laughter, partly at himself and partly at the situation — and this toned down the savagery. It was well remarked that he mixed so much that was picturesque and grotesque in his abuse, that it seemed more like an utterance in a vision than vulgar invective. He had many faults, and they were not all pleasant ones; he was a man of many wants; he was extraordinarily tenacious, and weakly unreasonable as to his personal comforts, and this became a terrible tyranny for those who lived with him. Then people did not appreciate his intellectual scorn or sinister and furious vaticinations. He abused his knack of caricature and power of saying bitter things, and was remarkable for the impartiality with which he exercised that power; he may have been scornful and perhaps envious; but remember he was a Scot, peasant born, peasant bred — and dyspeptic. It was unfortunate that his wife, by reason of her caustic temper, was not qualified to influence the softer side of his charac-ter. — *My Confidences* (1896).

Bryan Waller Procter

Mr. Thomas Carlyle, when he was introduced by Edw. Irving to Mr. ——'s family (of which I almost formed a part), in 1823, was fresh from Scotland. He was then already author of the "Life of Schiller;" and his strong German tendencies were already formed. He had grave fea-tures, a brown florid complexion, and a simple, manly manner, not de-pending on cultivation so much as on the internal thoughts which gave it motion and character. I found him very sensible and pleasant; having some peculiar opinions, indeed, with which, it must be owned, I did not much disagree....

Mr. Carlyle's style, which is at first repulsive, becomes in the end very attractive. His humour, although grave, is not saturnine: some of his graver epigrams, indeed, pierce at once to the very heart of a subject. He worships the hero; yet he is in general thoroughly radical. He loves the poor worker in letters, the peasant, the farmer with his horny hand, the plain speaker, the bold speaker; yet he has no pity for the negro, who, he says, should submit to slavery because he is not fit for freedom. It follows from this, that the man must remain poor who has not obvious means to achieve riches, and that oppression and misfortune are reasonable decrees of fate, against which our feelings should not cavil or rebel. — "Recollections of Men of Letters" in *An Autobiographical Fragment* (1877).

LORD CHESTERFIELD

Sir John Hawkins

Nature, it must be owned, had endowed him with fine parts, and these he cultivated with all the industry usually practiced by such as prefer the semblance of what is really fit, just, lovely, honourable, to the qualities themselves; thus he had eloquence without learning, complaisance without friendship, and gallantry without love....

His dissimulation, deep and refined as it was, did not lead him to profess any sincere regard to virtue or religion: the grosser immoralities he affects to speak of with abhorrence; but such as might be practised without the loss of health and reputation he seemed to think there was no law against. He was therefore, if secret, vain in his amours, and though, setting aside his mien, his person had little to recommend it, for he was low of stature, had coarse features, and a cadaverous complexion.... He was also long-visaged and long-necked, but from the shoulders to the waist very short, which a wit once observing, said, he was a giant cut down, alluding to the practice of cutting down ships of war to render them more active. — *The Life of Samuel Johnson, LL.D.* (1787).

John, Lord Hervey

Lord Chesterfield was allowed by everybody to have more conversable entertaining table-wit than any man of his time; his propensity to ridicule, in which he indulged himself with infinite humour and no distinction, and with inexhaustible spirits and no discretion, made him sought and feared, liked and not loved, by most of his acquaintance; no sex, no relation, no rank, no power, no profession, no friendship, no obligation, was a shield from those pointed glittering weapons, that seemed to shine only to a stander-by, but cut deep in those they touched. All his acquaintance were indifferently the objects of his satire, and served promiscuously to feed that voracious appetite for abuse that made him fall on everything that came in his way, and treat every one of his companions in rotation at the expense of the rest. I remember two lines in a satire of Boileau's that fit him exactly: — "Mais c'est un petit fou qui se croit tout permis, / Et qui pour un bon mot va perdre vingt amis." And as his lordship, for want of principle, often sacrificed his character to his interest, so by these means he as often, for want of prudence, sacrificed his interest to his vanity. With a person as disagreeable as it was possible for a human figure to be without being deformed, he affected following many women of the first beauty and the most in fashion; and, if you would have taken his word for it, not without success; whilst in fact and in truth he never gained any one above the venal rank of those whom an Adonis or a Vulcan might be equally well with, for an equal sum of money. He was very short, disproportioned, thick, and clumsily made; had a broad, rough-featured, ugly face, with black teeth, and a head big enough for a Polyphemus. One Ben Ashurst, who said few good things, though admired for many, told Lord Chesterfield once that he was like a stunted giant — which was a humourous idea and really apposite. Such a thing would disconcert Lord Chesterfield as much as it would have done anybody who had neither his wit nor his assurance on other occasions; for though he could attack vigorously, he could defend but weakly, his quickness never showing itself in reply, any more than his understanding in argument. — *Memoirs of the Reign of George the Second* (1848).

G.K. CHESTERTON

Holbrook Jackson

I first beheld him on a Yorkshire moor far from his natural element, which is London.... He was staying at the house of a Bradford merchant adjoining the moor, and I was to meet him there. It was April, and raining. I trudged through the damp furze and heather up to the house only to find that the object of my pilgrimage had disappeared without leaving a trace behind him. No alarm was felt, as this was one of his habits.... Therefore I adjourned with the lady of the house and Mrs Chesterton to an upper hall, where a noble latticed window commanded a wide vista of the moor. I peered into the wild, half hoping that I should first behold the great form of Gilbert Chesterton looming over the bare brow of a new large faith.

You see my imagination was somewhat overwrought, and I was not to be thus gratified. G.K.C. did not fill the high horizon of the far wold, he did not burst upon our ken like a titan gradually growing bigger as he came nearer into our vision. His coming was not melodramatic; it was, on the contrary, quite simple, quite idyllic, and quite characteristic. In fact, he did not come at all, rather was it that our eyes, and later our herald, went to him. For quite near to the house we espied him, hatless and negligently clad in a Norfolk suit of homespun, leaning in the rain against a budding tree, absorbed in the pages of a little red book.

This was a more fitting vision. It suited admirably his unaffected, careless, and altogether childlike genius. He came into the house shortly afterwards and consumed tea and cake like any mortal and talked that talk of Olympus with the abandonment and irresistibility of a child. I found his largeness wonderfully proportionate, even, as is so rarely the case with massive men, to his head. This is amply in keeping with the rest of his person. He wears a tangled mass of light brown hair prematurely streaked with grey, and a slight moustache. His grey-blue eyes laugh happily as his full lips unload themselves of a constant flow of self-amused and piquant words. Like Dr Johnson, whom he resembles so much in form, he is a great talker. But while I looked at him I was not reminded of the lexicographer, but of Balzac. And as his monologue rolled on and we laughed and wondered, I found myself carried away to a studio in France, where the head of Chesterton became one with the head of Rodin's conception of France's greatest literary genius.

Since then I have seen G.K.C. many times. I have seen him standing upon platforms defending the peoples' pleasures against the inroads of Puritanism. I have seen him addressing men from a pulpit, and on one memorable occasion at Clifford's Inn Hall I saw him defending the probability of the liquefication of the blood of St Januarius in the teeth of a pyrotechnic heckling from Bernard Shaw. Again I have seen his vast person dominating the staring throng in Fleet Street like a superman; and I have seen the traffic of Ludgate Circus held up for him, as he strolled by in cloak and sombrero like a brigand of Adelphi drama or a Spanish hidalgo by Velasquez, oblivious of critical 'bus-driver and wonder-struck multitude.

But best is it to see him in his favourite habitat of Bohemian Soho. There in certain obscure yet excellent French restaurants, with Hilaire Belloc and other writers and talkers, he may be seen, sitting behind a tall tankard of lager or a flagon of Chianti, eternally unravelling the mysterious tangle of living ideas; now rising mountainously on his feet to overshadow the company with weighty argument, anon brandishing a wine-bottle as he insists upon defending some controversial point until "we break the furniture"; and always chuckling at his own wit and the sallies of others, as he fights the battle of ideas with indefatigable and unconquerable good-humour. — *Romance and Reality* (1912).

Frank Swinnerton

Charles Masterman ... has told me how Chesterton used to sit writing his articles in a Fleet Street cafe, sampling and mixing a terrible conjunction of drinks, while many waiters hovered about him, partly in awe, and partly in case he should leave the restaurant without paying for what he had had. One day — I do not know whether Chesterton was present or absent — the head waiter approached Masterman. 'Your friend,' he whispered admiringly, 'he very clever man. He sit and laugh. And then he write. And then he laugh at what he write.' It has always been essential to Chesterton that he should be amused by what he wrote, and by what he said in public. I have heard him laugh so much at a debate that he gave himself hiccups for the rest of the evening.

In early days he was very nearly as big as he afterwards became, but whereas in mature years his much-thinned hair straggled untidily, like a blown wisp of steam, it was then solid and well brushed. A feature of it was a Whistlerian white plume in the centre; and anybody who sees an old photograph of Chesterton will there find the plume as neat and trim as brush could make it. Presently he grew more like Porthos; and then like Dr Johnson; and at last like that portrait by Velasquez of Don

Alessandro del Borro which is at present to be seen in Berlin. His gigantic aspect became a matter of common reference. The story of the man who gave up his seat to three ladies was associated with him. Finally a serious illness contracted his figure and forced him to live less strenuously than he had done....

Upon the public platform he swayed his large bulk from side to side; but he did not gesticulate. His speech was prefaced and accompanied by a curious sort of humming, such as one may hear when glee singers give each other the note before starting to sing. He pronounced the word 'I' (without egotism) as if it were 'Ayee,' and drawled, not in the highly gentlemanly manner which Americans believe to be the English accent, and which many Englishmen call the Oxford accent, but in a manner peculiar to himself and either attractive or the reverse according to one's taste (to me attractive). As he talked, and as he invented amusing fancies, he punctuated his talk with little breathless grunts or last gasps of laughter, so that he gave the impression — what with the drawl and the breathless grunts — of speaking very slowly indeed. He also gave the impression of speaking without any effort whatever, without raising his voice, or becoming intimidated by his audience or by lack of material to fill the time allotted to him, or feeling anything but sweet charity towards all those — even Jews, politicians, and sophisticates — whom he felt compelled to denounce. To those, accordingly, who care more for character than for opinion, more for talent than for fashion, Chesterton remains one of the great figures of our time. For the rest, and for those easily made impatient by his habit — they call it 'trick' — of antithesis, he was merely an ingenious and snort-provoking creature. He certainly lived behind the times; but whether that is a sin or only a misfortune I shall not now attempt to determine. — *The Georgian Literary Scene* (1935).

WINSTON CHURCHILL

Mark Twain

... Winston Churchill, son of Lord Randolph Churchill and nephew of a duke. I had met him at Sir Gilbert Parker's seven years before, when he was twenty-three years old, and had met him and introduced him to his lecture audience a year later in New York, when he had come over to tell of the lively experiences he had had as a war correspondent in the South African War, and in one or two wars on the Himalayan frontier of India.

Sir Gilbert Parker said, "Do you remember the dinner here seven years ago?"

"Yes," I said, "I remember it."

"Do you remember what Sir William Vernon Harcourt said about you?"

"No."

"Well, you didn't hear it. You and Churchill went up on the top floor to have a smoke and a talk, and Harcourt wondered what the result would be. He said that whichever of you got the floor first would keep it to the end, without a break; he believed you, being old and experienced, would get it and that Churchill's lungs would have a half-hour's rest for the first time in five years. When you two came down, by and by, Sir William asked Churchill if he had had a good time, and he answered eagerly, 'Yes.' Then he asked you if you had had a good time. You hesitated, then said without eagerness, 'I have had a smoke.' "
— *Mark Twain in Eruption*, ed. Bernard DeVoto (1940).

SAMUEL TAYLOR COLERIDGE

Thomas Carlyle

I have seen many other curiosities. Not the least of these I reckon Coleridge, the Kantean metaphysician and quondam Lake poet. I will tell you all about our interview *when we meet*. Figure a fat flabby incurvated personage, at once short, rotund and relaxed, with a watery mouth, a snuffy nose, a pair of strange brown timid yet earnest looking eyes, a high tapering brow, and a great bush of grey hair — you will have some faint idea of Coleridge. He is a kind, good soul, full of religion and affection, and poetry and animal magnetism. His cardinal sin is that he wants *will*; he has no resolution, he shrinks from pain or labour in any of its shapes. His very attitude bespeaks this: he never straightens his knee joints, he stoops with his fat ill shapen shoulders, and in walking he does not tread but shovel and slide — my father would call it *skluiffing*. He is also always busied to keep by strong and frequent inhalations the water of his mouth from overflowing; and his eyes have a look of anxious impotence; he would do with all his heart, but he knows he dare not. The conversation of the man is much as I antici-pated. A forest of thoughts; some true, many false, most part dubious, all of them ingenious in some degree, often in a high degree. But there is no method in his talk; he wanders like a man sailing among many cur-rents, withersoever his lazy mind directs him—; and what is more un-pleasant he preaches, or rather soliloquizes: he cannot speak; he can only "tal-k" (so he names it). Hence I found him unprofitable, even tedious: but we parted very good friends I promising to go back and see him some other evening—a promise I fully intend to keep.... I reckon him a man of great and useless genius—a strange not at all a great man. — From a letter to John A. Carlyle, 24 June 1824.

Coleridge is a steam-engine of a hundred horses power—with the boiler burst. His talk is resplendent with imagery and the shows of thought; you listen as to an oracle, and find yourself no jot the wiser. He is without beginning or middle or end. A round fat oily yet impatient little man, his mind seems totally beyond his own controul; He speaks incessantly, not thinking or imagining or remembering, but combining all these processes into one; as a rich and lazy housewife might mingle her soup and fish and beef and custard into one unspeakable mass and present it trueheartedly to her astonished guests. — From a letter to Thomas Murray, 24 August 1824.

Coleridge is a mass of richest spices, putrified into a dunghill: I never hear his *tawlk*, without feeling ready to worship him and toss him in a blanket. — From a letter to John A. Carlyle, 22 January 1825.

The good man, he was now getting old, towards sixty perhaps; and gave you the idea of a life that had been full of sufferings; a life heavy-laden, half-vanquished, still swimming painfully in seas of mani-fold physical and other bewilderment. Brow and head were round, and of massive weight, but the face was flabby and irresolute. The deep eyes, of a light hazel, were as full of sorrow as of inspiration; confused pain looked mildly from them, as in a kind of mild astonishment. The whole figure and air, good and amiable otherwise, might be called flabby and irresolute; expressive of weakness under possibility of strength. He hung loosely on his limbs, with knees bent, in stooping attitude; in walking, he rather shuffled than decisively stept; and a lady once remarked, he never could fix which side of the garden-walk would suit him best, but continually shifted, in corkscrew fashion, and kept trying both. A heavy-laden, high-aspiring and surely much-suffering man. His voice, naturally soft and good, had contracted itself into a plaintive snuffle and singsong; he spoke as if preaching—you would have said, preaching earnestly and also hopelessly the weightiest things. I still recollect his 'object' and 'subject', terms of continual recurrence in the Kantean province; and how he sung and snuffled them into 'om-m-mject' and 'sum-m-mject', with a kind of solemn shake or quaver, as he rolled along. No talk, in his century or any other, could be more surprising. — *Life of John Sterling* (1851).

Ralph Waldo Emerson

From London, on the 5th August [1833], I went to Highgate, and wrote a note to Mr. Coleridge, requesting leave to pay my respects to him. It was near noon. Mr. Coleridge sent a verbal message that he was in bed, but if I would call after one o'clock, he would see me. I returned at one, and he appeared, a short, thick old man, with bright blue eyes and fine clear complexion, leaning on his cane. He took snuff freely, which presently soiled his cravat and neat black suit. He asked whether I knew [Washington] Allston, and spoke warmly of his merits and doings when he knew him in Rome; what a master of the Titian-esque he was, etc., etc. He spoke of Dr. Channing. It was an unspeakable misfortune that he should have turned out a Unitarian after all. On this, he burst into a declamation on the folly and ignorance of Unitarianism — its high unreasonableness.... When he stopped to take breath, I interposed, that, "whilst I highly valued all his explanation, I was bound to tell him that I was born and bred a Unitarian." "Yes," he said, "I supposed so;" and continued as before....

I was in his company for about an hour, but find it impossible to recall the largest part of his discourse, which was often like so many printed paragraphs in his books — perhaps the same — so readily did he fall into certain commonplaces. As I might have foreseen, the visit was rather a spectacle than a conversation, of no use beyond the satisfaction of my curiosity. He was old and pre-occupied, and could not bend to a new companion and think with him. — *English Traits* (1856).

Samuel C. Hall

It is a rare privilege to have known such a man. The influence of one so truly good as well as great cannot have been transitory. It is a joy to me now — nearly fifty years after his departure. I seem to hear the melodious voice, and look upon the gentle, gracious, and loving countenance of "the old man eloquent," as I write this Memory....

I have listened to him more than once for above an hour, of course without putting in a single word; I would as soon have attempted a song while a nightingale was singing. There was rarely much change of countenance; his face, when I knew him, was overladen with flesh, and its expression impaired; yet to me it was so tender, and gentle, and gracious, and loving, that I could have knelt at the old man's feet almost in adoration. My own hair is white now; yet I have much the same feeling as I had then, whenever the form of the venerable man rises in memory before me. Yet I cannot recall — and I believe could not recall at the time, so as to preserve as a cherished thing in my remembrance — a single sentence of the many sentences I heard him utter. In his "Table Talk" there is a world of wisdom, but that is only a collection of scraps, chance-gathered. If any left his presence unsatisfied, it resulted rather from the superabundance than the paucity of the feast. And probably there has never been an author who was less of an egotist: it was never of himself he talked; he was always under the influence of that divine precept, "It is more blessed to give than to receive."

I can recall many evening rambles with him over the high lands that look down on London; but the memory I cherish most is linked with a crowded street, where the clumsy and coarse jostled the old man eloquent, as if he had been earthy, of the earth. It was in the Strand: he pointed out to me the window of a room in the office of the *Morning Post* where he had consumed much midnight oil; and then for half an hour he talked of the sorrowful joy he had often felt when, leaving the office as day was dawning, he heard the song of a caged lark that sung his orisons from the lattice of an artisan who was rising to begin his labour as the poet was pacing homewards to rest after his work all night. Thirty years had passed, but that forgotten melody — that dear bird's song — gave him then as much true pleasure as when, to his wearied head and heart, it was the matin hymn of nature....

At the time I speak of he was growing corpulent and heavy; being seldom free from pain, he moved apparently with difficulty, yet liked to walk, with shuffling gait, up and down and about the room as he talked, pausing now and then as if oppressed by suffering.

I need not say that I was a silent listener during the evenings to which I refer, when there were present some of those who "teach us from their urns;" but I was free to gaze on the venerable man — one of the humblest, and one of the most fervid, perhaps, of the worshippers by whom he was surrounded, and to treasure in memory the poet's gracious and loving looks — the "thick waving silver hair" — the still, clear blue eyes; and on such occasions I used to leave him as if I were in a waking dream, trying to recall, here and there, a sentence of the many weighty and mellifluous sentences I had heard — seldom with success — and feeling at the moment as I had been surfeited with honey.

May I not now lament that I did not foresee a time when I might be called upon to write concerning this good and great and most lovable man? How much I might have enriched these pages — now but weak records of the impressions I received!

Many famous men have described the personal appearance of the poet. The best portrait of him is, I think, from the pen of Words-worth: —

> A noticeable man, with large, grey eyes,
> And a *pale* face that seemed, undoubtedly,
> As if a *blooming* face it ought to be;
> Heavy his low-hung lip did oft appear,
> Depress'd by weight of moving phantasy;
> Profound his forehead was, though not severe.

... But the earliest word-portrait we have of him was drawn by Wordsworth's sister in 1797: — "At first I thought him very plain; that is, for about three minutes. He is pale, thin, has a wide mouth, thick lips, longish, loose-growing, half-curling, rough black hair. His eye is large and full, and not dark, but grey, such an eye as would receive from a heavy soul the dullest expression; but it speaks every emotion of his animated mind. He has fine dark eyebrows, and an overhanging fore-head." — *A Book of Memories* (1877).

William Hazlitt

Coleridge had agreed to come over and see my father, according to the curtesy of the country ... but, in the meantime, I had gone to hear him preach the Sunday after his arrival.... On the Tuesday following, the half-inspired speaker came. I was called down into the room where he was, and went half-hoping, half-afraid. He received me very graciously, and I listened for a long time without uttering a word. I did not suffer in his opinion by my silence. "For those two hours," he after-wards was pleased to say, "he was conversing with William Hazlitt's forehead!" His appearance was different from what I had anticipated from seeing him before. At a distance, and in the dim light of the chapel, there was to me a strange wildness in his aspect, a dusky obscu-rity, and I thought him pitted with the small-pox. His complexion was at that time clear, and even bright — "As are the children of yon azure sheen." His forehead was broad and high, light as if built of ivory, with large projecting eyebrows and his eyes rolling beneath them, like a sea with darkened lustre.... His mouth was gross, voluptuous, open, elo-quent; his chin good-humoured and round; but his nose, the rudder of the face, the index of the will, was small, feeble, nothing — like what he has done. It might seem that the genius of his face as from a height surveyed and projected him (with sufficient capacity and huge aspiration) into the world unknown of thought and imagination, with nothing to support or guide his veering purpose, as if Columbus had launched his adventurous course for the New World in a scallop, without oars or compass. So at least I comment on it after the event. Coleridge, in his person, was rather above the common size, inclining to the corpulent, or like Lord Hamlet, "somewhat fat and pursy." His hair (now, alas! gray) was then black and glossy as a raven's, and fell in smooth masses over his forehead. — "My First Acquaintance with Poets."

Leigh Hunt

Coleridge was as little fitted for action as Lamb, but on a different account. His person was of a good height, but as sluggish and solid as the other's was light and fragile. He had, perhaps, suffered it to grow old before its time, for want of exercise. His hair was white at fifty; and as he generally dressed in black, and had a very tranquil demeanor, his appearance was gentlemanly, and for several years before his death was reverend. Nevertheless, there was something invincibly young in the look of his face. It was round and fresh-coloured, with agreeable features, and an open, indolent, good-natured mouth. This boy-like expression was very becoming in one who dreamed and speculated as he did when he was really a boy, and who passed his life apart from the rest of the world, with a book, and his flowers. His forehead was prodigious — a great piece of placid marble; and his fine eyes, in which all the activity of his mind seemed to concentrate, moved under it with a sprightly ease, as if it was pastime to them to carry all that thought. — *Autobiography* (1859).

John Keats

Last Sunday I took a Walk towards highgate and in the lane that winds by the side of Lord Mansfield's park I met Mr Green our Demonstrator at Guy's in conversation with Coleridge — I joined them, after enquiring by a look whether it would be agreeable — I walked with him at his alderman-after-dinner pace for near two miles I suppose. In those two Miles he broached a thousand things — let me see if I can give you a list — Nightingales, Poetry — on Poetical Sensation — Metaphysics — Different genera and species of Dreams — Nightmare — a dream accompanied by a sense of touch — single and double touch — A dream related — First and second consciousness — the difference explained between will and Volition — so many metaphysicians from a want of smoking and second consciousness — Monsters — the Kraken — Mermaids — Southey believes in them — Southey's belief too much diluted — A Ghost story — Good morning — I heard his voice as he came towards me — I heard it as he moved away — I had heard it all the interval — if it may be called so. He was civil enough to ask me to call on him at Highgate. [See John Keats — Samuel Taylor Coleridge for Coleridge's version of this meeting.] — From a letter to George and Georgiana Keats, 14 February–3 May 1819.

Charles MacFarlane

The philosopher and bard arrived, with his laudanum bottle in his pocket, ate very little dinner, sipped a glass or two of wine, took another glass suspected to have been nearly all diluted laudanum, and then went off at score into a monologue which lasted the remainder of the dinner, the whole of the dessert, and for nearly an hour after. Nobody interrupted him, as nobody could have cut across his torrent of talk without being washed away. Lord Dover, who had had former experience, seemed to enjoy it all; but not so the impatient, irritable Lord Ward; he liked to talk himself, and no man could better take his share at that exercise. As he took a hasty departure, he said: "Well! I have heard of the *summum bonum* before, and now I know what is the *summum bore-em!*"

I never could boast of a surplus stock of patience; I never could have understood the half of Coleridge's ultra–German, transcendental philosophy, but I could find high poetry in it, and could have listened to it — in the winter season when nights are long — from sunset till midnight. I met him but seldom, and then not in his best days — far from that; but each time I was astonished and delighted while I was with him, and left him with a perhaps unpleasant bewilderment or swimming of the head, but with an innermost persuasion that I had been, not talking with, but hearing talk, a wondrous man. — *Reminiscences of a Literary Life* (1917).

Bryan Waller Procter

Samuel Taylor Coleridge was like the Rhine, "That exulting and abounding river." He was full of words, full of thought; yielding both in an unfailing flow, that delighted many, and perplexed a few of his hearers. He was a man of prodigious miscellaneous reading, always ready to communicate all he knew. From Alpha to Omega, all was familiar to him.... He went from flower to flower, throughout the whole garden of learning, like the butterfly or the bee, — most like the bee. He talked with everybody, about anything. He was so full of information that it was a relief to him to part with some portion of it to others. It was like laying down part of his burden.... Coleridge had a weighty head, dreaming grey eyes, full, sensual lips, and a look and manner which were entirely wanting in firmness and decision. His motions also appeared weak and undecided, and his voice had nothing of the sharpness or ring of a resolute man. When he spoke his words were thick and slow, and when he read poetry his utterance was altogether a chant.

One day, when dining with some lawyers, he had been more than usually eloquent and full of talk. His perpetual interruptions were resented by one of the guests, who said to his neighbour, "I'll stop this fellow;" and thereupon addressed the master of the house with "G——, I've not forgotten my promise to give you the extract from 'The Pandects.' It was the ninth chapter that you were alluding to. It begins: "Ac veteres quidam philosophi.' " "Pardon me, sir," interposed Coleridge, "there I think you are in error. The ninth chapter begins in this way, 'Incident saepe causae,' etc." It was in vain to refer to anything on the supposition that the poet was ignorant, for he really had some acquaintance with every subject. I imagine that no man had ever read so many books and at the same time had digested so much.

Coleridge was prodigal of his words, which in fact he could with difficulty suppress; but he seldom talked of himself or of his affairs. He was very speculative, very theological, very metaphysical, and not infrequently threw in some little pungent sentence, characteristic of the defects of some of his acquaintance. In illustration of his unfailing talk, I will give an account of one of his days, when I was present. He had come from Highgate to London, for the sole purpose of consulting a friend about his son Hartley ("our dear Hartley"), towards whom he expressed, and I have no doubt felt, much anxiety. He arrived about one or two o'clock, in the midst of a conversation, which immediately began to interest him. He struck into the middle of the talk very soon, and held the "ear of the house" until dinner made its appearance about four o'clock. He then talked all through the dinner, all the afternoon, all the evening, with scarcely a single interruption. He expatiated on this subject and on that; he drew fine distinctions; he made subtle criticisms. He descended to anecdotes, historical, logical, rhetorical; he dealt with law, medicine, and divinity, until, at last, five minutes before eight o'clock, the servant came in and announced that the Highgate stage was at the corner of the street, and was waiting to convey Mr. Coleridge home. Coleridge immediately started up oblivious of all time, and said, in a hurried voice, "My dear Z——, I will come to you some other day, and talk to you about our dear Hartley." He had quite forgotten his son and everybody else, in the delight of having such an enraptured audience. — "Recollections of Men of Letters" in *An Autobiographical Fragment* (1877).

Samuel Rogers

Coleridge was a marvellous talker. One morning, when Hookham Frere also breakfasted with me, Coleridge talked for three hours without intermission about poetry, and so admirably that I wish every word he uttered had been written down. But sometimes his harangues were quite unintelligible, not only to myself, but to others. Wordsworth and I called upon him one forenoon, when he was in a lodging off Pall Mall. He talked uninterruptedly for about two hours, during which Wordsworth listened to him with profound attention, every now and then nodding his head as if in assent. On quitting the lodging, I said to Wordsworth, 'Well, for my own part, I could not make head or tail of Coleridge's oration: pray, did you understand it?' 'Not one syllable of it,' was Wordsworth's reply. — *Recollections of the Table-Talk of Samuel Rogers* (1856).

Himself

I am remarkably fond of beans and bacon; and this fondness I attribute to my father having given me a penny for having eat a large quantity of beans on Saturday. For the other boys did not like them, and as it was an economic food, my father thought that my attachment and penchant for it ought to be encouraged. My father was very fond of me, and I was my mother's darling: in consequence I was very miserable. For Molly, who had nursed my brother Francis, and was immoderately fond of him, hated me because my mother took more notice of me than of Frank, and Frank hated me because my mother gave me now and then a bit of cake, when he had none, — quite forgetting that for one bit of cake which I had and he had not, he had twenty sops in the pan, and pieces of bread and butter with sugar on them from Molly, from whom I received only thumps and ill names.

So I became fretful and timorous, and a tell-tale; and the schoolboys drove me from play, and were always tormenting me, and hence I took no pleasure in boyish sports, but read incessantly. My father's sister kept an *every-thing* shop at Crediton — and there I read through all the gilt-cover little books that could be had at that time, and likewise all the uncovered tales of *Tom Hickathrift, Jack the Giant-killer,* etc. and etc. etc. — and I used to lie by the wall, and *mope* — and my spirits used to come upon me suddenly, and in a flood — and then I was accustomed to run up and down the church-yard, and act over all I had been reading on the docks, the nettles, and the rank-grass. At six years old I remember to have read *Belisarius, Robinson Crusoe,* and *Philip Quarll* — and then I found the *Arabian Nights'* entertainments — one tale of which (the tale of a man who was compelled to seek for a pure virgin) made so deep an impression on me (I had read it in the evening while my mother was mending stockings) that I was haunted by spectres whenever I was in the dark — and I distinctly remember the anxious and fearful eagerness with which I used to watch the window in which the books lay — and whenever the sun lay upon them, I would seize it, carry it by the wall, and bask, and read. My father found out the effect which these books had produced — and burnt them. So I became a *dreamer* — and acquired an indisposition to all bodily activity — and I was fretful, and inordinately passionate, and as I could not play at any thing, and was slothful, I was despised and hated by the boys; and because I could read and spell, and had, I may truly say, a memory and understanding forced into almost an unnatural ripeness, I was flattered and wondered at by all the old women — and so I became very vain, and despised most of the boys that were at all near my own age, and before I was eight years old I was a *character*: sensibility, imagination, vanity, sloth, and feelings of deep and bitter contempt for almost all who traversed the orbit of my understanding were even then prominent and manifest. — From a letter to Thomas Poole, 9 October 1797.

WILKIE COLLINS

Rudolph Lehmann

I can see him now as I used to see him in those early, unforgotten days: a neat figure of a cheerful plumpness, very small feet and hands, a full brown beard, a high and rounded forehead, a small nose not naturally intended to support a pair of large spectacles behind which his eyes shone with humour and friendship; not by any means the sort of man imagination would have pictured as the creator of Count Fosco and the inventor of the terrors of *Armadale* and the absorbing mystery of *The Moonstone.* — Quoted by John Lehmann in *Ancestors and Friends* (1962).

John Lothrop Motley

P.S. — I forgot to say that another of [John] Forster's guests [besides Charles Dickens] was Wilkie Collins (the 'Woman in White's' author). He is a little man, with black hair, a large white forehead, large spectacles, and small features. He is very unaffected, vivacious, and agreable. — From a letter to his mother, 15 March 1861.

JOSEPH CONRAD

Ford Madox Ford

He was small rather than large in height; very broad in the shoulder and long in the arm; dark in complexion with black hair and a clipped black beard. He had the gestures of a Frenchman who shrugs his shoulders frequently. When you had really secured his attention he would insert a monocle into his right eye and scrutinise your face from very near as a watchmaker looks into the works of a watch. He entered a room with his head held high, rather stiffly and with a haughty manner, moving his head once semicircularly. In this one movement he had expressed to himself the room and its contents; his haughtiness was due to his determination to master that room, not to dominate its occupants, his chief passion being the realisation of aspects to himself. — *Joseph Conrad: A Personal Remembrance* (1924).

John Galsworthy

It was in March 1893 that I first met Conrad on board the English sailing ship "Torrens" in Adelaide Harbour. He was superintending the stowage of cargo. Very dark he looked in the burning sunlight — tanned, with a peaked brown beard, almost black hair, and dark brown eyes, over which the lids were deeply folded. He was thin, not tall, his arms very long, his shoulders broad, his head set rather forward. He spoke to me with a strong foreign accent. He seemed to me strange on an English ship. For fifty-six days I sailed in his company — *Castles in Spain* (1927).

Bertrand Russell

I made the acquaintance of Joseph Conrad in September 1913, through our common friend Lady Ottoline Morell. I had been for many years an admirer of his books, but should not have ventured to seek acquaintance without an introduction. I traveled down to his house near Ashford in Kent in a state of somewhat anxious expectation. My first impression was one of surprise. He spoke English with a very strong foreign accent, and nothing in his demeanor in any way suggested the sea. He was an aristocratic Polish gentleman to his finger tips. His feeling for the sea, and for England, was one of romantic love—love from a certain distance, sufficient to leave the romance untarnished....

He was, as anyone may see from his books, a very rigid moralist and politically far from sympathetic with revolutionaries. He and I were in most of our opinions by no means in agreement, but in something very fundamental we were extraordinarily at one.

My relation to Joseph Conrad was unlike any other that I have ever had. I saw him seldom, and not over a long period of years. In the outworks of our lives, we were almost strangers, but we shared a certain outlook on human life and human destiny, which, from the very first, made a bond of extreme strength. —*Portraits From Memory* (1956).

H.G. Wells

At first he impressed me, as he impressed Henry James, as the strangest of creatures. He was rather short and round-shouldered with his head as it were sunken into his body. He had a dark retreating face with a very carefully trimmed and pointed beard, a trouble-wrinkled forehead and very troubled dark eyes, and the gestures of his hands and arms were from the shoulders and very Oriental indeed. He reminded people of Du Maurier's Svengali and, in the nautical trimness of his costume, of Cutliffe Hyne's Captain Kettle. He spoke English strangely. Not badly altogether; he would supplement his vocabulary—especially if he were discussing cultural or political matters—with French words; but with certain oddities. He had learnt to read English long before he spoke it and he had formed wrong sound impressions of many familiar words; he had for example acquired an incurable tendency to pronounce the last *e* in these and those. He would say, "*Wat* shall we do with *thesa* things?" And he was always incalculable about the use of "shall" and "will." When he talked of seafaring his terminology was excellent but when he turned to less familiar topics he was often at a loss for phrases.

Yet he wove an extraordinarily rich descriptive English prose, a new sort of English of his own, conspicuously and almost necessarily free from stereotyped expressions and hack phrases, in which foreign turns and phrases interlaced with unusual native words unusually used. And I think it was this fine, fresh, careful, slightly exotic quality about his prose, that "foreign" flavour which the normal Anglo-Saxon mind habitually associates with culture, that blinded criticism to the essentially sentimental and melodramatic character of the stories he told. His deepest theme is the simple terror of strange places, of the jungle, of night, of the incalculable sea; as a mariner his life was surely a perpetual anxiety about miscalculations, about the hidden structural vices of his ship, about shifting cargo and untrustworthy men; he laid bare with an air of discovery what most adventurers, travellers and sailors habitually suppress. Another primary topic with him — best treated in that amazingly good story *Amy Foster*, a sort of caricature autobiography, was the feeling of being incurably "foreign." He pursued a phantom "honour" — in *Lord Jim* for instance; his humour in *The Nigger of the Narcissus*, is dismal, and you may search his work from end to end and find little tenderness and no trace of experienced love or affection. But he had set himself to be a great writer, an artist in words, and to achieve all the recognition and distinction that he imagined should go with that ambition, he had gone literary with a singleness and intensity of purpose that made the kindred concentration of Henry James seem lax and large and pale. — *Experiment in Autobiography* (1934).

JAMES FENIMORE COOPER

Samuel C. Hall

Of the group around [Paris] there was one who left an impression on my memory — Fenimore Cooper. He "stalked" about the *salon* — a tall, stalwart man, with the unmistakeable air of self-confidence I have noticed in many Americans; as if it were a prime thought that independence was to be maintained by a seeming indifference to the opinions of on-lookers — a sensation that vanishes, however, when the demeanor that has given rise to it is found but the rough shell of a sweet kernel; for Americans are among the most socially generous of mankind. I had other and better opportunities of seeing Fenimore Cooper afterward: but in that *salon*, jostled by *petits maîtres*, he was out of place—as much so as an Indian cross-bow would have been among a collection of Minié rifles. [Bryan Waller] Procter, in 1828, wrote of him: "He has a dogged, discontented look, and seems ready to affront or be affronted. His eye is rather deep-set, dull, and with little motion." He describes Cooper as rude even to coarseness in English society. That is not my experience of the author of "The Spy"—the originator of the class of sea-fictions—to whom the reading world owes a large debt. He was certainly the opposite of "genial," and seemed to think it good taste and sound judgment to be condescending to his equals....

I met Cooper often during my residence at Paris in 1831. I have referred to him elsewhere. He seemed to me the *beau-idéal*—let the term be translated at will—of an American citizen, and gave me, more than any other man I have ever seen, the idea of a Puritan of our own Commonwealth days, with a bearing that might perhaps be termed stern, and certainly was not cordial: a firm step, a massive head and figure, and commanding look. He was not a man to whom one would readily apply the adjective "lovable"; but he seemed eminently calculated to extort respect, or even—if circumstances should make it his object to do so—to inspire fear. —*Retrospect of a Long Life* (1883).

STEPHEN CRANE

H.G. Wells

A very important acquaintance of my early Sandgate time ... was the American Stephen Crane.... He was a lean, blond, slow-speaking, perceptive, fragile, tuberculous being, too adventurous to be temperate with anything and impracticable to an extreme degree. He liked to sit and talk, sagely and deeply. How he managed ever to get to the seats of war to which he was sent I cannot imagine. I don't think he got very deeply into them. But he got deeply enough into them to shatter his health completely.

In Greece he met and married an energetic lady who had been sent out by some American newspaper as the first woman war correspondent. With, perhaps, excessive vigour she set out to give the ailing young husband a real good time. Morton Frewen (the wealthy father of Clare Sheridan) lent them a very old and beautiful house, Brede House near Rye and there they inaugurated a life of gay extravagance and open hospitality....

That was the setting in which I remember Crane. He was profoundly weary and ill, if I had been wise enough to see it, but I thought him sulky and reserved. He was essentially the helpless artist; he wasn't the master of his party, he wasn't the master of his home; his life was altogether out of control; he was being carried along. What he was still clinging to, but with a dwindling zest, was artistry. He had intense receptiveness to vivid work; he had an inevitably right instinct for the word in his stories; but he had no critical chatter. We compared our impressions of various contemporaries. "That's Great," he'd say or simply "*Gaw!*" Was so and so "any good"? So and so was "no good." ...

One night Mrs. Crane came to us. He had had a haemorrhage from his lungs and he had tried to conceal it from her. He "didn't want anyone to bother." Would I help get a doctor?

There was a bicycle in the place and my last clear memory of that fantastic Brede House party is riding out of the cold skirts of a wintry night into a drizzling dawn along a wet road to call up a doctor in Rye.

That crisis passed, but he died later in the new year, 1900. He did his utmost to conceal his symptoms and get on with his dying. Only at the end did his wife wake up to what was coming. She made a great effort to get him to Baden-Baden. She conveyed him silent and sunken and stoical to Fokestone by car, regardless of expense, she had chartered a special train to wait for him at Boulogne and he died almost as soon as he arrived in Germany. — *Experiment in Autobiography* (1934).

THOMAS DE QUINCEY

Thomas Carlyle

What do you think too? I am an acquaintance almost a friend of — The Opium-Eater's! Poor Dequincey! He is essentially a gentle and genial little soul; only that the Liver is diseased, and the "I-ety" egoism is strong and both together sometimes overset his balance. Poor soul! One of the most perfect *gentlemen* I have ever seen; and yet here he is living in *lodgings*, with two of his little children (writing for bread in the paltriest of all newspapers) while his wife with other two resides in

Westmoreland, — as a kind of "hostage" to his creditors! — From a letter to James Johnston, 19 November 1827.

A much stranger visitor was here last Wednesday-night: Thomas De Quincey the Opium-eater in person with his two children, and sat till midnight! The week before I half accidentally met him one night at Gordon's: he grew pale as ashes at my entrance; but we soon recovered him again; and kept him in flowing talk to a late hour. He is one of the smallest men you ever in your life beheld; but with a most gentle and sensible face, only that the teeth are destroyed by opium, and the little bit of an under-lip projects like a shelf. He speaks with a slow sad and soft voice, in the *politest* manner I have almost ever witnessed; and with great gracefulness and sense, were it not that he seems decidedly given to *prosing*. Poor little fellow! It might soften a very hard heart to see him so courteous, yet so weak and poor; retiring *home* with his two children to a miserable lodging-house, and writing all day for the King of Donkies, the Proprietor of the Saturday Post. I lent him Jean Paul's *Autobiography* which I got lately from Hamburg, and advised him to translate it for Blackwood, that so he might raise a few pounds and "fence off" the Genius of Hunger yet a little while. Poor little De Quincey! He is an innocent man; and, as you said, extremely *washable* away. — From a letter to John A. Carlyle, 29 November 1827.

As for De Quincey, I have not seen him this winter; and no man, except Bailiffs, it appears, has for the last eighteen months: he is said to be in the uttermost unaidable embarrassment; bankrupt in purse, and as nearly as possible in mind. I used to like him well, as one of the prettiest Talkers I ever heard; of great, indeed of diseased *acuteness*, not without depth, of a fine sense too, but of no breadth, no justness, weak, diffuse, supersensitive; on the whole, a perverted, ineffectual man. — From a letter to John Stuart Mill, 18 April 1833.

Poor De Quincey, whom I wished to know, was reported to tremble at the thought of such a thing; and did fly pale as ashes, poor little soul, the first time we actually met. He was a pretty little creature, full of wire-drawn ingenuities, bankrupt enthusiasms, bankrupt pride, with the finest silver-toned low voice, and most elaborate gently-winding courtesies and ingenuities in conversation. "What wouldn't one give to have him in a box, and take him out to talk!" That was Her [Jane Welsh Carlyle's] criticism of him, and it was right good. A bright, ready, and melodious talker, but in the end an inconclusive and long-winded. One of the smallest man figures I ever saw; shaped like a pair of tongs, and hardly above five feet in all. When he sate, you would have taken him, by candlelight, for the beautifullest little child; blue-eyed, sparkling face, had there not been a something, too, which said "Eccovi — this child has been in hell." After leaving Edinburgh I never saw him, hardly ever heard of him. His fate, owing to opium, etc., was hard and sore, poor fine-strung weak creature, launched *so* into the literary career of ambition and mother of dead dogs. — *Reminiscences* (1881).

George Gilfillan

Conceive a small, pale-faced, wo-begone, and attenuated man, opening the door of his room in —— street, advancing towards you with hurried movement, and half-recognising glance; saluting you in low and hesitating tones, asking you to be seated; and after he has taken a seat opposite you, but without looking you in the face, beginning to pour into your willing ear, a stream of learning and wisdom as long as you are content to listen, or to lend him the slighest cue. Who is it? 'Tis De Quincey, the celebrated Opium-eater, the friend and interpreter of Coleridge and Wordsworth, the sounder of metaphysic depths, and the dreamer of imaginative dreams, the most learned and most singular man alive, the most gifted of scholars, the most scholar-like of men of genius. He has come from his desk, where he has been prosecuting his profound researches, or, peradventure, inditing a lively paper for "Tait," or a recondite paper for "Blackwood." Your first feeling, as he enters, is, Can this be he? Is this the distinguished scholar? Is this the impassioned autobiographer? Is this the man who has recorded such gorgeous visions, seen by him while shut up in the Patmos of a laudanum phial? His head — how can it carry all he knows? His brow is singular in shape, but not particularly large or prominent: where has nature expressed his majestic intellect? His eyes — they sparkle not, they shine not, they are lustreless: nay, they have a slight habit — the one of occasionally looking in a different direction from the other; there is nothing else particular about them; there is not even the glare which lights up sometimes dull eyes into eloquence; and yet, even at first, the *tout ensemble* strikes you as that of no common man, and you say, ere he has opened his lips, "He is either mad or inspired."

But sit and listen to him; hear his small, thin, yet piercing voice, winding out so distinctly his subtleties of thought and feeling; his long and strange sentences, evolving like a piece of complicated music, and including everything in their comprehensive sweep; his interminable digressions, striking off at every possible angle from the main stream of his discourse, and ever returning to it again; his quotations from favourite authors, so perpetual and so appropriate; his recitation of passages from the poets in a tone of tremulous earnestness; his vast stores of learning, peeping out every now and then through the loopholes of his small and searching talk; his occasional bursts of enthusiasm; his rich collection of anecdote; his uniform urbanity and willingness to allow you your full share in the conversation. Witness all this for an hour together, and you will say at the close, "This is the best living image of Burke and Coleridge — this is an extraordinary man." You sit and listen, and, as the evening steals on, his sentences get longer and longer, and yet your inclination to weary gets less and less. Your attention is fixed by hooks of steel, and at three in the morning you rise unsatiated. You leave him on his way to his desk, to study till peep of dawn; and, going home, your dreams are haunted by the curious man, and you seem still to hear him, with his deep, low voice, out-Kanting Kant, or out-mystifying Coleridge, or demolishing some ricketty literary reputation, or quoting, in his deep and quiet under-tone, some of the burning words of Shelley or Wordsworth. — *First and Second Galleries of Literary Portraits* (1854).

Charles MacFarlane

I forget, at the moment, the quantity [of laudanum] to which De Quincey carried his daily dose — I know it was very high; but I also believe that, for the sake of a startling effect, he made it much more than it really was. He could do nothing without this stimulant. When invited out, he carried his laudanum bottle with him to dinner-table and supper-table. This used greatly to annoy John Wilson, his frequent host, and at that time the most jovial of poets and of men.

"Hang you, De Quincey!" he would say. "Can't you take your whiskey toddy like a Christian man, and leave your d——d opium slops to infidel Turks, Persians, and Chinamen?" — *Reminiscences of a Literary Life* (1917).

Henry Crabb Robinson

JUNE 17th [1812] ... At four o'clock dined in the hall with De Quincey, who was very civil to me, and invited me cordially to visit his cottage in Cumberland. De Quincey is, like myself, an enthusiast for Wordsworth; his person is small, his complexion fair, and his air and manner those of a sickly, enfeebled man. From which circumstances his sensibility, which I have no doubt is genuine, is in danger of being mistaken for a pulling and womanly weakness. At least, coarser and more robustly healthful persons will think so. His conversation is sensible, and I *suppose* him to be a man of information on general subjects....

FEB. 12th [1814] ... De Quincey came by appointment, and we went together to Lamb, with whom we drank tea and stayed till eleven. This was contrary to my intention, and the evening was rather dull. De Quincey is a dry, solemn man, whose conversation does not flow readily, though he speaks well enough and like a sensible man. He is too much a disciple and admirer to have anything of his own. But he is still an amiable man, and, though it is an effort to keep up a conversation with him on general subjects, he is an interesting companion....

MAY 23rd [1814] ... As I was about to leave chambers De Quincey called on me and stayed several hours.... De Quincey is a tedious proser though a sensible man. He wearies by the uniformity of his homilies, and he has no measure in his talk. His admiration of Wordsworth is not the only interesting trait in his character, I believe, had I knowledge enough of him to take an interest in his character.

OCT. 31st [1821] ... I then called on De Quincey — a visit of duty. De Quincey is a tiresome man, though certainly of great talent; he is necessitous and will be in great distress soon, for his talents are not marketable. He is in ill-health, is querulous, very strongly impressed with his own excellence, and prone to despise others. But I cannot shun him, situated as he is — he is in search of and has a prospect of literary employ.... — *The Diary of Henry Crabb Robinson.*

CHARLES DICKENS

Richard Henry Dana

Disappointed in Dickens's appearance. (We have heard him called 'the handsomest man in London, etc.') He is of middle height (under if anything) with a large expressive eye, regular nose, matted, curling, wet-looking black hair, a dissipated looking mouth with a vulgar draw to it, a muddy, olive complexion, stubby fingers and a hand by no means patrician. A hearty off hand manner, far from well bred and a rapid, dashing way of talking. He looks wide awake, 'up to everything,' full of cleverness, with quick feelings and great ardor. You admire him and there is a fascination about him which keeps your eye on him, yet you cannot get over the impression that he is a low bred man.

Tom Appleton says, 'Take the genius out of his face and there are a thousand London shop keepers about the theatres and eating houses who look exactly like him.' He has what I suppose to be the true Cockney cut. — From Dana's diary, 26 January 1842.

Frederick Locker-Lampson

Dickens had much social tact; he was genial and manly; he had a strong personality; he could say "No," but I should think he had infinitely greater pleasure in saying "Yes." He was a jovial fellow, with a most elastic spirit, and apparently an exhaustless vitality. I am told he was an adept at brewing stiff punch, but sparing in his own libations. He favoured convivial philanthropy — indeed, he was the first person to preach the deep spiritual significance of the Christmas goose. He boiled the hot water and potatoes at picnics, was adroit at conjuring and otherwise amusing the young people. Indeed, Dickens entered heart and soul into everything he did; he was a keen man of business, active and practical. He told me that genuine appreciation of his works was as fresh and precious to him then (1869) as it had been thirty years before; indeed, he was still so sensitive to neglect that, in a railway carriage, if his opposite neighbour were reading one of his novels, he did not dare to watch him, lest he should see the book thrown aside with indifference.

His appearance was attractive; he was not conventionally gentlemanlike-looking — I should have been disappointed if he had been so: he was something better. I shall not quickly forget him at Macaulay's funeral, as he walked among the subdued-looking clericals and staid men of mark; there was a stride in his gait and a roll; he had a seafaring complexion and air, and a huge white tie.

Dickens was fond of dress; he owned that he had the primeval savage's love for bright positive colours. I consoled him with the assurance that it was the poet side of his nature that was so gratified.

Dickens had, as indeed I have already remarked, a wonderfully animated countenance. There was an eager look in his bright eyes, and his manners were as free from *mauvaise honte* as from unseasonable familiarity. He told stories with real dramatic effect; he gave one at my table, as related by [Samuel] Rogers (who made story-telling a fine art), of the English and French duellists who agreed to fight with pistols, the candles being extinguished, in a small room. The brave but humane Englishman, unwilling to shed blood, gropes his way to the fire-place, and discharges his weapon up the chimney; when, lo and behold! whom should he bring down but the dastardly Frenchman, who had crept thither for safety! Dickens said that Rogers's postscript was not the worst part of the story — "When I tell that in Paris, I always put the Englishman up the chimney!" Dickens mimicked Rogers's calm, low-pitched, drawling voice and dry biting manner very comically. — *My Confidences* (1896).

John Lothrop Motley

The only very distinguished literary person that I have seen of late for the first time is Dickens. I met him last week at a dinner at John Forster's. I had never even seen him before, for he never goes now into fashionable company. He looks about the age of Longfellow. His hair is not much grizzled and is thick, although the crown of his head is getting bald. His features are good, the nose rather high, the eyes largish, greyish and very expressive. He wears a moustache and beard, and dresses at dinner in exactly the same uniform which every man in London or the civilised world is bound to wear, as much as the inmates of a penitentiary are restricted to theirs. I mention this because I had heard that he was odd and extravagant in his costume. I liked him exceedingly. We sat next each other at table, and I found him genial, sympathetic, agreeable, unaffected, with plenty of light easy talk and touch-and-go fun without any effort or humbug of any kind. He spoke with great interest of many of his Boston friends, particularly of Longfellow, Wendell Holmes, Felton, Sumner, and Tom Appleton. — From a letter to his mother, 15 March 1861.

Henry Crabb Robinson

Dickens is a fine writer and excellent man. It is to be lamented that he is ambitious of living genteely and giving dinners to the rich. With an income of three or four thousand a year, and sometimes much more, he may at length, it is to be feared, leave his children to be maintained by the public. He is delicate in his appearance and some slight tendency to be a fop. He is liberal in his opinions, charitable, and a good chairman at public dinners. — *Diary* (1967).

Mark Twain

The [Langdon] family went to the Dickens reading and I accompanied them.... Mr. Dickens read scenes from his printed books. From my distance he was a small and slender figure, rather fancifully dressed, and striking and picturesque in appearance. He wore a black velvet coat with a large and glaring red flower in the buttonhole. He stood under a red upholstered shed behind whose slant was a row of strong lights — just such an arrangement as artists use to concentrate a strong light upon a great picture. Dickens's audience sat in a pleasant twilight, while he performed in the powerful light cast upon him from the concealed lamps. He read with great force and animation, in the lively passages, and with stirring effect. It will be understood that he did not merely read but also acted. His reading of the storm scene in which Steerforth lost his life was so full of energetic action that his house was carried off its feet, so to speak. — *The Autobiography of Mark Twain*, ed. Charles Neider (1959).

William Wordsworth

[Having met Dickens on one occasion in 1843, Wordsworth was asked how he had liked the famous novelist.] Why, I am not much given to turn critic on people I meet; but, as you ask me, I will candidly avow that I thought him a very talkative, vulgar young person, — but I dare say he may be very clever. Mind, I don't want to say a word against him, for I have never read a line he has written. — *Life of Dickens* by R. Shelton Mackenzie (1870).

JOHN DONNE

Izaak Walton

He was of Stature moderately tall, of a strait and equally-proportioned body, to which all his words and actions gave an unexpressible addition of Comeliness.

The melancholy and pleasant humor, were in him so contempered, that each gave advantage to the other, and made his Company one of the delights of Mankind....

His aspect was chearful, and such, as gave a silent testimony of a clear knowing soul, and of a Conscience at peace with it self.

His melting eye, shewed that he had a soft heart, full of noble compassion; of too brave a soul to offer injuries, and too much a Christian not to pardon them in others. — *Lives* (1675).

/

THEODORE DREISER

Bennett Cerf

We went to the baseball game, Dreiser and I. He was a dour, sulky, unpleasant man. He got bored about the fifth or sixth inning and said, "Come on, let's get out of here," so I had to leave. I remember it was a close game and I was outraged, but I had to go with him....

The year before I arrived, Liveright had published Theodore Dreiser's *A Book About Myself*, with no success, but Dreiser was hard at work on *An American Tragedy*, which was published shortly after I left. He was one of the most churlish, disagreeable men I ever met in my life, always thinking that everybody was cheating him. He'd come in about every three months to examine the ledger to see whether his royalty statements were correct.

We soon discovered Dreiser didn't know what he was doing. He'd make a great pretense of checking, but he was just trying to scare us into being honest. He'd make little marks against all the items he'd examined and then he'd go out for lunch and we'd rub all the marks off, and when he came back he wouldn't ever notice....

In 1925, just after I left, Liveright had published Dreiser's *An American Tragedy*. It was a big hit and almost immediately became a best seller. [Horace] Liveright by this time was casting an envious eye on Hollywood, which was becoming bigger and bigger, and he was made to order for it. He decided he was going out there to look over the terrain. Before he left he said to Dreiser, "I think I can sell *American Tragedy* while I'm there." Dreiser said it was ridiculous to think that anyone could sell Hollywood a story about a young man who gets an office girl pregnant and then meets a society girl and drowns the office girl.

So Horace said, "I'll make a deal with you, Dreiser. The first fifty thousand dollars I get for your book in Hollywood, you get complete. After that, we go fifty-fifty."

Dreiser said, "You won't get a dollar for it. Nobody will make that picture, Horace."

Horace said, "Watch me!"

So they shook hands. In those days fifty thousand dollars was a lot of money for movie rights. But Horace sold *American Tragedy* for eighty-five thousand dollars! When he came back, of course, Horace had to boast about his triumph, and I was a very good person to tell, because I was always appreciative. So he called me up and said, "What do you think I got for *American Tragedy*? Eighty-five thousand dollars! Wait till I tell Dreiser!"

I said, "Gee, I'd like to be there."

He said, "I'm taking him to lunch next Thursday at the Ritz, and I'd like you to come and watch Dreiser when I tell him."

So the three of us went to the Ritz....

Finally after we had finished our meal, before the coffee came, Horace said, "Dreiser, I sold *American Tragedy*."

Dreiser said, "Oh, come on."

Horace said, "I did."

Finally Dreiser said, "Well, what did you get for it?"

Horace said, "Eighty-five thousand dollars."

It took a few moments for this to sink in, and then Dreiser let out a cry of triumph. He exulted, "What I'm going to do with that money!" He took a pencil out of his pocket and began writing on the tablecloth. He said, "I'm going to pay off the mortgage on my place up in Croton and I'm going to get an automobile," and so on.

Horace listened for a minute, then reminded Dreiser, "You know, you're not getting the whole eighty-five thousand. Remember our deal? You get fifty and then we split the thirty-five. You're going to get sixty-seven thousand, five hundred."

Dreiser put down his pencil and looked at Liveright. He said, "Do you mean to tell me you're going to take seventeen thousand, five hundred dollars of *my* money?"

Horace said, "Dreiser, that was the deal we made. You didn't think I'd sell your book at all."

Just at this moment the waiter brought the coffee in. Suddenly Dreiser seized his cup and threw the steaming coffee in Liveright's face. It was shocking. Horace jumped up, coffee streaming down his shirt front. Luckily it didn't hit him in the eyes. Dreiser got up from the table without a word and marched out of the restaurant. Horace, always the showman, always gallant, stood there mopping himself up, and retained enough of his equilibrium to say, "Bennett, let this be a lesson to you. Every author is a son of a bitch." — *At Random: The Reminiscences of Bennett Cerf* (1977).

JOHN DRYDEN

William Congreve

He was of a Nature exceedingly Humane and Compassionate; easily forgiving Injuries, and capable of a prompt and sincere Reconciliation with them who had offended him.

Such a Temperament is the only solid Foundation of all moral Virtues, and sociable Endowments. His Friendship, where he profess'd it, went much beyond his Professions; and I have been told of strong and generous Instances of it by the Persons themselves who received them: Tho' his Hereditary Income was little more than a bare Competency.

As his Reading had been very extensive, so was he very happy in a Memory tenacious of everything that he had read. He was not more possess'd of Knowledge, than he was Communicative of it. But then his Communication of it was by no means pedantick, or impos'd upon the Conversation; but just such, and went so far as by the natural Turns of the Discourse in which he was engag'd it was necessarily promoted or required. He was extream ready and gentle in his Correction of the Errors of any Writer, who thought fit to consult him; and full as ready and patient to admit of the Reprehension of others, in respect of his own Oversight or Mistakes. He was of very easie, I may say of very pleasing Access: But something slow, and as it were diffident in his Advances to others. He had something in his Nature that abhorr'd Intrusion into any Society whatsoever. Indeed it is to be regretted, that he was rather blameable in the other Extreme: For, by that means, he was Personally less known, and, consequently his Character might become liable both to Misapprehensions and Misrepresentations. To the best of my Knowledge and Observation, he was, of all the Men that I ever knew, one of the most Modest, and the most Easily to be discountenanced in his Approaches, either to his Superiors or his Equals. — From the dedication to the Duke of Newcastle prefixed to Dryden's collected plays (1717).

Alexander Pope

I saw Mr. Dryden when I was about twelve years old. This bust [by Peter Scheemaker] is like him. I remember his face, for I looked upon him with the greatest veneration even then, and observed him very particularly.

Dryden lived in Gerrard Street, and used most commonly to write in the ground-room next the street.

Dryden was not a very genteel man. He was intimate with none but poetical men. He was said to be a very good man by all that knew him. He was as plump as Mr. Pitt, of a fresh colour, and a down look — and not very conversible. — Spence's *Observations, Anecdotes, and Characters of Books and Men* (1966).

Himself

I know I am not fitted by nature to write comedy: I want that gaiety of humour which is required to it. My conversation is slow and dull; my humour saturnine and reserved; in short, I am none of those who endeavour to break jests in company, or make reparties. — "Defence of an Essay of Dramatic Poesy."

GEORGE ELIOT

Frederick Locker-Lampson

Nature had disguised George Eliot's apparently stoical, yet really vehement and sensitive, spirit, and her soaring genius, in a homely and insignificant form. Her countenance was equine — she was rather like a horse; and her head had been intended for a much longer body — she was not a tall woman. She wore her hair in not pleasing, out-of-fashion loops, coming down on either side of her face, so hiding her ears; and her garments concealed her outline — they gave her a waist like a milestone. You will see her at her very best in the portrait by Sir Frederic Burton. To my mind George Eliot was a plain woman.

She had a measured way of conversing; restrained, but impressive. When I happened to call she was nearly always seated in the chimney corner on a low chair, and she bent forward when she spoke. As she often discussed abstract subjects, she might have been thought pedantic, especially as her language was sprinkled with a scientific terminology; but I do not think she was a bit of a pedant. Then, though she had a very gentle voice and manner, there was, every now and then, just a suspicion of meek satire in her talk.

Her sentences unwound themselves very neatly and completely, leaving the impression of past reflection and present readiness; she spoke exceedingly well, but not with all the simplicity and *verve*, the happy *abandon* of certain practised women of the world; however, it was in a way that was far more interesting. I have been told she was most agreeable *en tête-à-tête*; that when surrounded by admirers she was apt to become oratorical — a different woman. She did not strike me as witty or markedly humorous; she was too much in earnest: she spoke as if with a sense of responsibility, and one cannot be exactly captivating when one is doing that. Madame de Sable might have said of her, 'elle s'écouta en parlant.' She was a good listener.

I ought to say that during all the time I knew her, George Eliot appeared to be suffering from feeble health, and without doubt this affected her whole bearing. — *My Confidences* (1896).

T.S. ELIOT

Virginia Woolf

I was interrupted somewhere on this page by the arrival of Mr Eliot. Mr Eliot is well expressed by his name — a polished, cultivated, elaborate young American, talking so slow, that each word seems to have special finish allotted it. But beneath the surface, it is fairly evident that he is very intellectual, intolerant, with strong views of his own, & a poetic creed. I'm sorry to say that this sets up Ezra Pound & Wyndham Lewis as great poets, or in the current phrase "very interesting" writers. He admires Mr Joyce immensely. He produced 3 or 4 poems for us to look at — the fruit of two years, since he works all day in a Bank, & in his reasonable way thinks regular work good for people of nervous constitutions. I became more or less conscious of a very intricate & highly organised framework of poetic belief; owing to his caution, & his excessive care in the use of language we did not discover much about it. I think he believes in "living phrases" & their difference from dead ones; in writing with extreme care, in observing all syntax & grammar; & so making this new poetry flower on the stem of the oldest — *Diary*, 15 November 1918.

RALPH WALDO EMERSON

Arthur Hugh Clough

He came to Oxford just at the end of Lent term, and stayed three days. Everybody liked him, and as the orthodox mostly had never heard of him, they did not suspect him; he is the quietest, plainest, unobtrusivest man possible; will talk, but will rarely *discourse* to more than a single person, and wholly declines 'roaring'. He is very Yankee to look at, lank and sallow, and not quite without the twang; but his looks and voice are pleasing nevertheless, and give you the impression of perfect intellectual cultivation, as completely as would any great scientific man in England — Faraday or Owen for instance, more in their way perhaps than in that of Wordsworth or Carlyle. I have been with him a great deal; for he came over to Paris and was there a month, during which we dined together daily; and since that I have seen him often in London, and finally here. One thing that struck everybody is that he is much less Emersonian than his Essays. There is no dogmatism or arbitrariness or positiveness about him. — From a letter to Thomas Arnold, 16 July 1848.

William Dean Howells

I think it was Emerson himself who opened his door to me, for I have a vision of the fine old man standing tall on his threshold, with the card [from Hawthorne] in his hand, and looking from it to me with a vague serenity, while I waited a moment on the door-step below him. He must then have been about sixty, but I remember nothing of age in his aspect, though I have called him an old man. His hair, I am sure, was still entirely dark, and his face had a kind of marble youthfulness, chiselled to a delicate intelligence by the highest and noblest thinking that any man has done. There was a strange charm in Emerson's eyes, which I felt then and always, something like that I saw in Lincoln's, but shyer, but sweeter and less sad. His smile was the very sweetest I have ever beheld, and the contour of the mask and the line of the profile were in keeping with this incomparable sweetness of the mouth, at once grave and quaint, though quaint is not quite the word for it either, but subtly, not unkindly arch, which again is not the word....

I do not know in just what sort he made me welcome, but I am aware of sitting with him in his study or library, and of his presently speaking of Hawthorne, whom I probably celebrated as I best could, and whom he praised for his personal excellence, and for his fine qualities as a neighbor. "But his last book," he added, reflectively, "is a mere mush," and I perceived that this great man was no better equipped to judge an artistic fiction than the groundlings who were then crying out upon the indefinite close of the *Marble Faun*....

Emerson had, in fact, a defective sense as to specific pieces of literature; he praised extravagantly, and in the wrong place, especially among the new things, and he failed to see the worth of much that was fine and precious beside the line of his fancy....

He questioned me about what I had seen of Concord, and whom besides Hawthorne I had met, and when I told him only Thoreau, he asked me if I knew the poems of Mr. William Henry Channing. I have known them since, and felt their quality, which I have gladly owned a genuine and original poetry; but I answered then truly that I knew them only from Poe's criticisms: cruel and spiteful things which I should be ashamed of enjoying as I once did.

"Whose criticisms?" asked Emerson.

"Poe's," I said again.

"Oh," he cried out, after a moment, as if he had returned from a far search for my meaning, "*you mean the jingle-man!*"

I do not know why this should have put me to such confusion, but if I had written the criticisms myself I do not think I could have been more abashed. Perhaps I felt an edge of reproof, of admonition, in a characterization of Poe which the world will hardly agree with; though I do not agree with the world about him, myself, in its admiration. — *Literary Friends and Acquaintance* (1900).

Frederick Lehmann

Robert Chambers had given me a letter for Ralph Waldo Emerson, which made him ask me to spend a day with him at Concord. He seemed to me the beau ideal of a contented and virtuous sage. Placidity and serenity were to my mind the chief characteristics of his face and manner. His conversation flowed without the slightest effort, copiously and harmoniously. He took me all over Concord, pointing out all the lions of the war of independence. He seemed proud of the wealth of his New England orchard, the apple trees having done specially well that year. All his surroundings, not only his family but his house and furniture seemed to fit Emerson, and left upon me the very pleasant impression of my having come in contact with a master mind living in refined frugality. Among others, Emerson had asked Hawthorne to meet me. As usual, he hardly ever spoke, and I only remember him breaking his apparent vow of silence when appealed to by a Mr Bradford, who, after a fiery denunciation of the South and having come to the end of his peroration, passionately turned to his silent listener with the words: 'Don't you agree with me?' Then Hawthorne astonished him by uttering the monosyllable 'No', after which he again relapsed into silence.

Emerson told me that Hawthorne's increased taciturnity caused much anxiety to his family. My recollection of him is of one gloomy and much troubled, while I shall always think of Emerson as pellucid and at peace. – Quoted by John Lehmann in *Ancestors and Friends* (1962).

Herman Melville

I have heard Emerson since I have been here [in Boston]. Say what they will, he's a great man....

Nay, I do not oscillate in Emerson's rainbow, but prefer rather to hang myself in mine own halter than swing in any other man's swing. Yet I think Emerson is more than a brilliant fellow. Be his stuff begged, borrowed, or stolen, or of his own domestic manufacture he is an uncommon man. Swear he is a humbug – then is he no common humbug. Lay it down that had not Sir Thomas Browne lived, Emerson would not have mystified.... No one is his own sire. – I was very agreeably disappointed in Mr Emerson. I had heard of him as full of transcendentalisms, myths & oracular gibberish; I had only glanced at a book of his once in Putnam's store – that was all I knew of him, till I heard him lecture. – To my surprise, I found him quite intelligible, tho' to say truth, they told me that that night he was unusually plain. – Now, there is a something about every man elevated above mediocrity, which is, for the most part, instinctuly perceptible. This I see in Mr Emerson. And, frankly, for the sake of the argument, let us call him a fool; – then had I rather be a fool than a wise man. – I love all men who *dive*. Any fish can swim near the surface, but it takes a great whale to go down stairs five miles or more; & if he dont attain the bottom, why, all the lead in Galena [Illinois – famous for its lead mines] can't fashion the plumet that will. I'm not talking of Mr Emerson now – but of the whole corps of thought-divers, that have been diving & coming up again with bloodshot eyes since the world began.

I could readily see in Emerson, notwithstanding his merit, a gaping flaw. It was, the insinuation, that had he lived in those days when the world was made, he might have offered some valuable suggestions. These men are all cracked right across the brow. And never will the pullers-down be able to cope with the builders-up....

I was going to say something more – It was this. – You complain that Emerson tho' a denizen of the land of gingerbread, is above munching a plain cake in company of jolly fellows, & swiging off his ale like you & me. Ah, my dear sir, that's his misfortune, not his fault. His belly, sir, is in his chest, & his brains descend down into his neck, & offer an obstacle to a draught of ale or a mouthful of cake. — From two letters to Evert A. Duyckinck, 24 February and 3 March 1849.

JOHN EVELYN

Samuel Pepys

By water to Deptford, and there made a visit to Mr. Evelings, who, among other things, showed me most excellent painting in little — in distemper, Indian Incke — water colours — graveing; and above all, the whole secret of Mezzo Tinto and the manner of it, which is very pretty, and good things done with it. He read to me very much also of his discourse he hath been many years and now is about, about Guardenage; which will be a most noble and pleasant piece. He read me part of a play or two of his making, very good, but not as he conceits them, I think, to be. He showed me his *Hortus hyemalis*; leaves laid up in a book of several plants, kept dry, which preserve Colour however, and look very finely, better than any herball. In fine, a most excellent person he is, and must be allowed a little for a little conceitedness; but he may well be so, being a man so much above others. He read me, though with too much gusto, some little poems of his own, that were not transcendent, yet one or two very pretty Epigrams: among others, of a lady looking in at a grate and being pecked at by an Eagle that was there. — *Diary*, 5 November 1665.

HENRY FIELDING

Samuel Johnson and James Boswell

Fielding being mentioned, Johnson exclaimed, 'he was a blockhead;' and upon my expressing my astonishment at so strange an assertion, he said, 'What I mean by his being a blockhead is that he was a barren rascal.' BOSWELL. 'Will you not allow, Sir, that he draws very natural pictures of human life?' JOHNSON. 'Why, Sir, it is of very low life. [Samuel] Richardson used to say, that had he not known who Fielding was, he should have believed he was an ostler. Sir, there is more knowledge of the heart in one letter of Richardson's, than in all "Tom Jones". I, indeed, never read "Joseph Andrews" '. ERSKINE. 'Surely, Sir, Richardson is very tedious.' JOHNSON. 'Why, Sir, if you were to read Richardson for the story, your impatience would be so much fretted that you would hang yourself. But you must read him for the sentiment, and consider the story as only giving occasion to the sentiment.' — I have already given my opinion of Fielding; but I cannot refrain from repeating here my wonder at Johnson's excessive and unaccountable depreciation of one of the best writers that England has produced. — Boswell's *Life of Samuel Johnson* (1791).

Dr. Charles Burney

Johnson's severity against Fielding did not arise from any viciousness in his style, but from his loose life, and the profligacy of almost all his male characters. Who would venture to read one of his novels aloud to modest women? His novels are *male* amusements, and very amusing they certainly are. — Fielding's conversation was coarse, and so tinctured with the rank weeds of *the Garden*, that it would now be thought only fit for a brothel. — Boswell's *Life of Samuel Johnson* (1791).

Lady Mary Wortley Montagu

I am sorry for H. Fielding's death, not only as I shall read no more of his writings, but I believe he lost more than others, as no man enjoyed life more than he did, though few had less reason to do so, the highest of his preferment being raking in the lowest sinks of vice and misery. I should think it a nobler and less nauseous employment to be one of the staff-officers that conduct nocturnal weddings. His happy constitution (even when he had, with great pains, half demolished it) made him forget everything when he was before a venison pasty, or over a flask of champagne; and I am persuaded he has known more happy moments than any prince upon earth. His natural spirits gave him rapture with his cook-maid, and cheerfulness when he was fluxing in a garret. There was a great similitude between his character and that of Sir Richard Steele. He had the advantage both in learning and, in my opinion, genius: They both agreed in wanting money in spite of all their friends, and would have wanted it, if their hereditary lands had been as extensive as their imagination; yet each of them [was] so formed for happiness, it is pity he was not immortal. — From a letter to the Countess of Bute, 22 September 1755.

F. SCOTT FITZGERALD

Herbert Gorman

One morning near noon from my second-floor window I heard the shrill honking of a motor-horn and a few minutes later a porter knocked to inform me that friends of mine waited below. I went down to the side-entrance of the hotel and there was Scott Fitzgerald in a small open French car (a Citroen, I believe) with Mrs. Dorothy Parker seated beside him. He jumped over the side of his *voiture* and greeted me with enthusiasm.

At this time Scott was about thirty years old but he seemed much younger, in actions as well as appearance. He was dressed in wrinkled white trousers, a white sports-shirt open at the neck and a pair of soiled white sneakers; his face, neck and arms were rather ruddy than tanned and his hair appeared bleached by the bright sun of the Esterel. There was a Golden Boy aspect about him. He was extremely active, jumping about constantly and making elaborate gestures....

The second encounter I desire to recall has been fragmentarily adumbrated (at second-hand through Edmund Wilson) in Arthur Mizener's *The Far Side of Paradise*. I believe this meeting took place in 1928, although it may have been almost a year later. Memory sometimes shuffles the years when the birth-sign-posts exceed sixty. Anyway, the meeting place was Adrienne Monnier's apartment on the rue de l'Odéon on the Left Bank in Paris and the occasion was a dinner in honor of Miss Sylvia Beach, the original publisher of James Joyce's *Ulysses*. Joyce and I had walked some distance from the *bistro* where we indulged often in our two Pernods before dining and we were somewhat tardy when we arrived at Mademoiselle Monnier's apartment. Over the charming period furniture, paintings, marvellous silkwork and bibelots a blur of voices greeted us and the first persons we saw were Zelda and Scott Fitzgerald. Joyce stiffened slightly as though he were about to run the gauntlet. We were greeted by Adrienne and Sylvia, waved to by Nora Joyce who had arrived (as she generally did) with my wife before us and immediately approached by Scott. He rushed forward, sank upon one knee and kissed Joyce's hand. To me he gave a bright and happy greeting as though we had parted but yesterday. During the dinner (a very fine one, by the way) he called several times across the table to Joyce such remarks as "How does it feel to be a great genius, Sir?" and "I am so excited at seeing you, Sir, that I could weep." ...

As Nora, my wife, Joyce and I drove away in a squeaking taxi he explained what had made him stiffen slightly at the unexpected sight of Scott. It was not dislike. It was something else altogether. It was fear. It appeared that sometime before Scott had called upon Joyce while he was living on the sixth floor of the apartment-house at 2, Square Robiac, just off the long winding rue de Grenelle. Scott may have been drinking but I think his deportment, as Joyce described it, was not particularly due to any artificial exhilaration. They were a sincere part of the man himself and betrayed his indubitable worship of actual greatness in letters. He had kissed Joyce's hand then, enlarged upon Nora Joyce's beauty, and, finally, darted through an open window to the stone balcony outside, jumped up on the eighteen-inch-wide parapet and threatened to fling himself to the cobbled thoroughfare below unless Nora declared that she loved him, too. Nora declared hastily that she did and Joyce, always a fearful man where heights were concerned, recovered from a near-fainting lapse. "I think he must be mad," added Joyce to me after relating the tale. "He'll do himself some injury some day."—"Glimpses of F. Scott Fitzgerald," *Fitzgerald/Hemingway Annual 1973*, ed. Matthew J. Bruccoli.

Ernest Hemingway

When I knew Scott in Paris and on the Riviera he had never slept with another woman than Zelda. This is the straight gen.

She was unfaithful to him first with a young French naval flying officer.

That was the first thing that busted Scott up. Then she was crazy (Scyzophrenic; you look up the spelling. I've mis-spelled and it is too far to the dictionary in Mary's room) for a long time and nobody knew it. She was insanely jealous of Scott's work and any time he would work hard she would bust it up. This wasn't difficult as he was a much more than potential rummy. What saved him was that he couldnt drink. He had no tolerance for alcohol and would pass out cold at the number of drinks that would just make you feel good. He enjoyed passing out cold too because it made him the center of attention. Without meaning to be he was a terrific exhibitionist and as time went on he became a nastier and nastier drunk....

Scott after he got to be a really nasty drunk used to be very bad. I would go out to dinner with him and he would insult people and I would have to square it to keep him from being beaten up. He could never fight a lick on the best day he ever lived and he got so he liked to hit people and I would have to take over. This is one small sample of how it was in Paris. I lived over a saw-mill on the second floor of a Pavillion. My landlord lived on the first floor. Coming up to see us with young Scotty [Fitzgerald's daughter] he had her make pe-pee on the floor at the foot of the stairs just outside the landlord's door. It ran in under the door and the landlord came out and very nicely told Scott there was a toilet under the stairs. He thought the child had been caught short.

"I know there is you son of a bitch," Scott said. "And I'll take you and shove your head in it."

There were hundreds and hundreds like that. But when, after one awful night when I had to give a large sum to the doorman at the Plaza to square something really awful Scott had done, I told him I couldn't ever go out and eat with him any more unless he would promise not to be horrible to people, or make an effort not to be anyway, he was able to write that thing about how he spoke with the authority of failure and I with the authority of etc. and so we would never be able to sit at table together again. A fairly smug version.

Zelda ruined him all right because every time he would get straightened out she would get him on the booze. But Harvey he used to seem to love to be humiliated and, of course, to humiliate whoever he was with. I've seen him do things you could hardly forgive a legitimate crazy for doing. At the start he used to be terribly contrite afterwards. Finally he didn't remember. He was always generous and he could be so damned nice sober....

When I first knew him he was very good looking in a too pretty way and every time he took a drink his face would change a little and after four drinks the skin would be drawn and it would look like a death's head. — From a letter to Harvey Breit, 18 August 1954.

Gertrude Stein

Taste has nothing to do with sentences, contended Gertrude Stein. She also added that Fitzgerald was the only one of the younger writers who wrote naturally in sentences.

Gertrude Stein and Fitzgerald are very peculiar in their relation to each other. Gertrude Stein had been very much impressed by This

Side of Paradise. She read it when it came out and before she knew any of the young american writers. She said of it that it was this book that really created for the public the new generation. She has never changed her opinion about this. She thinks this equally true of *The Great Gatsby*. She thinks Fitzgerald will be read when many of his well known contemporaries are forgotten. Fitzgerald always says that he thinks Gertrude Stein says these things just to annoy him by making him think that she means them, and he adds in his favourite way, and her doing it is the cruellest thing I ever heard. They always however have a very good time when they meet. — *The Autobiography of Alice B. Toklas* (1933).

BENJAMIN FRANKLIN

James Boswell

Sir John [Pringle], though a most worthy man, has a peculiar sour manner. Franklin again is all jollity and pleasantry. I said to myself: Here is a prime contrast: acid and alkali. — *Journal*, 15 September 1769.

Manasseh Cutler

Dr. Franklin lives in Market Street, between Second and Third Streets, but his house stands up a court-yard at some distance from the street. We found him in his Garden, sitting upon a grass plat under a very large Mulberry, with several other gentlemen and two or three ladies.... When I entered his house, I felt as if I was going to be introduced to the presence of an European Monarch. But how were my ideas changed, when I saw a short, fat, trunched old man, in a plain Quaker dress, bald pate, and short white locks, sitting without his hat under the tree, and, as Mr. [Eldridge] Gerry introduced me, rose from his chair, took me by the hand, expressed his joy to see me, welcomed me to the city, and begged me to seat myself close to him. His voice was low, but his countenance open, frank, and pleasing. He instantly reminded me of old Captain [John] Cummings, for he is nearly of his pitch, and no more of the air of superiority about him. I delivered him my letters. After he had read them, he took me again by the hand, and, with the usual compliments, introduced me to the other gentlemen of the company, who were most of them members of the Convention. Here we entered into a free conversation, and spent our time most agreeably until it was dark. The tea-table was spread under the tree, and Mrs. Bache, a very gross and rather homely lady, who is the only daughter of the Doctor and lives with him, served it out to the company. She had three of her children about her, over whom she seemed to have no kind of command, but who appeared to be excessively fond of their Grandpapa. — From Cutler's journal for July 1787, *Life of Rev. Manasseh Cutler*, ed. W.P. Cutler and J.P. Cutler (1888).

THOMAS FULLER

Anonymous

He was of Stature somewhat Tall, exceeding the meane, with a proportionable bigness to become it, but no way inclining to Corpulency: of an exact Straightnesse of the whole Body, and a perfect Symmetry in every part thereof. He was a Sanguine constitution, which beautified his Face with a pleasant Ruddinesse, but of so Grave and serious an aspect, that it Awed and Discountenanced the smiling Attracts of that complexion. His Head Adorned with a comely Light-Coloured Haire, which was so, by Nature exactly Curled (an Ornament enough of it self in this Age to Denominate a handsome person, and wherfore all Skill and Art is used) but not suffered to overgrow to any length unseeming his modesty and Profession.

His Gate and Walking was very upright and graceful, becoming his well shapen Bulke: aproaching something near to that we terme Majesticall; but that the Doctor was so well known to be void of any affectation or pride. Nay so Regardlesse was he of himselfe in his Garb and Rayment, in which no doubt his Vanity would have appeared, as well as in his stately pace: that it was with some trouble to himselfe, to be either Neat or Decent; it matter'd not for the outside, while he thought himself never too Curious and Nice in the Dresses of his mind. — *The Life of that Reverend Divine, and Learned Historian Dr. Thomas Fuller* (1661).

EDWARD GIBBON

Fanny Burney

Fat and ill-constructed, Mr. Gibbon has cheeks of such prodigious chubbiness that they envelop his nose so completely as to render it, in profile, absolutely invisible. His look and manner are placidly mild, but rather effeminate; his voice — for he was speaking to Sir Joshua [Reynolds] at a little distance — is gentle, but of studied precision of accent. Yet, with these Brodignatious cheeks, his neat little feet are of a miniature description; and with these, as soon as I turned round, he hastily described a quaint sort of circle, with small quick steps, and a dapper gait, as if to mark the alacrity of his approach, and then stopping short, when full face to me, he made so singularly profound a bow that — though hardly able to keep my gravity — I felt myself blush deeply at its undue, but palpably intended, obsequiousness.

This demonstration, however, over, his sense of politeness, or project of flattery, was satisfied; for he spoke not a word, though his gallant advance seemed to indicate a design of bestowing upon me a little rhetorical touch of a compliment. But, as all eyes in the room were suddenly cast upon us both, it is possible he partook a little himself of the embarrassment he could not but see that he occasioned; and was, therefore, unwilling, or unprepared, to hold forth so publicly upon — he scarcely, perhaps, knew what! for, unless my partial Sir Joshua should just then have poured it into his ears, how little is it likely Mr. Gibbon should have heard of Evelina! — From a letter to Samuel Crisp (n.d.); *Literature in Letters*, ed. James P. Holcombe (1866).

George Colman

The learned Gibbon was a curious counter-balance to the learned, (may I not say *less* learned?) [Samuel] Johnson. Their manners and taste, both in writing and conversation, were as different as their habiliments. On the day I first sat down with Johnson, in his rusty brown, and his black worsteds, Gibbon was placed opposite to me in a suit of flower'd velvet, with a bag and sword. Each had his measured phraseology; and Johnson's famous parallel, between Dryden and Pope, might be loosely parodied, in reference to himself and Gibbon. — Johnson's style was grand, and Gibbon's elegant; the stateliness of the former was sometimes pedantick, and the polish of the latter was occasionally finical. Johnson march'd to kettle-drums and trumpets; Gibbon moved to flutes and haut-boys; — Johnson hew'd passages through the Alps, while Gibbon levell'd walks through parks and gardens. — Maul'd as I had been by Johnson, Gibbon pour'd balm upon my bruises, by condescending, once or twice, in the course of the evening, to talk with me; — the great historian was light and playful, suiting his matter to the capacity of the boy; — but it was done *more suâ*; — still his mannerism prevail'd; — still he tapp'd his snuff-box, — still he smirk'd, and smiled; and rounded his periods with the same air of good-breeding, as if he were conversing with men. — His mouth, mellifluous as Plato's, was a round hole, nearly in the centre of his visage. — *Random Records* (1830).

Edmond Malone

Mr. Gibbon, the historian, is so exceedingly indolent that he never even pares his nails. His servant, while Gibbon is reading, takes up one of his hands, and when he has performed the operation lays it down, and then manages the other — the patient in the meanwhile scarcely knowing what is going on, and quietly pursuing his studies.

The picture of him painted by Sir J. Reynolds, and the prints made from it, are as like the original as it is possible to be. When he was introduced to a blind French lady, the servant happening to stretch out her mistress's hand to lay hold of the historian's cheek, she thought, upon feeling its rounded contour, that some trick was being played upon her with the *sitting* part of a child, and exclaimed, "Fidonc!"

Mr. Gibbon is very replete with anecdotes, and tells them with great happiness and fluency. — *Life of Edmond Malone* by Sir James Prior (1860).

Himself

This was my birthday, on which I entered into the 26th year of my age. This gave me occasion to look a little into myself, and consider impartially my good and bad qualities. It appeared to me, upon this enquiry, that my character was virtuous, incapable of a base action, and formed for generous ones; but that it was proud, violent, and disagreeable in society. These qualities I must endeavour to cultivate, extirpate, or restrain, according to their different tendency. Wit I have none. My imagination is rather strong than pleasing. My memory both capacious and retentive. The shining qualities of my understanding are extensiveness and penetration; but I want both quickness and exactness. As to my situation in life, tho' I may sometimes repine at it, it perhaps is the best adapted to my character. I can command all the conveniences of life, and I can command too that independence, (that first earthly blessing), which is hardly to be met with in a higher or lower fortune. — *Journal*, 8 May 1763.

OLIVER GOLDSMITH

Dr. James Beattie

A poor fretful creature, eaten up with affectation and envy. He was the only person I ever knew who acknowledged himself to be envious. In [Samuel] Johnson's presence he was quiet enough; but in his absence expressed great uneasiness in hearing him praised. He envied even the dead; he could not bear that Shakespeare should be so much admired as he is. There might, however, be something like magnanimity in envying Shakespeare and Dr. Johnson; as in Julius Caesar's weeping to think that at an age at which he had done so little, Alexander should have done so much. But surely Goldsmith had no occasion to envy me; which, however, he certainly did, for he owned it (though, when we met, he was always very civil); and I received undoubted information that he seldom missed an opportunity of speaking ill of me behind my back. Goldsmith's common conversation was a strange mixture of absurdity and silliness; of silliness so great, as to make me sometimes think that he affected it. Yet he was a genius of no mean rank: somebody, who knew him well, called him *an inspired idiot*. — From a letter to Sir William Forbes, 10 July 1788, *Life and Writings* (1824).

James Boswell

At this time [1763] I think he had published nothing with his name, though it was pretty generally known that one *Dr. Goldsmith* was the author of *An Enquiry into the present State of polite Learning in Europe*, and of *The Citizen of the World*, a series of letters supposed to be written from London by a chinese. No man had the art of displaying with more advantage as a writer, whatever literary acquisitions he made. '*Nihil quod tetigit non ornavit.*' His mind resembled a fertile, but thin soil. There was a quick, but not a strong vegetation, of whatever chanced to be thrown upon it. No deep root could be struck. The oak of the forest did not grow there; but the elegant shrubbery and the fragrant parterre appeared in gay succession. It has been generally circulated and believed that he was a mere fool in conversation; but, in truth, this has been greatly exaggerated. He had, no doubt, a more than common share of that hurry of ideas which we often find in his countrymen, and which sometimes produces a laughable confusion in expressing them. He was very much what the French call *un étourdi*, and from vanity and an eager desire of being conspicuous wherever he was, he frequently talked carelessly without knowledge of the subject, or even without thought. His person was short, his countenance coarse and vulgar, his deportment that of a scholar aukwardly affecting the easy gentleman. Those who were in any way distinguished, excited envy in him to so ridiculous an excess, that the instances of it are hardly credible. When accompanying two beautiful young ladies with their mother on a tour in France, he was seriously angry that more attention was paid to them than to him; and once at the exhibition of the *Fantoccini* in London, when those who sat next him observed with what dexterity a puppet was made to toss a pike, he could not bear that it should have such praise, and exclaimed with some warmth, 'Pshaw! I can do it better myself.' (He went home with Mr. Burke to supper; and broke his shin by attempting to exhibit to the company how much better he could jump over a stick than the puppets.)

He, I am afraid, had no settled system of any sort, so that his conduct must not be strictly scrutinised; but his affections were social and generous, and when he had money he gave it away very liberally. His desire of imaginary consequence predominated over his attention to truth. When he began to rise into notice, he said he had a brother who was Dean of Durham, a fiction so easily detected, that it is wonderful how he should have been so inconsiderate as to hazard it. He boasted to me at this time of the power of his pen in commanding money, which I believe was true in a certain degree, though in the instance he gave he was by no means correct. He told me that he had sold a novel for four hundred pounds. This was his *Vicar of Wakefield*. But Johnson informed me, that he had made the bargain for Goldsmith, and the price was sixty pounds. — Boswell's *Life of Samuel Johnson* (1791).

Goldsmith's incessant desire of being conspicuous in company, was the occasion of his sometimes appearing to such disadvantage as one should hardly have supposed possible in a man of his genius. When his literary reputation had risen deservedly high, and his society was much courted, he became very jealous of the extraordinary attention which was every where paid to Johnson. One evening, in a circle of wits, he found fault with me for talking of Johnson as entitled to the honour of unquestionable superiority. 'Sir, (said he,) you are for making a monarchy of what should be a republick.'

He was still more mortified, when talking in a company with fluent vivacity, and, as he flattered himself, to the admiration of all who were present; a German who sat next him, and perceived Johnson rolling himself, as if about to speak, suddenly stopped him, saying, 'Stay, stay, — Toctor Shonson is going to say something.' This was, no doubt, very provoking, especially to one so irritable as Goldsmith, who frequently mentioned it with strong expressions of indignation.

It may also be observed, that Goldsmith was sometimes content to be treated with an easy familiarity, but, upon occasions, would be consequential and important. An instance of this occurred in a small particular. Johnson had a way of contracting the names of his friends; as Beauclerk, Beau; Boswell, Bozzy; Langton, Lanky; Murphy, Mur; Sheridan, Sherry. I remember one day, when Tom Davies was telling that Dr. Johnson said, 'We are all in labour for a name to *Goldy's* play,' Goldsmith seemed displeased that such liberty should be taken with his name, and said, 'I have often desired him not to call me *Goldy*.'... Goldsmith, however, was often very fortunate in his witty contests, even when he entered the lists with Johnson himself. Sir Joshua Reynolds was in company with them one day, when Goldsmith said, that he thought he could write a good fable, mentioned the simplicity which that kind of composition requires, and observed, that in most fables the animals introduced seldom talk in character. 'For instance, (said he,) the fable of the little fishes, who saw birds fly over their heads, and envying them, petitioned Jupiter to be changed into birds. The skill (continued he,) consists in making them talk like little fishes.' While he indulged himself in this fanciful reverie, he observed Johnson shaking his sides, and laughing. Upon which he smartly proceeded, 'Why, Dr. Johnson, this is not so easy as you seem to think; for if you were to make little fishes talk, they would talk like WHALES.' — Boswell's *Life of Samuel Johnson* (1791).

Samuel Johnson

Goldsmith should not be for ever attempting to shine in conversation: he has not temper for it, he is so much mortified when he fails. Sir, a game of jokes is composed partly of skill, partly of chance. A man may be beat at times by one who has not the tenth part of his wit. Now Goldsmith's putting himself against another, is like a man laying a hundred to one who cannot spare the hundred. It is not worth a man's while. A man should not lay a hundred to one, unless he can easily spare it, though he has a hundred chances for him: he can get but a guinea, and he may lose a hundred. Goldsmith is in this state. When he contends, if he gets the better, it is a very little addition to a man of his literary reputation: if he does not get the better, he is miserably vexed.... The misfortune of Goldsmith in conversation is this: he goes on without knowing how he is to get off. His genius is great, but his knowledge is small. As they say of a generous man, it is a pity he is not rich, we may say of Goldsmith, it is a pity he is not knowing. He would not keep his knowledge to himself....

When people find a man of the most distinguished abilities as a writer, their inferiour while he is with them, it must be highly gratifying to them. What Goldsmith comically says of himself is very true, — he always gets the better when he argues alone; meaning, that he is master of a subject in his study, and can write well upon it; but when he comes into company, grows confused, and unable to talk.... Sir, he is so much afraid of being unnoticed, that he often talks merely lest you should forget that he is in the company....

Goldsmith had no settled notions upon any subject; so he talked always at random. It seemed to be his intention to blurt out whatever was in his mind, and see what would become of it. He was angry too, when catched in an absurdity; but it did not prevent him from falling into another the next minute. I remember [Anthony] Chamier, after talking with him for some time, said, 'Well, I do believe he wrote this poem himself [*The Traveller*]: and, let me tell you, that is believing a great deal.'... No man was more foolish when he had not a pen in his hand, or more wise when he had. — Boswell's *Life of Samuel Johnson* (1791).

THOMAS GRAY

Samuel Johnson

Sir, I do not think Gray a first-rate poet. He has not a bold imagination, nor much command of words. The obscurity in which he has involved himself will not persuade us that he is sublime. His Elegy in a Church-yard has a happy selection of images, but I don't like what are called his great things. His Ode which begins "Ruin seize thee, ruthless King,/ Confusion on thy banners wait!" has been celebrated for its abruptness, and plunging into the subject all at once. But such arts as these have no merit, unless when they are original. We admire them only once; and this abruptness has nothing new in it. We have had it often before....

Sir, he was dull in company, dull in his closet, dull everywhere. He was dull in a new way, and that made many people think him GREAT. He was a mechanical poet. — Boswell's *Life of Samuel Johnson* (1791).

Himself

As I am recommending myself to your love, methinks I ought to send you my picture (for I am no more what I was, some circumstances excepted, which I hope I need not particularize to you); you must add then, to your former ideas, two years of age, reasonable quantity of dulness, a great deal of silence, and something that rather resembles, than is, thinking; a confused notion of many strange and fine things that have swum before my eyes for some time, a want of love for general society, indeed an inability to it. On the good side you may add a sensibility for what others feel, and indulgence for their faults or weaknesses, a love of truth, and detestation of every thing else. Then you have to deduct a little impertinence, a little laughter, a great deal of pride, and some spirits. These are all the alterations I know of, you perhaps may find more. — From a letter to Richard West, 21 April 1741.

HORACE GREELEY

Mark Twain

I met Mr. Greeley only once and then by accident. It was in 1871, in the (old) *Tribune* office. I climbed one or two flights of stairs and went to the wrong room. I was seeking Colonel John Hay and I really knew my way and only lost it by my carelessness. I rapped lightly on the door, pushed it open and stepped in. There sat Mr. Greeley, busy writing, with his back to me. I think his coat was off. But I knew who it was, anyway. It was not a pleasant situation, for he had the reputation of being pretty plain with strangers who interrupted his train of thought. The interview was brief. Before I could pull myself together and back out, he whirled around and glared at me through his great spectacles and said:

"Well, what in hell do *you* want!"

"I was looking for a gentlem——"

"Don't keep them in stock — clear out!"

I could have made a very neat retort but didn't, for I was flurried and didn't think of it till I was downstairs. — *Mark Twain in Eruption*, ed. Bernard DeVoto (1940).

THOMAS HARDY

Hamlin Garland

He was in his late prime at this time [1899] and made a powerful impression on me. He was small and blond, with a fine head and full brown beard, more like a studious country doctor than a novelist, and his wife was equally plain. "We were both essentially country folk," he said. "My house is outside Dorchester which is only a little city. I am a justice of the peace," he added, with a faint smile. "I am hardly ever in London. I came up this time on my wife's account."

His lack of humor, his blunt, plain speech, his scientific outlook on the world all reminded me of [John] Burroughs. His clothing was about like that which Burroughs wore when he came to town.

He spoke of America rather wistfully. "I'd like to see it," he said. "I have a great many readers over there and feel very friendly toward them, but I fear I shall never see them."

"You would be royally received."

"I know, I know! I'm afraid of that. I am afraid of New York. It's too rackety over there." — *Roadside Meetings* (1930).

Henry W. Nevinson

He was not large or countrified or robust. He was spare and straight in figure, hands white and soft and loose-skinned, face grey-white like delicate wax, lined with thin wrinkles, thoughtful and pathetic and profoundly sad, showing little of power or rage or physical courage; eyes bluish-grey, already whitening, head rather bald, but fringed with soft light hair, the eyebrows and moustache of the same colour and thin texture. He sat quite silent at first, and took little notice of the conversation. Then he began to talk, always with simple and quiet unconscious modesty, attempting no phrase or eloquence such as [George] Meredith delighted in, but just stating his opinion or telling some reminiscence or story — always a little shyly like a country cousin among quick-witted Londoners. Indeed, at a later meeting he told me that when among Londoners he at first felt overcome by their wit and knowledge, but afterwards he perceived they usually had only three ideas which they repeated. — P.E.N. Books (1941).

BRET HARTE

Hamlin Garland

One afternoon [in London] as [Israel] Zangwill and I were having tea at Joseph Hatton's house, my attention was drawn to a man whose appearance was almost precisely that of the typical English clubman of the American stage. He was tall, and his hair parted in the middle was white. He wore gray-striped trousers, a cutaway coat over a fancy vest, and above his polished shoes glowed lavender spats. In his hand he carried a pair of yellow gloves.

"Who is that?" I asked of Zangwill.

"Don't you know who that is?" he asked. "That is your noble compatriot, Francis Bret Harte."

"Bret Harte!" I started at him in amazement. Could that dandy, that be-monocled, be-spatted old beau be the author of "The Luck of Roaring Camp" and "Two Men of Sandy Bar"? As I stared, I recalled Joaquin Miller in his little cottage high on the hills above Oakland, and marveled at the changes which the years had wrought in his expatriate fellow. I said to Zangwill, "I have a letter to Harte from [William Dean] Howells — present me."

Zangwill led me over to Harte and introduced me as an American writer with a note from Howells. Harte was politely interested. "Come and see me on Thursday," he said, and gave me his address which was near Lancaster Gate.

Although courteous, his manner was not winning and I hesitated about making the call. However, it was easier to go than to excuse myself, and on the afternoon he had named, I found my way to his "bachelor apartments" in Lancaster Gate. They seemed to me very ladylike, spic and span, and very dainty in coloring, with chairs of the gilded, spindle-legged perilous sort which women adore; and when Harte came in to greet me he was almost as aristocratic as the room. He was wearing the same suit with the same fancy vest but with a different tie, and from his vest dangled an English eyeglass. His whole appearance was that of an elderly fop whose life had been one of self-indulgent ease. His eyes were clouded with yellow, and beneath them the skin was puffed and wrinkled. Although affable and polite he looked and spoke like a burned-out London sport. I was saddened by this decay of a brilliant and powerful novelist. — *Roadside Meetings* (1930).

William Dean Howells

He was then [1871], as always, a child of extreme fashion as to his clothes and the cut of his beard, which he wore in a mustache and the drooping side whiskers of the day, and his jovial physiognomy was as winning as his voice, with its straight nose, and fascinating forward thrust of the under lip, its fine eyes, and good forehead, then thickly crowned with the black hair which grew early white, while his mustache remained dark: the most enviable and consoling effect possible in the universal mortal necessity of either aging or dying. He was, as one could not help seeing, thickly pitted, but after the first glance one forgot this, so that a lady who met him for the first time could say to him, "Mr. Harte, aren't you afraid to go about in the cars so recklessly when there is this scare about smallpox?" "No, madam," he said, in that rich note of his, with an irony touched by pseudo-pathos, "I bear a charmed life."...

As for Harte's talk, it was mostly ironical, not to the extreme of satire, but tempered to an agreeable coolness even for things he admired. He did not apparently care to hear himself praised, but he could very accurately and perfectly mark his discernment of excellence in others. He was at times a keen observer of nature, and again not, apparently....

You never could be sure of Harte; he could only by chance be caught in earnest about anything or anybody....

He was a tease, as every sweet and fine wit is apt to be, but his teasing was of the quality of a caress, so much kindness went with it. — *Harper's Magazine* (December 1903).

Mark Twain

Bret Harte was one of the pleasantest men I have ever known. He was also one of the unpleasantest men I have ever known. He was showy, meretricious, insincere; and he constantly advertised these qualities in his dress. He was distinctly pretty, in spite of the fact that his face was badly pitted with smallpox. In the days when he could afford it — and in the days when he couldn't — his clothes always exceeded the fashion by a shade or two. He was always conspicuously a little more intensely fashionable than the fashionablest of the rest of the community. He had good taste in clothes. With all his conspicuousness there was never anything really loud nor offensive about them. They always had a single smart little accent, effectively located and that accent would have distinguished Harte from any other of the ultra-fashionables. Oftenest it was his necktie. Always it was of a single color, and intense. Most frequently, perhaps, it was crimson — a flash of flame under his chin; or it was indigo blue and as hot and vivid as if one of those splendid and luminous Brazilian butterflies had lighted there. Harte's dainty self-complacencies extended to his carriage and gait. His carriage was graceful and easy, his gait was of the mincing sort, but was the right gait for him, for an unaffected one would not have harmonized with the rest of the man and the clothes.

He hadn't a sincere fiber in him. I think he was incapable of emotion, for I think he had nothing to feel with. I think his heart was merely a pump and had no other function....

In the early days I liked Bret Harte, and so did the others, but by and by I got over it; so also did the others. He couldn't keep a friend permanently. He was bad, distinctly bad; he had no feeling, and he had no conscience. His wife was all that a good woman, a good wife, a good mother, and a good friend, can be; but when he went to Europe as consul he left her and his little children behind, and never came back again from that time until his death, twenty-six years later.

He was an incorrigible borrower of money; he borrowed from all his friends; if he ever repaid a loan the incident failed to pass into history. He was always ready to give his note but the matter ended there....

[During a stay of a] fortnight at our house Harte made himself liberally entertaining at breakfast, at luncheon, at dinner, and in the billiard room — which was our workshop — with smart and bright sarcasms leveled at everything on the place; and for Mrs. Clemens's sake I endured it all until the last day; then, in the billiard room he contributed the last feather; it seemed to be a slight and vague and veiled satirical remark with Mrs. Clemens for a target; he denied that she was meant, and I might have accepted the denial if I had been in a friendly mood but I was not, and was too strongly moved to give his reasonings a fair hearing. I said in substance this:

"Harte, your wife is all that is fine and lovable and lovely, and I exhaust praise when I say she is Mrs. Clemens's peer—but in all ways you are a shabby husband to her, and you often speak sarcastically, not to say sneeringly, of her, just as you are constantly doing in the case of other women; but your privilege ends there; you must spare Mrs. Clemens. It does not become you to sneer at all; you are not charged anything here for the bed you sleep in, yet you have been very smartly and wittily sarcastic about it, whereas you ought to have been more reserved in that matter, remembering that you have not owned a bed of your own for ten years; you have made sarcastic remarks about the furniture of the bedroom and about the table ware and about the servants and about the carriage and the sleigh and the coachman's livery—in fact about every detail of the house and half of its occupants; you have spoken of all these matters contemptuously, in your unwholesome desire to be witty, but this does not become you; you are barred from these criticisms by your situation and circumstances; you have a talent and a reputation which would enable you to support your family most respectably and independently if you were not a born bummer and tramp; you are a loafer and an idler, and you go clothed in rags, with not a whole shred on you except your inflamed red tie, and *it* isn't paid for; nine-tenths of your income is borrowed money—money which, in fact, is stolen, since you never intended to rapay any of it; you sponge upon your hard-working widowed sister for bread and shelter in the mechanics' boarding-house which she keeps; latterly you have not ventured to show your face in her neighborhood because of the creditors who are on watch for you. Where have you lived? Nobody knows. Your own people do not know. But I know. You have lived in the Jersey woods and marshes, and have supported yourself as do the other tramps; you have confessed it without a blush; you sneer at everything in this house, but you ought to be more tender, remembering that everything in it was honestly come by and has been paid for."

Harte owed me fifteen hundred dollars at that time; later he owed me three thousand. He offered me his note, but I was not keeping a museum and didn't take it.—*Mark Twain in Eruption*, ed. Bernard DeVoto (1940).

Himself

The style of criticism which my lecture—or rather myself as a lecturer—has received, of which I send you a specimen, culminated this morning in an editorial in the 'Republican' which I shall send you, but have not with me at present. I certainly never expected to be mainly criticised for being what *I am not*, a handsome fop, but this assertion is at the bottom of all the criticism. They may be right—I dare say they are — in asserting that I am no orator, have no special faculty for speaking — no fire, dramatic earnestness, or expression, but when they intimate that I am running on my good looks — save the mark! — I confess I get hopelessly furious. You will be amused to hear that my gold 'studs' have again become 'diamonds,' my worn-out shirts 'faultless linen,' my haggard face that of a 'Spanish-looking exquisite,' by habitual quiet and 'used-up' way, 'gentle and elegant languor.' — From a letter to his wife, 19 October 1873.

NATHANIEL HAWTHORNE

Samuel C. Hall

There are but few other distinguished Americans with whom I have been acquainted; among them, however, I must name Hawthorne — not long ago removed from us. He was a handsome man, of good "presence;" reserved — nay, painfully "shy," and apparently utterly unconscious of his *status* in society. He was, as is known, a most estimable gentleman. Those who knew him intimately depose to the high qualities of his mind and heart. Generous in all his sympathies, of a nature earnestly affectionate, a disposition naturally and emphatically good, he was dearly loved and is truly mourned by the widow and children who survive him. — *A Book of Memories* (1877).

William Dean Howells

The door was opened to my ring by a tall handsome boy whom I suppose to have been Mr. Julian Hawthorne; and the next moment I found myself in the presence of the romancer, who entered from some room beyond. He advanced carrying his head with a heavy forward droop, and with a pace for which I decided that the word would be *pondering*. It was the pace of a bulky man of fifty, and his head was that beautiful head we all know from the many pictures of it. But Hawthorne's *look* was different from that of any picture of him that I have seen. It was sombre and brooding, as the look of such a poet should have been; it was the look of a man who had dealt faithfully and therefore sorrowfully with that problem of evil which forever attracted, forever evaded Hawthorne. It was by no means troubled; it was full of a dark repose. Others who knew him better and saw him oftener were familiar with other aspects, and I remember that one night at Longfellow's table, when one of the guests happened to speak of the photograph of Hawthorne which hung in a corner of the room, Lowell said, after a glance at it, "Yes, it's good; but it hasn't his fine *accipitral* look."

In the face that confronted me, however, there was nothing of keen alertness; but only a sort of quiet, patient intelligence, for which I seek the right word in vain. It was a very regular face, with beautiful eyes; the mustache, still entirely dark, was dense over the fine mouth. Hawthorne was dressed in black, and he had a certain effect which I remember, of seeming to have on a black cravat with no visible collar. He was such a man that if I had ignorantly met him anywhere I would have instantly felt him to be a personage....

After tea, he showed me a bookcase, where there were a few books toppling about on the half-filled shelves, and said, coldly, "This is my library." I knew that men were his books, and though I myself cared for books so much, I found it fit and fine that he should care so little, or seem to care so little. Some of his own romances were among the volumes on these shelves, and when I put my finger on the *Blithedale Romance* and said that I preferred that to the others, his face lighted up, and he said that he believed the Germans liked that best too.

Upon the whole we parted such good friends that when I offered to take leave he asked me how long I was to be in Concord, and not only bade me come to see him again, but said he would give me a card to Emerson, if I liked. I answered, of course, that I should like it beyond all things; and he wrote on the back of his card something which I found, when I got away, to be, "I find this young man worthy." The quaintness, the little stiffness of it, if one pleases to call it so, was amusing to one who was not without his sense of humor, but the kindness filled me to the throat with joy. In fact, I entirely liked Hawthorne. He had been as cordial as so shy a man could show himself; and I perceived, with the repose that nothing else can give, the entire sincerity of his soul.

Nothing could have been further from the behavior of this very great man than any sort of posing, apparently, or a wish to affect me with a sense of his greatness. I saw that he was as much abashed by our encounter as I was; he was visibly shy to the point of discomfort, but in no ignoble sense was he conscious, and as nearly as he could with one so much his younger he made an absolute equality between us. My memory of him is without alloy one of the finest pleasures of my life. — *Literary Friends and Acquaintance* (1900).

John Lothrop Motley

I hear, by the way, that Hawthorne is about to publish a new novel. I know that he wrote one in Rome, and I hope it will be as beautiful and as successful as his other works. We liked him very much. He is the most bashful man I believe that ever lived, certainly the most bashful American, *mauvaise honte* not being one of our national traits, but he is a very sincere, unsophisticated, kind-hearted person, and looks the man of genius he undoubtedly is. — From a letter to his father, 29 December 1859.

[Also see Ralph Waldo Emerson — Frederick Lehmann.]

WILLIAM HAZLITT

Thomas Carlyle

William Hazzlitt takes his punch and oysters and rackets and whore at regular intervals; escaping from bailiffs as he best can, and writing when they grow unguidable by any other means. He has married (for the second time, his first spouse and the taylor's daughter being both alive): I never saw him, or wished to [remainder of page missing. Hazlitt had divorced his first wife, Sarah Stoddart, in 1822. He was in love with the daughter of his landlord, a tailor, from 1820 to 1823; his *Liber Amoris* (1823) tells the story. He married his second wife, a Mrs. Bridgwater in 1824.] — From a letter to Thomas Murray, 24 August 1824.

Samuel Taylor Coleridge

William Hazlitt is a thinking, observant, original man, of great power as a Painter of Character-Portraits, and far more in the manner of the old Painters than any living Artist, but the objects must be *before* him; he has no imaginative memory. So much for his intellectuals. His manners are 99 in 100 singularly repulsive; brow-hanging, shoe-contemplative, strange.... He is, I verily believe kindly-natured; is very fond of, attentive to, and patient with children; but he is jealous, gloomy, and of an irritable pride. With all this, there is much good in him. He is disinterested; an enthusiastic lover of the great men who have been before us; he says things that are his own, in a way of his own; and though from habitual shyness, and the outside and bearskin at least, of misanthropy, he is strangely confused and dark in his conversation, and delivers himself of almost all his conceptions with a Forceps, yet he says more than any man I ever knew (yourself only excepted) that is his own in a way of his own; and oftentimes when he has warmed his mind, and the synovial juice has come out and spread over his joints, he will gallop for half an hour together with real eloquence. He sends well-headed and well-feathered Thoughts straight forwards to the mark with a Twang of the Boswtring. If you could recommend him as a portrait-painter, I should be glad. To be your Companion, he is, in my opinion, utterly unfit. His own health is fitful. — From a letter to Thomas Wedgwood, 16 September 1803.

Samuel C. Hall

I did not like Hazlitt: nobody did. He was out of place at the genial gatherings at Highgate; though he was often there: for genial he certainly was not. He wrote with a pen dipped in gall, and had a singularly harsh and ungentle look; seeming indeed as if his sole business in life was to seek for faults. He was a leading literary and art critic of his time; but he has left to posterity little either to guide or instruct. I recall him as a small, mean-looking, unprepossessing man; but I do not quite accept [Benjamin Robert] Haydon's estimate of him — "a singular compound of malice, candor, cowardice, genius, purity, vice, democracy, and conceit." Lamb said of him, that he was, "in his natural state, one of the wisest and finest spirits breathing." I prefer the portrait of De Quincey: "He smiled upon no man!" — *Retrospect of a Long Life* (1883).

Charles Lamb

I should belie my own conscience, if I said less than that I think W.H. to be, in his natural and healthy state, one of the wisest and finest spirits breathing. So far from being ashamed of that intimacy, which was betwixt us, it is my boast that I was able for so many years to have preserved it entire; and I think I shall go to my grave without finding, or expecting to find such a companion. — From an open letter to Robert Southey, October 1823.

P.G. Patmore

For depth, force, and variety of intellectual expression, a finer head and face than Hazlitt's were never seen. I speak of them when his countenance was not dimmed and obscured by illness, or clouded and deformed by those fearful indications of internal passion which he never even attempted to conceal. The expression of Hazlitt's face, when anything was said in his presence that seriously offended him, or when any peculiarly painful recollection passed across his mind, was truly awful—more so than can be conceived as within the capacity of the human countenance; except, perhaps, by those who have witnessed Edmund Kean's last scene of *Sir Giles Overreach* from the front of the pit. But when he was in good health, and in a tolerable humour with himself and the world, his face was more truly and entirely answerable to the intellect that spoke through it, than any other I ever saw, either in life or on canvas; and its crowning portion, the brow and forehead, was, to my thinking, quite unequalled, for mingling capacity and beauty.

For those who desire a more particular description, I will add, that Hazlitt's features, though not cast in any received classical mould, were regular in their formation, perfectly consonant with each other, and so finely "chiselled" (as the phrase is), that they produced a much more prominent and striking effect than their scale of size might have led one to expect. The forehead, as I have hinted, was magnificent; the nose precisely that (combining strength with lightness and elegance) which physiognomists have assigned as evidence of a fine and highly cultivated taste; though there was a peculiar character about the nostrils, like that observable in those of a fiery and unruly horse. The mouth, from its ever-changing form and character, could scarcely be described, except as to its astonishingly varied power of expression, which was equal to, and greatly resembled, that of Edmund Kean. His eyes, I should say, were not good. They were never brilliant, and there was a furtive and at times a sinister look about them, as they glanced suspiciously from under their overhanging brows, that conveyed a very unpleasant impression to those who did not know him. And they were seldom directed frankly and fairly towards you; as if he were afraid that you might read in them what was passing in his mind concerning you. His head was nobly formed and placed; with (until the last few years of his life) a profusion of coal-black hair, richly curled; and his person was of the middle height, rather slight, but well formed and put together.

Yet all these advantages were worse than thrown away, by the strange and ungainly manner that at times accompanied them. Hazlitt entered a room as if he had been brought back to it in custody; he shuffled sidelong to the nearest chair, sat himself down upon one corner of it, dropped his hat and his eyes upon the floor, and, after having exhausted his stock of conventional small-talk in the words "It's a fine day" (whether it was so or not), seemed to resign himself moodily to his fate. And if the talk did not take a turn that roused or pleased him, thus he would sit, silent and half-absorbed, for half an hour or half a minute, as the case might be, and then get up suddenly, with a "Well, good morning," shuffle back to the door, and blunder his way out, audibly muttering curses on his folly, for willingly putting himself in the way of becoming the laughing-stock of — the servants! for it was of *that* class and intellectual grade of persons that Hazlitt alone stood in awe. Of the few private houses to which his inclinations ever led him, he perfectly well knew that, even if there had been (which, as we have seen there was not) anything unusual or *outre* in his appearance, his intellectual pretensions would alone have been thought of. But there was no reaching the drawing-room without running the gauntlet of the servants' hall; and this it was that crushed and confounded him. I am satisfied that Hazlitt never entered a room — scarcely ever his own — that he was not writhing under the feelings engendered during his passage to it; and that he never knocked at a door without fearing that it might be opened by a new servant, who would wonder what so "strange" a person could want with their master or mistress. — *My Friends and Acquaintance* (1854).

Bryan Waller Procter

His talk (when not political) was principally on books and on such anecdotes as brought out the characters of individual men. In these last he always allowed small facts and involuntary actions to have their full share of weight. He himself had no books, and he never borrowed them, except for temporary reference. All his works were made out of "the carver's brain." There was nothing that he refused to discuss. Although encumbered by some prejudices (which he knew and admitted), he would argue all subjects candidly....

No man was competent to write upon Hazlitt who did not know him personally. Some things of which he has been accused were referable merely to temporary humour or irritability, which was not frequent, and which was laid aside in an hour. At other times (by far the greater portion of his life) he was a candid and reasonable man. He felt the injuries and slanders, however, which were spit forth upon him acutely; and resented them. He was not one of those easy, comfortable, and so-called "good-natured" men, who are simply inaccessible to strong emotions, and from whom the minor ills of life fall off, without disturbing them, like rain from a pent-house top.

His essays are full of thought; full of delicate perceptions. They do not speak of matters which he has merely seen or remembered, but enter into the rights and wrongs of persons; into the meaning and logic of things; into causes and results; into motives and indications of character. He is, in short, not a *raconteur* but a reasoner. This will be observed in almost all his numerous essays. If he is often ostentatious, that is to say, if he accumulates image upon image, reason upon reason, it is simply that he is more in earnest than other writers.

In addition to these general qualities, how felicitous are many of his obiter remarks! They deserve to be enshrined by some abler workman than myself....

My first meeting with Mr. Hazlitt took place at the house of Leigh Hunt, where I met him at supper. I expected to see a severe, defiant-looking being. I met a grave man, diffident, almost awkward in manner, whose appearance did not impress me with much respect. He had a quick, restless eye, however, which opened eagerly when any good or bright observation was made; and I found at the conclusion of the evening, that when any question arose, the most sensible reply always came from him. Although the process was not too obvious, he always seemed to have reasoned with himself before he uttered a sentence. And the reader of his essays will recollect that the same process is observable there....

I saw a great deal of Hazlitt during the last twelve or thirteen years of his stormy, anxious, uncomfortable life.... I went to visit him very often during his late *breakfasts* (when he drank tea of an astounding strength), not unfrequently also at the Fives Court, and at other persons' houses; and once I dined with him. This (an unparalleled occurrence) was in York Street, when some friend had sent him a couple of Dorking fowls, of which he suddnely invited me to partake. I went, expecting the usual sort of dinner; but it was limited solely to the fowls and bread. He drank nothing but water, and there was nothing but water to drink. He offered to send for some porter for me, but being out of health at the time, I declined, and escaped soon after dinner to a coffee-house, where I strengthened myself with a few glasses of wine.

Do I mention this spare entertainment as a charge against Hazlitt? Oh no, I do not; on the contrary, I was sure that the matter had never entered into his mind. He drank water only, and lived plainly, and not unreasonably assumed that what sufficed for himself was sufficient for others. He had nothing that was parsimonious or mean in his character, and I believe that he never thought of eating or drinking, except when hunger or thirst reminded him of these wants. With the exception of a very rare dinner or supper with a friend or intimate, his time was generally spent alone. After a late breakfast he took his quire of foolscap paper, and commenced writing (in a large hand almost as large as text) his day's work. I never saw any rough draft or copy. He wrote readily—not very swiftly, perhaps, but easily, as if he had made up his mind—the manuscript that I believe went to the printer. In his latter years he dined generally at the Southampton Coffee-house, in Southampton Buildings, and was much interested by the saying of people whom he met there; and would often repeat and comment on them when they served to develop character.

Hazlitt was of the middle size, with eager, expressive eyes; near which his black hair, sprinkled sparely with grey, curled round in wiry, resolute manner. His grey eyes, not remarkable in colour, expanded into great expression when occasion demanded it. Being very shy, however, they often evaded your steadfast look. They never (as has been asserted by some one) had a sinister expression; but they sometimes flamed with indignant glances, when their owner was moved to anger; like the eyes of other angry men. At home, his style of dress (or undress) was perhaps slovenly, because there was no one to please; but he always presented a very clean and neat appearance when he went abroad. His mode of walking was loose, weak and unsteady; although his arms displayed strength, which he used to put forth when he played at racquets with Martin Burney and others. He played in the old Fives Court (now pulled down) in St. Martin's Street; and occasionally exhibited impatience when the game went against him....

He lived mainly alone—the life of a solitary thinker. This gave originality to some of his essays; sometimes it deprived him of the advantage of comparing his opinions with those of others. —"Recollections of Men of Letters" in *An Autobiographical Fragment* (1877).

Henry Crabb Robinson

JUNE 15th [1815] ... I called on Wordsworth for the first time at his lodgings. He was luckily at home, and I spent the forenoon with him, walking. We talked about Hazlitt in consequence of a malignant attack on Wordsworth by him in Sunday's *Examiner*. Wordsworth that very day called on [Leigh] Hunt, who, in a manly way, asked whether Wordsworth had seen the paper of the morning, saying, if he had, he should consider his call as a higher honour. He disclaimed the article. The attack by Hazlitt was a note in which, after honouring Milton for being a consistent patriot, he sneered at Wordsworth as the author of 'paltry sonnets upon the royal fortitude,' etc. and insinuated that he had left out the Female Vagrant, a poem describing the miseries of war sustained by the poor. This led to Wordsworth's mentioning the cause of his coolness towards Hazlitt. It appears that Hazlitt, when at Keswick, narrowly escaped being ducked by the populace, and probably sent to prison for some gross attacks on women. He even whipped one woman, *more puerorum*, for not yielding to his wishes. The populace were incensed against him and pursued him, but he escaped to Wordsworth, who took him into his house at midnight, gave him clothes and money (from three to five pounds). Since that time Wordsworth, though he never refused to meet Hazlitt when by accident they came together, did not choose that with his knowledge he should be invited. In consequence, Lamb never asked Hazlitt while Wordsworth was in town, which probably provoked Hazlitt, and which Lamb himself disproved of. But Lamb, who needs very little indulgence for himself, is very indulgent towards others, and rather reproaches Wordsworth for being inveterate against Hazlitt....

OCT. 2nd [1830] ... I found [Walter Savage] Landor at my lodgings. He told me ... of the death of William Hazlitt, a man for whom I once had kindness, and whom I have served as a friend. But for many years I have ceased to feel any respect for him and even to speak with him. I resented his ill-treatment of Wordsworth, etc. He was a very able man. He had a certain honesty about him in politics, but it was the honest hatred of the tyranny of the powerful in which so much of envy is blended with better feelings. He was precisely the *Jacobin* so admirably described by [Edmund] Burke in his *Reflections [on the Revolution in France]*. He was a gross sensualist, and was always in great poverty. He therefore was indelicate in money matters. His prose writings I have always read with great delight. It is more than thirty years since I assisted him to find a publisher for his first book. He used to say to Miss [Mary] Lamb that he should always feel a kindness towards me, for I was the first man who found out that there was anything in him....

OCT. 7th [1830] ... [Charles Armitage] Brown related anecdotes of Hazlitt's personal cowardice, as well as of his slovenliness, and says he was the worst-tempered man he ever knew. — *Diary*.

Thomas Noon Talfourd

In person, Mr. Hazlitt was of the middle size, with a handsome and eager countenance, worn by sickness and thought; and dark hair, which had curled stiffly over the temples, and was only of late years sprinkled with grey. His gait was slouching and awkard, and his dress neglected; but when he began to talk, he could not be mistaken for a common man. In the company of persons with whom he was not familiar, his bashfulness was painful; but when he became entirely at ease, and entered on a favourite topic, no one's conversation was ever more delightful. He did not talk for effect — to dazzle, or surprise, or annoy — but with the most simple and honest desire to make his view of the subject entirely apprehended by his hearer. There was sometimes an obvious struggle to do this to his own satisfaction; he seemed labouring to drag his thought to light from its deep lurking place; and with modest distrust of that power of expression which he had found so late in life, he often betrayed a fear that he had failed to make himself understood, and recurred to the subject again and again, that he might be assured he had succeeded. In argument, he was candid and liberal; there was nothing about him pragmatical or exclusive; he never drove a principle to its utmost possible consequences, but, like Locksley, "allowed for the wind." For some years previous to his death, he observed an entire abstinence from fermented liquors, which he had once quaffed with the proper relish he had for all the good things of his life, but which he courageously resigned when he found the indulgence perilous to his health and faculties. The cheerfulness with which he made this sacrifice always appeared to us one of the most amiable traits in his character. He had no censure for others, who, with the same motive, were less wise or less resolute; nor did he think he had earned, by his own constancy, any right to intrude advice which he knew, if wanted, must be unavailing. Nor did he profess to be a convert to the general system of abstinence, which was advocated by one of his kindest and staunchest friends; he avowed that he yielded to necessity; and instead of avoiding the sight of that which he could no longer taste, he was seldom so happy as when he sat with friends at their wine, participating in the sociality of the time, and realising his own past enjoyment in that of his companions, without regret and without envy. Like Dr. Johnson, he made himself a poor amends for the loss of wine by drinking tea, not so largely, indeed, as the hero of Boswell, but at least of equal potency — for he might have challenged Mrs. Thrale and all her sex to make stronger tea than his own. — "Thoughts upon the Intellectual Character of the late William Hazlitt" in *List of the Writings of William Hazlitt and Leigh Hunt*, by Alexander Ireland (1868).

ERNEST HEMINGWAY

Lillian Hellman

It was in those pre–Moscow Paris weeks that I had first met Ernest Hemingway, although his bride-to-be, Martha Gellhorn — we didn't know then that she was to marry him, and I doubt that she was sure of it, either — had crossed on the boat with Dorothy Parker, her husband Alan Campbell, and me. Martha spent a good deal of her time in the boat's gymnasium, where, Dottie said, all of Ernest's ladies began their basic training for the life partnership.

I liked Ernest. It would have been hard for a woman not to like him if he wanted you to, tried for it. He had just come out of Spain — this was the second year of the Spanish Civil War — and had come up to Paris for a holiday before he and Martha returned to Spain....

One night after dinner, when we usually parted, the Campbells and I, led by Ernest, moved around Paris from whiskey to scrambled eggs to their old acquaintances at the Deux Magots or Lilas to a place with blaring, bad jazz. By that time I was drunk and headachy and left a note with a waiter saying goodnight.

I had been asleep for two or three hours when there was a loud pounding on the hotel door. Ernest was there with a bottle of Scotch and a package. He was in good humor and we had a large drink of Scotch from his bottle, a talk about my coming to Spain after Moscow, some conversation I didn't understand about the women in his life, and then he threw the package on my bed.

He said, "The proofs of *To Have and Have Not*. Want to read them? Right now?"

It wasn't that I was so young that year, it was that I was younger than I should have been about respected literary men and I had forgotten that I had told him earlier that evening that when I worked at Liveright's I had swiped the first copy of *In Our Time* as it came from the printer, sitting with it at the office at eight o'clock the next morning so anxious to talk about the book that I had forgotten other people wouldn't be there at that hour, and had paced up and down the street, and then run up and down the stairs, until Horace [Liveright] and Julian Messner and Tom Smith finally arrived.

So I was pleased to be sitting up in bed, fighting a hangover, flattered that Ernest had brought his new book for my opinion. He sat by the window, drinking, looking through a magazine, mostly watching me as I read the book. I wanted him to go away and leave the book, but when it was good, which wasn't always, I forgot about him. And it was good, and suddenly very strange, right before I rubbed my eyes and turned off the lamp as daylight came in the window. I went back and reread two or three pages.

"There are missing pages in these proofs."

Ernest said, "Where?"

He came to the bed and I showed him what I thought was a puzzling jump in story and in meaning.

"Nothing is missing. What made you say that?" His voice had changed, not to sharpness, but to a tone one would use with an annoying child or an intrusive stranger, and these many years later I can still hear the change. I tried to say why I thought what I thought, but I got out only half sentences and even those stopped when he kissed me on the forehead, picked up the page proofs and walked out the door. I was puzzled and hurt and, after a minute, angry. I followed him into the hall and stood staring at him as he waited for the elevator.

He came back toward me, pulled me within arm's length, and said, "I wish I could sleep with you, but I can't because there's somebody else. I hope you understand." He smiled at me, patted my head, went down in the elevator, and I was so surprised that I stood in the hall until it was too late to run down the steps and say — Say what? So I went to wake Dottie in the room next to mine. She shook her head at me for a long time.

"You mean I shouldn't have read it or I shouldn't have said anything?"

"Oh, who wouldn't? How were you supposed to know that Max Perkins persuaded him the book was too long and Ernest wouldn't let Max cut it so he made the cuts himself and they're bad, evidently, and you guessed it. And you've only just met Ernest and nobody told you, poor girl, that you're not allowed to think a comma could be in the wrong place, or that the book isn't the greatest written in our time although that's hard to follow, isn't it, because his previous book was always the greatest?"

I said, "What was that about not sleeping with me? Who asked him? Who the hell even thought about him?"

"Revenge, Lilly. Made him feel better. And if that's all he ever says or does you'll be lucky, because he's not a man who forgives people much." — *An Unfinished Woman: A Memoir* (1969).

James Joyce

We [Joyce and his wife] were with him just before he went to Africa. He promised us a living lion. Fortunately we escaped that. But we would like to have the book he has written. He's a good writer, Hemingway. He writes as he is. We like him. He's a big, powerful peasant, as strong as a buffalo. A sportsman. And ready to live the life he writes about. He would never have written it if his body had not allowed him to live it. But giants of his sort are truly modest; there is

much more behind Hemingway's form than people know. — Quoted by
Richard Ellman in *James Joyce* (1959).

Robert McAlmon

The night I checked in at the hotel [in Rapallo, Italy] I encountered Ernest Hemingway and his wife, Hadley, and also Henry (Mike)
Strater, a painter, and his wife. I had never heard of any of them
before. Hemingway was a Middle Western American who worked for a
Canadian newspaper, and he was a type outside my experience. At times
he was deliberately hard-boiled, case-hardened, and old; at other times
he was the hurt, sensitive boy, defensive, suspicions lurking in his
peering analytic glances at the person with whom he was talking. He
approached a cafe with a small-boy, tough-guy swagger, and before
strangers of whom he was uncertain a potential snarl of scorn played on
his large-lipped, rather loose mouth....

A year or so later the lot of us were in Paris at the same time, and
after a trip to London I talked of going to Spain, Hemingway wanted
much to see a bullfight, and after a week of talking about it we headed
toward Spain. Hemingway and Hadley had a fondness for pet names.
Beery-poppa (Hemingway) said a loving good-by to Feather-kitty (Hadley), Bumby (their baby), and Waxen-puppy (their dog), and he and I,
well lubricated with whisky, got on the train.

The next day, on the way to Madrid, our train stopped at a way-
side station for a time. On the track beside us was a flatcar, upon which
lay the maggot-eaten corpse of a dog. I, feeling none too hale and
hearty, looked away, but Hemingway gave a dissertation on facing
reality. It seemed that he had seen in the war the stacked corpses of
men, maggot-eaten in a similar way. He advised a detached and scientific attitude toward the corpse of the dog. He tenderly explained that
we of our generation must inure ourselves to the sight of grim reality. I
recalled that Ezra Pound had talked once of Hemingway's "self-
hardening process." At last he said, "Hell, Mac, you write like a realist.
Are you going to go romantic on us?"

The day that we were to see our first bullfight we agreed that the
horse part of it might bother us, so we had a few drinks before taking
our seats. We took a bottle of whisky with us, with the understanding
that, if shocked, we would gulp down a quantity to calm ourselves. My
reactions to the bullfight were not at all what I had anticipated. At first
it seemed totally unreal, like something happening on the screen. The
first bull charged into the ring with tremendous violence. When the
horses were brought in, it charged head on and lifted the first horse over
its head. But the horns did not penetrate.

Instead of a shock of disgust, I rose in my seat and let out a yell. Things were happening too quickly for my mind to consider the horse's suffering. Later, however, when one of the horses was galloping in hysteria around the ring, treading on its own entrails, I decidedly didn't like it. I have since discovered that many hardened Spanish *aficionados*, and in one case I knew of, the brother of a bullfighter, had to look the other way on such occasions. Hemingway became at once an *aficionado*, that is, a passionate bullfight fan or enthusiast, intent upon learning all about the art. If I suspect that his need to love the art of bullfighting came from Gertrude Stein's praise of it, as well as from his belief in the value of "self-hardening," it is only because his bullfight book (*Death in the Afternoon*) adopts such a belligerent attitude in the defense of bull-fighting. There are countless English and Americans who were bull-fight enthusiasts many years before that summer of 1924 when Heming-way and I both saw our first, but he made it into a literary or artistic experience....

Before leaving Paris, Hemingway had been much of a shadow-boxer. As he approached a cafe he would prance about, sparring at shadows, his lips moving, calling his imaginary opponents's bluff. Upon returning from Spain, he substituted shadow-bullfighting for shadow-boxing. The amount of imaginary cape work and sword thrusts he made in those days was formidable. Later he went to Key West and went in for barracuda fishing, and I wonder if he took then to shadow-barra-cuda-fishing, or coming back from Africa he would shadow-lion-hunt. He has a boy's need to be a tough guy, a swell boxer, a strong man. — *Being Geniuses Together* (1938).

Samuel Putnam

My first meeting with Ernest Hemingway did not take place on the Left Bank but in Chicago, and, curiously enough, in North Wells Street, up several flights in a ramshackle old building where a certain interminable and indescribably tedious but, so it appeared, very impor-tant bankruptcy hearing was in progress, if progress is the word. I was covering the case for my paper, and among the other reporters present was a mild-mannered, inconspicuous young chap who came up and introduced himself as Hemingway and who stated that he represented the *Toronto Star*.

This was in the early 'twenties. The author of *The Sun Also Rises* and *A Farewell to Arms* was as yet practically unheard of in the literary world; he had had some poems published in Miss Monroe's magazine, that was about all....

The next time I saw Hemingway was shortly after *The Sun Also*

Rises had appeared. He was now well on the road to being a famous author and in the process had succeeded in conferring, also, a dubious fame upon the American expatriate colony of Montparnasse. As we sat over our drinks at the Deux-Magots it did not take me long to discover that the somewhat shy and youthful reporter whom I had met in Chicago had vanished and that in his place was a literary celebrity. It was not that he was in the least pompous or conceited; I cannot conceive of that with Hemingway, ever. He was, rather, the exuberant young man who has made a fine start and is agreeably conscious and proud of the fact; you could not help liking him for it. He gave you the impression of a certain tense seriousness with regard to the writer's trade; it was as if he was determined not to spoil his start and to work like hell, as he put it, to see that this did not happen. In typical Hemingway language and with all the Hemingway nonchalance, he proceeded to deliver to a highly appreciative audience of one a brief, informal, but extremely revealing lecture on the art of writing.

Work — that was the thing he stressed most of all: the writer must work — and work and work — at his job. Apothegms dropped from his lips as from those of a brilliant sophomore doing his best not to appear too brilliant, even to the extent of resorting to a copybook triteness. "Easy writing makes hard reading." That was one of the things he said which I have always remembered. He said it a number of times.

"The first and most important thing of all, at least for writers today, is to strip language clean, to lay it bare down to the bone, and that takes work."

Has he been influenced in this respect by Gertrude Stein? He admitted that he had learned something from her, but was not too enthusiastic. Similarly, as to Ezra Pound he was rather pleasantly, and youthfully, patronizing. Then, with charming simplicity and without being "interviewed," he went on to speak of his "influences." Chief among these, he assured me, was the Old Testament in the King James version. "That's how I learned to write," he said, "by reading the Bible."... I asked if he would put Shakespeare alongside the Bible as a model for writers.

"Yes, Shakespeare — but above all, the Old Testament. That's all any writer needs."

How had he come to write *The Sun Also Rises?*

"Oh, I don't know. I was just knocking around with the bunch and I tried to put it down. If you're a writer, you write; and if you're a good writer, you write about things you know."

Would he say, as some of the critics were saying, that his novel was an expression of postwar disillusionment?

"The war played hell with a lot of us."

"The 'Lost Generation'?" I suggested.

"Don't take what Gertie says too seriously," he advised. "How the hell are you going to be lost when you've never been found?"

"What do you try to do in writing, anyway?"

"Put down what I see and what I feel in the best and simplest way I can tell it."...

So much for the literary side. This, after all, proved to be the minor part of the conversation, or of Hemingway's monologue, perhaps I should way. He talked of hunting and fishing and drinking. Especially of drinking, which he regarded, apparently, as something of a big-game exploit. Here, sitting opposite me now, was the creator of that character who had uttered the famous dictum about the bottle as "a sovereign means of direct action." He sat there, talking on and on, and brilliantly, of flying, skiing, boxing, bull-fighting. The "three most exciting things in life," he gravely informed me, were flying, skiing, and sexual intercourse. Only, he did not say sexual intercourse but used the short and not unlovely word.

Here was one writer who could talk as well as write, and very much as he wrote. Or was it that he wrote as he talked, especially in a work like *The Sun Also Rises*? He was so effective an oral narrator, without any of the usual more or less self-conscious attributes of the "good conversationalist," that one was quite content to surrender and drift as one does with the stream of his prose, which, like all prose at its best, has something of the effect of an enchantment, as incantation, of a primitive and rhythmic magic. — *Paris Was Our Mistress* (1947).

Gertrude Stein

The first thing that happened when we were back in Paris was Hemingway with a letter of introduction from Sherwood Anderson.

I remember very well the impression I had of Hemingway that first afternoon. He was an extraordinarily good-looking young man, twenty-three years old. It was not long after that that everybody was twenty-six. It became the period of being twenty-six....

So Hemingway was twenty-three, rather foreign looking, with passionately interested, rather than interesting eyes. He sat in front of Gertrude Stein and listened and looked.

They talked then, and more and more, a great deal together. He asked her to come and spend an evening in their apartment and look at his work. Hemingway had then and has always a very good instinct for finding apartments in strange but pleasing localities and good femmes de ménage and good food. This his first apartment was just off the place du Tertre. We spent the evening there and he and Gertrude Stein went over all the writing he had done up to that time. He had begun the novel that it was inevitable he would begin and there were the little poems afterwards printed by [Robert] McAlmon in the Contract Edition. Gertrude Stein rather liked the poems, they were direct, Kiplingesque, but the novel she found wanting. There is a great deal of description in this, she said, and not particularly good description. Begin over again and concentrate, she said....

Gertrude Stein and Sherwood Anderson are very funny on the subject of Hemingway. The last time that Sherwood was in Paris they often talked about him. Hemingway had been formed by the two of them and they were both a little proud and a little ashamed of the work of their minds. Hemingway had at one moment, when he had repudiated Sherwood Anderson and all his works, written him a letter in the name of american literature which he, Hemingway, in company with his contemporaries was about to save, telling Sherwood just what he, Hemingway thought about Sherwood's work, and, that thinking, was in no sense complimentary. When Sherwood came to Paris Hemingway naturally was afraid. Sherwood as naturally was not.

As I say he and Gertrude Stein were endlessly amusing on the subject. They admitted that Hemingway was yellow, he is, Gertrude Stein insisted, just like the flat-boat men on the Mississippi river as described by Mark Twain. But what a book, they both agreed, would be the real story of Hemingway, not those he writes but the confessions of the real Ernest Hemingway. It would be for another audience than the audience Hemingway now has but it would be very wonderful. And then they both agreed that they have a weakness for Hemingway because he is such a good pupil. He is a rotten pupil, I protested. You don't understand, they both said, it is so flattering to have a pupil who does it without understanding it, in other words he takes training and anybody who takes training is a favourite pupil. They both admit it to be a weakness....

In the meantime McAlmon had printed the three poems and ten stories of Hemingway and William Bird had printed In Our Time and Hemingway was getting to be known. He and George Antheil and everybody else and Harold Loeb was once more in Paris. Hemingway had become a writer. He was also a shadow-boxer, thanks to Sherwood, and he heard about bull-fighting from me. I have always loved spanish dancing and spanish bull-fighting and I loved to show the photographs of bull-fighters and bull-fighting. I also loved to show the photograph where Gertrude Stein and I were in the front row and had our picture taken there accidentally. In these days Hemingway was teaching some young chap how to box. The boy did not know how, but by accident he knocked Hemingway out. I believe this sometimes happens. At any rate in these days Hemingway although a sportsman was easily tired. He used to get quite worn out walking from his house to ours. But then he had been worn by the war. Even now he is, As Hélène says all men are, fragile. Recently a robust friend of his said to Gertrude Stein, Ernest is very fragile, whenever he does anything sporting something breaks, his arm, his leg, or his head.

In those early days Hemingway liked all his contemporaries except Cummings. He accused Cummings of having copied everything, not from anybody but from somebody. Gertrude Stein who had been much impressed by The Enormous Room said that Cummings did not copy, he was the natural heir of the New England tradition with its aridity and its sterility, but also with its individuality. They disagreed about this. They also disagreed about Sherwood Anderson. Gertrude Stein contended that Sherwood Anderson had a genius for using a sentence to convey a direct emotion, this was in the great american tradition, and that really except Sherwood there was no one in America who could write a clear and passionate sentence. Hemingway did not believe this, he did not like Sherwood's taste. — *The Autobiography of Alice B. Toklas* (1933).

John Steinbeck

[Early reports said that Hemingway had died from the accidental discharge of a shotgun while he was cleaning it.] The first thing we heard of Ernest Hemingway's death was a call from the London Daily Mail, asking me to comment on it. And quite privately, although something of this sort might have been expected, I find it shocking. He had only one theme — only one. A man contends with the forces of the world, called fate, and meets them with courage. Surely a man has a right to remove his own life but you'll find no such possibility in any of H's heros. The sad thing is that I think he would have hated accident much more than suicide. He was an incredibly vain man. An accident while cleaning a gun would have violated everything he was vain about. To shoot yourself with a shot gun in the head is almost impossible unless it is planned. Most such deaths happen when a gun falls, and then the wound is usually in the abdomen. A practiced man does not load a gun while cleaning it. Indeed a hunting man would never have a loaded gun in the house....

But apart from all that — he has had the most profound effect on writing — more than anyone I can think of. He has not a vestige of humor. It's a strange life. Always he tried to prove something. And you only try to prove what you aren't sure of. He was the critics' darling because he never changed style, theme nor story. He made no experiments in thinking nor in emotion. A little like [Robert] Capa, he created an ideal image of himself and then tried to live it. I am saddened at his death. I never knew him well, met him a very few times and he was always pleasant and kind to me although I am told that privately he spoke very disparagingly of my efforts. But then he thought of other living writers, not as contemporaries but as antagonists. He really cared about his immortality as though he weren't sure of it. And there's little doubt that he has it. — From a letter to Pascal Covici, July 1961.

LEIGH HUNT

Thomas Carlyle

Hunt and the Hunts, as you have heard, live only in the next street from us. Hunt is always ready to go and walk with me, or sit and talk with me to all lengths if I want him. He comes in once a week (when invited, for he is very modest), takes a cup of tea, and sits discoursing in his brisk, fanciful way till supper time, and then cheerfully eats a cup of porridge (to sugar only), which he praises to the skies, and vows he will make his supper of at home. He is a man of thoroughly London make, such as you could not find elsewhere, and I think about the *best* possible to be made of his sort: an airy, crotchety, most copious clever talker, with an honest undercurrent of reason too, but unfortunately not the deepest, not the most practical — or rather it is the most *un*practical ever man dealt in. His hair is grizzled, eyes black-hazel, complexion of the clearest dusky brown; a thin glimmer of a smile plays over a face of cast-iron gravity. He never laughs — can only titter, which I think indicates his worst deficiency. His house excels all you have ever read of — a *poetical Tinkerdom*, without parallel even in literature. In his family room, where are a sickly large wife and a whole shoal of well-conditioned wild children, you will find half a dozen old rickety chairs gathered from half a dozen different hucksters, and all seemingly engaged, and just pausing, in a violent *hornpipe*. On these and around them and over the dusty table and ragged carpet lie all kinds of litter — books, papers, egg-shells, scissors, and last night when I was there the torn heart of a half-quartern loaf. His own room above stairs, into which alone I strive to enter, he keeps cleaner. It has only two chairs, a bookcase, and a writing-table; yet the noble Hunt receives you in his

Tinkerdom in the spirit of a king, apologises for nothing, places you in the best seat, takes a window-sill himself if there is no other, and there folding closer his loose-flowing 'muslin cloud' of a printed nightgown in which he always writes, commences the liveliest dialogue on philosophy and the prospects of man (who is to be beyond measure 'happy' yet); which again he will courteously terminate the moment you are bound to go: a most interesting, pitiable, lovable man, to be used kindly but with discretion. After all, it is perhaps rather a comfort to be near honest, friendly people — at least, an honest, friendly man of that sort. — From a letter to Alexander Carlyle, 27 June 1834.

Charles Dickens

His life was in several respects, a life of trouble, though his cheerfulness was such that he was, upon the whole, happier than some men who have had fewer griefs to wrestle with.... Leigh Hunt's was an essentially human nature, rich and inclusive.... It has been said occasionally that Leigh Hunt was a weak man. He had, it is true, particular weaknesses, as evinced in his want of business knowledge, and in a certain hesitation of judgment on some points, which his son has aptly likened to the ultra deliberation of Hamlet, and which was the result of an extreme conscientiousness. But a man who had the courage to take his stand against power on behalf of right — who, in the midst of the sorest temptations, maintained his honesty unblemished by a single stain — who, in all public and private transactions, was the very soul of truth and honor — who never bartered his opinion or betrayed his friend — could not have been a weak man. — *All the Year Round* (24 December 1859).

Samuel C. Hall

I knew but little of Leigh Hunt when he was in his prime. I had met him, however, more than once, soon after his return from Italy, when he recommenced a career of letters which he had been induced to abandon, trusting to visionary hopes in the aid he was to derive from familiar intercourse with Byron. He was tall, but slightly formed, quiet and contemplative in gait and manner, yet apparently affected by momentary impulse; his countenance brisk and animated, receiving its expression chiefly from dark and brilliant eyes, but supplying unequivocal evidence of that mixed blood which he derived from the parent stock, to which his friend Hazlitt alluded in reference to his flow of animal spirits as well as to his descent, "he had tropical blood in his veins." His son Thornton (*Cornhill Magazine*) describes him "as in height about five feet ten inches, remarkably straight and upright in his carriage, with a firm step and a cheerful, almost dashing, approach." He had straight black hair, which he wore parted in the centre; a dark, but not pale complexion; black eyebrows, firmly marking the edge of a brow over which was a singularly upright, flat, white forehead, and under which beamed a pair of eyes, dark, brilliant, reflecting, gay, and kind, with a certain look of observant humour....

In conversation Leigh Hunt was always more than pleasing; he was "ever a special lover of books," as well as a devout worshipper of Nature; and his "talk" mingled, often very sweetly, the simplicity of a child with the acquirements of a man of the world....

When I saw him last he was yielding to the universal conqueror. His loose and straggling white hair thinly scattered over a brow of manly intelligence: his eyes dimmed somewhat, but retaining that peculiar gentleness yet brilliancy which in his youth were likened to those of a gazelle; his earnest heart and vigorous mind outspeaking yet, in sentences eloquent and impressive; his form partially bent, but energetic and self-dependent, although by fits and starts — Leigh Hunt gave me the idea of a sturdy ruin, that "wears the mossy vest of time," but which, in assuming the graces that belong of right to age, was not oblivious of the power, and worth, and triumph enjoyed in manhood and in youth. — A Book of Memories (1877).

Nathaniel Hawthorne

When I reached home, at about half past two, I found Sophia [Hawthorne's wife] awaiting me anxiously; for Mrs. [Russell] Sturgis had notified Leigh Hunt that we were coming to visit him at Hammersmith, and she was to send her carriage for us at three o'clock. Barry Cornwall [the pen name of Bryan Waller Procter] had likewise written me a note, and a note of introduction to Leigh Hunt. At three, the carriage came; and though the sky looked very ominous, we drove off, and reached Hammersmith in half an hour, or little more — the latter part of the drive in a real gush and pour of rain. Mr. Hunt met us at the door of his little house; a very plain and shabby little house, in a contiguous range of others like it, with no view but an ugly village-street, and nothing beautiful inside or out. But Leigh Hunt is a beautiful and venerable old man, tall and slender, with a striking face, and the gentlest and most naturally courteous manners. He ushered us into his little study, or parlor, or both; a very mean room, with poor paper-hangings and carpet, few books, and an awful lack of upholstery; all which defects it is sad to see, because Leigh Hunt would so much enjoy all beautiful things, and would seem to be in his place among them; nor has he the grim dignity that makes nakedness the better robe.

He is a beautiful man. I never saw a finer face, either as to the cut of the features, or the expression, or that showed the play of feeling so well. At my first glimpse of his face, when he met us in the entry, I saw that he was old, his long hair being quite white, and his wrinkles many; an aged visage, in short. But as he talked, and became earnest in conversation, I ceased to see his age; and sometimes a flash of youth came out of his eyes, and illuminated his whole face. It was a really wonderful effect. I have never met an Englishman whose manners pleased me so well; with so little that was conventional, and yet perfect good-breeding, it being the growth of a kindly and sensitive nature, without any reference to rule. His eyes are dark, and very fine, and his voice accompanies them like music; — a very pleasant voice. He is exceedingly appreciative of what is passing among those who surround him. I felt that no effect of what he said — no flitting feeling in myself — escaped him; and, indeed, it rather confused me to see always a ripple on his face, responsive to any slightest breeze over my mind. His figure is very mobile; and as he talks, he folds his hands nervously, and betokens in many ways a nature delicate and immediately sensitive, quick to feel pleasure or pain. There is not an English trait in him, from head to foot, nor either intellectually or physically; no beef, no ale or stout; and this is the reason that the English have appreciated him no better, and that they leave this sweet and delicate poet poor, and with scanty laurels, in his old age. It is his American blood (his mother was a Pennsylvanian) that gives him whatever excellence he has — the fineness, subtlety, and grace that characterize him — and his person, too, is thoroughly American. I wonder that America has not appreciated him better, were it only for our own claims in him.

He loves dearly to be praised; that is, he loves sympathy as a flower likes sunshine; and in response to all that we said about his writings (and, for my part, I went quite to the extent of my conscience) his face shone, and he expressed great delight. He could not tell us, he said, the happiness that such appreciation gave him; it always took him by surprise, he remarked, for — perhaps because he cleaned his own boots, and performed other little ordinary offices for himself — he never was conscious of anything wonderful in his own person. And then he smiled. It is usually very difficult for me to praise a man to his face; but Mr. Hunt snuffs up the incense with such gracious satisfaction that it was comparatively easy to praise him; and then, too, we were the representatives of our country, and spoke for thousands. The rain poured, while we were talking, the lightning flashed, and the thunder broke; but I fancy it was really a sunny hour for Leigh Hunt. He, on his part, praised the Scarlet Letter; but I really do not think that I like to be praised *viva voce*; at least, I am glad when it is said and done with, though I will not say that my heart does not expand a little towards the man who rightly appreciates my books. But I am of somewhat sterner stuff and tougher fibre than Leigh Hunt; and the dark seclusion — the atmosphere without any oxygen of sympathy — in which I spent all the years of my youthful manhood — have enabled me to do almost as well without as with it.

Leigh Hunt must have suffered keenly in his life, and enjoyed keenly; keeping his feelings so much upon the surface as he does, and convenient for everybody to play upon. But happiness has greatly pre-dominated, no doubt. A light, mildly joyous nature, gentle, graceful, yet perhaps without that deepest grace that results from strength. I am inclined to imagine that he may be more beautiful, now, both in person and character, than in his earlier days; for the gravity of age sheds a venerable grace about him, after all, and gives a dignity which he may have lacked at first....

The sun shone out once, while we were talking, but was soon over-clouded; and it rained briskly again when we left his door. As we took leave he kissed Una's hand [Hawthorne's daughter]; for she had accompanied us, and sat listening earnestly, and looking very pretty, though saying not a word. He shook and grasped warmly both my hands, at parting; and seemed as much interested as if he had known us for years; and all this was genuine feeling, a quick, luxuriant growth out of his heart — a soil in which to sow flower-seeds, not acorns — but a true heart, nevertheless. His dress, by the by, was black, the coat buttoned up so high that I saw no sign of a shirt. His housemaid (my wife and Una say) was particularly slovenly in appearance. But Leigh Hunt himself is a beautiful object. — *Journals*, 5 October 1855.

William Hazlitt

We shall conclude the present article with a short notice of an individual ... whose merits we should descant at greater length, but that personal intimacy might be supposed to render us partial. It is well when personal intimacy produces this effect; and when the light, that dazzled us at a distance, does not on a closer inspection turn out an opaque substance. This is a charge that none of his friends will bring against Mr. Leigh Hunt. He improves upon acquaintance. The author translates admirably into the man. Indeed the very faults of his style are virtues in the individual. His natural gaiety and sprightliness of manner, his high animal spirits, and the *vinous* quality of his mind, produce an immediate fascination and intoxication in those who come in contact with him, and carry off in society whatever in his writings may to some seem flat and impertinent. From great sanguineness of temper, from great quickness and unsuspecting simplicity, he runs on to the public as he does at his own fireside, and talks about himself, forgetting that he is not always among friends. His look, his tone are required to point many things that he says: his frank, cordial manner reconciles you instantly to a little over-bearing, over-weening self-complacency. 'To be admired, he needs but to be seen': but perhaps he ought to be seen to be fully appreciated. No one ever sought his society who did not come away with a more favourable opinion of him: no one was ever disappointed, except those who had entertained idle prejudices against him. He sometimes trifles with his reader, or tires of a subject (from not being urged on by the stimulus of immediate sympathy) – but in conversation he is all life and animation, combining the vivacity of the schoolboy with the resources of the wit and the taste of the scholar. The personal character, the spontaneous impulses, do not appear to excuse the author, unless you are acquainted with his situation and habits – like some proud beauty who gives herself what we think strange airs and graces under a mask, but who is instantly forgiven when she shews her face. We have said that Lord Byron is a sublime coxcomb: why should we not say that Mr. Hunt is a delightful one? There is certainly an exuberance of satisfaction in his manner which is more than the strict logical premises warrant, and which dull and phlegmatic consitutions know nothing of, and cannot understand till they see it.... A light, familiar grace, and mild unpretending pathos are the characteristics of his more sportive or serious writings, whether in poetry or prose. A smile plays round the sparkling features of the one; a tear is ready to start from the thoughtful gaze of the other. He perhaps takes too little pains, and indulges in too much wayward caprice in both. A wit and a poet, Mr. Hunt is also distinguished by fineness of tact and sterling sense: he has only been a visionary in humanity, the fool of virtue. What then is the drawback to so many shining qualities, that has made them useless, or even hurtful to their owner? His crime is, to have been Editor of the *Examiner* ten years ago, when some allusion was made in it to the age of the present King, and though his Majesty has grown older, our luckless politician is no wiser than he was then! – *The Spirit of the Age* (1825).

Frederick Locker-Lampson

There are not a few misty portraits hanging in the gallery of my failing memory: Mr. Leigh Hunt's is one of them. I made his acquaintance in 1859 at No. 7 Cornwall Road, Hammersmith, where he lived, not wholly in the busy world, not quite beyond it. I walked thither with Mr. Joseph Severn, the painter friend of John Keats, and we found the man of letters seated in the corner of his poorly furnished parlour. It was a small room, in a small house, looking out on patches of small back gardens. There were one or two busts, and on the walls a few prints. Mr. Hunt had a book in his hand, and many books were lying about, on the table and under the table; there were books (shaggy books) and papers everywhere. By his side was a common white jug filled with yellow flowers.

Mr. Hunt was striking in appearance — tall, dark, grizzled, bright-eyed, and rather fantastically dressed in a sacerdotal-looking garment....

Mr. Hunt was most amiable: he discoursed about poetry as exhilaratingly as Ruskin does about art. He spoke of his own writings, and quite unaffectedly. It appeared to give him pleasure to do so. Perhaps if he had talked less about them it would have been because he thought the more.

He seemed proud of his old age, speaking with a smile of his *soixante et mille ans*. He gave me the impession of being rich in the milk of amiability and optimism. I do not think this was feigned, for I often heard of him as a benevolently minded man.

I could hardly realise that this was the Mr. Hunt who had written that underbred book about 'Bryon and his Contemporaries.' I suppose age and experience had mellowed him. I wish I had asked him about Byron; there is no doubt that he had been sorely tried by that unhappy creature. — *My Confidences* (1896).

Bryan Waller Procter

When I first visited Leigh Hunt (1817), he lived at No. 8, York Buildings, in the New Road. His house was small, and scantily furnished. In it was a tiny room, built out at the back of the drawing-room or first floor, which he appropriated as a study, and over the door of this was a line from the "Faery Queen" of Spenser, painted in gold letters. On a small table in this study, covered with humble green baize, Leigh Hunt sat and wrote his articles for the "Examiner" and "Indicator," and his verses. He had very few books, an edition of the Italian Poets in many volumes, Spenser's works, and the minor poems of Milton (edited by Warton) being, however, amongst them. I don't think that there was a Shakespeare. There were always a few cut flowers, in a glass of water, on the table.

Hunt was a little above the middle size, thin and lithe. His countenance was very genial and pleasant. His hair was black; his eyes were very dark, but he was short-sighted, and therefore perhaps it was that they had nothing of that fierce glance which black eyes so frequently possess. His mouth was expressive, but protruding; as is sometimes seen in half-caste Americans. It was shortly after my first visit that I met Charles Lamb, Hazlitt, [Thomas Love] Peacock, Walter Coulson, and others at supper there. Hunt never gave dinners, but his suppers of cold meat and salad were cheerful and pleasant; sometimes the cheerfulness (after a "wassail bowl") soared into noisy merriment. I remember one Christmas or New Year's evening, when we sat there till two or three o'clock in the morning, and when the jokes and stories and imitations so overcame me that I was nearly falling off my chair with laughter....

Leigh Hunt was always in trouble about money; but he was seldom sad, and never sour. The prospect of poverty did not make much impression on him who never possessed wealth. Otherwise he would probably have pursued some regular laborious employment. He deceived himself, when he said that he could not understand accounts. He had a good logical head and great quickness, but he liked the tasks to which he devoted his life. He liked to display his worship for Spenser, to criticise poetry, and to write of May-day and of rural pleasures. I believe that he seldom if ever undertook a task to which he was originally disinclined. There is no doubt that some of his voluntaries became wearisome before completion, but the work was always commenced because it was attractive to him.

Hunt had a crotchet or theory about social intercourse (between the sexes), to which he never made any converts. He was at one time too frequently harping on this subject. This used to irritate Hazlitt, who said, "D—— him; it's always coming out like a rash. Why doesn't he write a book about it, and get rid of it." Hunt did not press these opinions upon any one to a pitch of offence. He himself led a very domestic and correct life. And I am bound to say that, during an intimacy of many (forty) years, I never heard him utter an oath, although they were then very common; and I never heard from him an indelicate hint or allusion. Notwithstanding he indulged himself occasionally in pet words, some of which struck me as approaching almost to the vulgar. He was essentially a gentleman in conduct, in demeanour, in manner, in his consideration for others — indeed, in all things that constitute the material of a gentleman. He was very good tempered; thoroughly easy tempered. He saw hosts of writers, of less ability than himself, outstripping him on the road to future success, yet I never heard from him a word that could be construed into jealously or envy; not even a murmur....

He had no vanity, in the usually accepted meaning of the word. I mean, that he had not that exclusive vanity which rejects almost all things beyond self. He gave as well as received; no one more willingly. He accepted praise less as a mark of respect from others, than as a delight of which all are entitled to partake, such as spring weather, the scent of flowers, or the flavour of wine. It is difficult to explain this; it was like an absorbing property in the surface of the skin. Its possessor enjoys pleasure almost involuntarily, whilst another of colder or harder temperament is insensible to it. He had good, but not violent impulses. He was soon swayed, less by his convictions than by his affections. His mind had not much of the debating element in it. His smiles and tears were easy.

Yet Leigh Hunt was sometimes persistent in his opinions; especially in reference to books and music which he loved. But his comparative estimates of authors were perhaps sometimes at fault. He liked Milton more, and Spenser far more, than Shakespeare. I never saw a volume of that greatest of dramatists and poets in his house; but the beloved Spenser was always there, close at hand, for quotation or reference. I suspect that his reading was not very extensive, and that he therefore made up his mind upon too confined a view. He became a critic and a pronouncer of his own opinions too early. It is best to begin life by becoming a disciple. Hunt was never an under-graduate. He became a dispenser of praise and blame too soon after his departure from Christ's Hospital School. — "Recollections of Men of Letters" in *An Autobiographical Fragment* (1877).

Percy Bysshe Shelley

I had, last month, an unexpected letter from your friend, Leigh Hunt, whom I have since visited. He is indeed a most friendly, and excellent man. I have found few such as he appears to be in the world. He was so kind as to listen to the story of persecution which I am now enduring from a libidinous and vindictive woman, and to stand by me as yet by his counsel, and by his personal attentions to me. — From a letter to Lord Byron, 17 January 1817.

HENRY JAMES

Stopford Brooke

When he could not get the very word or adjective he wanted, it was most amusing to see him with one hand in the air, till he found it, when he flashed his hand down into the palm of the other and brought with a triumphant look the word he wanted, the exact word. Meanwhile when the word delayed, he piled up sentence after sentence and parenthetic side issues — till at last all was obscurity, and obscurity he thought was cleared when he discovered the elusive word he wanted. This was what his style became in his books. — *Diary*, 6 March 1916.

Anne Douglas Sedgwick

H.J. has shaved off his beard and is now clean-shaved, a rather stout, middle-aged man, with a large, regular, pale face, cold yet kind grey eyes, and something the look of a clever French priest in secular dress. He has a very hesitating yet decisive way of speaking — I mean the thought is decisive and the search of its expression give one an impression of fastidious choice; I liked him in the talk we had — all about dogs; he adores them. — *Anne Douglas Sedgwick* (1936).

Edith Wharton

While I was hesitating and peering out [of the motorcar] into the darkness James spied an ancient doddering man who had stopped in the rain to gaze at us. "Wait a moment, my dear — I'll ask him where we are"; and leaning out he signalled to the spectator.

"My good man, if you'll be good enough to come here, please; a little nearer — so," and as the old man came up: "My friend, to put it to you in two words, this lady and I have just arrived here from *Slough*; that is to say, to be more strictly accurate, we have recently *passed through* Slough on our way here, having actually motored to Windsor from Rye, which was our point of departure; and the darkness having overtaken us, we should be much obliged if you would tell us where we now are in relation, say, to the High Street, which, as you of course know, leads to the Castle, after leaving on the left hand the turn down to the railway station."

I was not surprised to have this extraordinary appeal met by silence, and a dazed expression on the old wrinkled face at the window; nor to have James go on: "In short" (his invariable prelude to a fresh series of explanatory ramifications), "in short, my good man, what I want to put to you in a word is this: supposing we have already (as I have reason to think we have) driven past the turn down to the railway station (which in that case, by the way, would probably not have been on our left hand, but on our right) where are we now in relation to ..."

"Oh, please," I interrupted, feeling myself utterly unable to sit through another parenthesis, "do ask him where the King's Road is."

"Ah — ? The King's Road? Just so! Quite right! Can you, as a matter of fact, my good man, tell us where, in relation to our present position, the King's Road exactly *is*?"

"Ye're in it," said the aged face at the window. — *A Backward Glance* (1934).

SAMUEL JOHNSON

James Boswell

His figure was large and well formed, and his countenance of the cast of an ancient statue; yet his appearance was rendered strange and somewhat uncouth, by convulsive cramps, by the scars of that distemper which it was once imagined the royal touch could cure, and by a slovenly mode of dress. He had the use only of one eye; yet so much does mind govern, and even supply the deficiency of organs, that his visual perceptions, as far as they extended, were uncommonly quick and accurate. So morbid was his temperament, that he never knew the natural joy of a free and vigourous use of his limbs; when he walked, it was like the struggling gait of one in fetters; when he rode, he had no command or direction of his horse, but was carried as if in a balloon. That with his constitiution and habits of life he should have lived seventy-five years, is a proof that an inherent vivida vis is a powerful preservative of the human frame....

At different times, he seemed a different man, in some respects; not, however, in any great or essential article, upon which he had fully employed his mind, and settled certain principles of duty, but only in his manners, and in the display of argument and fancy in his talk. He was prone to superstition, but not to credulity. Though his imagination might incline him to a belief of the marvelous and the mysterious, his vigorous reason examined the evidence with jealousy....

He was steady and inflexible in maintaining the obligations of religion and morality; both from a regard for the order of society, and from a veneration for the GREAT SOURCE of all order; correct, nay stern in his taste; hard to please, and easily offended; impetuous and irritable in his temper, but of a most humane and benevolent heart, which shewed itself not only in a most liberal charity, as far as his circumstances would allow, but in a thousand instances of active benevolence. He was afflicted with a bodily disease, which made him often restless and fretful; and with a constitutional melancholy, the clouds of which darkened the brightness of his fancy, and gave a gloomy cast to his whole course of thinking: we, therefore, ought not to wonder at his sallies of impatience and passion at any time; especially when provoked by obtrusive ignorance, or presuming petulance; and allowance must be made for his uttering hasty and satirical sallies even against his best friends.... He loved praise, when it was brought to him; but was too proud to seek for it. He was somewhat susceptible of flattery. As he was general and unconfined in his studies, he cannot be considered as master of any one particular science; but he had accumulated a vast and various collection of learning and knowledge, which was so arranged in his mind, as to be ever in readiness to be brought forth. But his superiority over other learned men consisted chiefly in what may be called the art of thinking, the art of using his mind; a certain continual power of seizing the useful substance of all that he knew, and exhibiting it in a clear and forcible manner; so that knowledge, which we often see to be no better than lumber in men of dull understanding, was, in him, true, evident, and acutal wisdom.... Though usually grave, and even awful in his deportment, he possessed uncommon and peculiar powers of wit and humour; he frequently indulged himself in colloquial pleasantry; and the heartiest merriment was often enjoyed in his company; with this great advantage, that, as it was entirely free from any poisonous tincture of vice or impiety, it was salutary to those who shared in it. He had accustomed himself to such accuracy in his common conversation, that he at all times expressed his thoughts with great force, and an elegant choice of language, the effect of which was aided by his having a loud voice, and a slow deliberate utterance. In him were united a most logical head with a most fertile imagination, which gave him an extraordinary advantage in arguing: for he could reason close or wide, as he saw best for the moment. Exulting in his intellectual strength and dexterity, he could, when he pleased, be the greatest sophist that ever contended in the lists of declamation; and, from a spirit of contradiction and a delight in shewing his powers, he would often maintain the wrong side with equal warmth and ingenuity; so that, when there was an audience, his real opinions could seldom be gathered from his talk; though when he was in company with a single friend, he would discuss a subject with genuine fairness; but he was too conscientious to make errour permanent and pernicious, by deliberately writing it; and, in all his numerous works, he earnestly inculcated what appeared to him to be the truth; his piety being constant, and the ruling principle of all his conduct.

Such was SAMUEL JOHNSON, a man whose talents, acquirements, and virtues were so extraordinary, that the more his character is considered the more he will be regarded by the present age, and by posterity, with admiration and reverence. — Boswell's *Life of Samuel Johnson* (1791).

Fanny Burney

Mrs. and Miss Thrale, Miss Owen, and Mr. Seward came long before *Lexiphanes*. Mrs. Thrale is a very pretty woman still; she is extremely lively and chatty; has no supercilious or pedantic airs, and is really gay and agreeable. Her daughter is about twelve years old, stiff and proud, I believe, or else shy and reserved: I don't yet know which....

My sister Burney was invited to meet and play to them. The conversation was supported with a good deal of vivacity (N.B. my father being at home) for about half an hour, and then Hetty and *Sukey*, for the first time *in public*, played a duet; and in the midst of this performance Dr. Johnson was announced. He is, indeed, very ill-favoured; is tall and stout; but stoops terribly; he is almost bent double. His mouth is almost constantly opening and shutting, as if he was chewing. He has a strange method of frequently twirling his fingers, and twisting his hands. His body is in continual agitation, *see-sawing* up and down; his feet are never a moment quiet; and, in short, his whole person is in *perpetual motion*. His dress, too, considering the times, and that he had meant to put on his *best becomes*, being engaged to dine in a large company, was as much out of the common road as his figure; he had a large wig, snuff-colour coat, and gold buttons, but no ruffles to his shirt, dirty fists, and black worsted stockings. He is shockingly near-sighted, and did not, till she held out her hand to him, even know Mrs. Thrale. He *poked his nose* over the keys of the harpsichord, till the duet was finished, and then my father introduced Hetty to him as an old acquaintance, and he cordially kissed her! When she was a little girl, he had made her a present of "*The Idler.*"

His attention, however, was not to be diverted five minutes from the books, as we were in the library; he pored over them, shelf by shelf, almost touching the backs of them with his eye-lashes, as he read their titles. At last, having fixed upon one, he began, without further cere- mony, to read to himself, all the time standing at a distance from the company. We were all very much provoked, as we perfectly languished to hear him talk; but it seems he is the most silent creature, when not particularly drawn out, in the world.

My sister then played another duet with my father; but Dr. Johnson was so deep in the *Encyclopédie* that, as he is very deaf, I ques- tion if he even knew what was going forward. When this was over, Mrs. Thrale, in a laughing manner, said, "Pray, Dr. Burney, can you tell me what that song was and whose, which Savoi sung last night at [Johann Christian] Bach's Concert, and which you did not hear?" My father con- fessed himself by no means so good a diviner, not having had time to consult the stars, though in the house of Sir Isaac Newton. However, wishing to draw Dr. Johnson into some conversation, he told him the question. The Doctor, seeing his drift, good-naturedly put away his book, and said very drolly, "And pray, Sir, *who is Bach?* is he a piper?" Many exclamations of surprise you will believe followed this question. — From a letter to Samuel Crisp, 27 and 28 March 1777.

Rev. Dr. Thomas Campbell

Johnson, you are the very man Lord Chesterfield describes: — a Hottentot indeed, and tho' your abilities are respectable, you never can be respected yourself. He has the aspect of an Idiot, without the faintest ray of sense gleaming from any one feature — with the most awkward garb, and unpowdered wig, on one side only of his head — he is for ever dancing the devil's jig, and sometimes he makes the most driveling effort to whistle some thought in his absent paroxisms.... His awkwardness at table is just what Chesterfield described, and his roughness of manners kept pace with that. — *A Diary of a Visit to England in 1775* (1947).

George Colman

On the day of my introduction [to Johnson], he was ask'd to dinner at my father's house, in Soho-square, and the Erudite Savage came a full hour before his time. I happen'd to be with my father, who was beginning his toilette, when it was announced to him that the Doctor had arrived. My sire, being one of the tributary princes who did homage to this monarch, was somewhat flurried; and, having dress'd himself hastily, took me with him into the drawing-room.

On our entrance, we found Johnson sitting in a *fauteuil* of rose-coloured satin, the arms and legs of which (of the chair, remember, not of the Doctor,) were of burnish'd gold; and the contrast of the man with the seat was very striking; — an unwash'd Coal-heaver in a *vis-à-vis* could not be much more misplaced than Johnson thus deposited. He was dress'd in a rusty suit of brown cloth *dittos*, with black worsted stockings; — his old yellow wig was of formidable dimensions; and the learned head which sustain'd it roll'd about in a seemingly paralytick motion; but, in the performance of its orbit, it inclined chiefly to one shoulder, — whether to the right or left, I cannot now remember; — a fault never to be forgiven by certain of the *Twaddleri*, who think these matters of the utmost importance.

He deign'd not to rise on our entrance; and we stood before him while he and my father talk'd. — There was soon a pause in the colloquy; and my father, making his advantage of it, took me by the hand, and said, — "Doctor Johnson, this is a little Colman." The Doctor bestow'd a slight ungracious glance upon me, and, continuing the rotary motion of his head, renew'd the previous conversation. — Again there was a pause; — and the anxious father, who had fail'd in his first effort, seized the opportunity for pushing his progeny, with — "This is my son, Doctor Johnson." The great man's contempt for me was now roused to wrath; — and, knitting his brows, he exclaim'd in a voice of thunder, "I *see* him, sir!" — he then fell back in his rose-colour'd satin *fauteuil*, as if giving himself up to meditation; implying that he would not be further plagued, either with an old fool or a young one.

The gigantick Johnson could not be easily thrown out at window, — particularly by my under-sized sire; — but he deserved to be "quoited down stairs, like a shove-groat shilling;" not exactly, perhaps, for his brutality to the boy, but for such an unprovoked insult to the father, of whose hospitalities he was partaking....

After this rude rebuff from the Doctor, I had the additional felicity to be placed next to him at dinner: — he was silent over his meal; but I observed that he was, as Shylock says of Lancelot Gobbo, "a huge feeder;" and during the display of his voracity, (which was worthy of *Bolt* Court,) the perspiration fell in copious drops from his visage upon the table-cloth: — the clumsiness of the bulky animal, his strange costume, his uncouth gestures, yet the dominion which he usurp'd withal, render'd his presence a phenomenon among gentlemen; — it was the incursion of a new species of Barbarian, — a *learned* Attila, King of the Huns, come to subjugate polish'd society. — *Random Records* (1830).

Rev. Dr. William Dodd

I spent yesterday afternoon with Johnson, the celebrated author of *The Rambler*, who is of all others the oddest and most peculiar fellow I ever saw. He is six feet high, and his eyes are distorted. He speaks roughly and loud, listens to no man's opinions, thoroughly pertinacious of his own. Good sense flows from him in all he utters, and he seems possessed of a prodigious fund of knowledge, which he is not at all reserved in communicating; but in a manner so obstinate, ungenteel, and boorish, as renders it disagreeable and dissatisfactory. In short, it is impossible for words to describe him. He seems often inattentive to what passes in company, and then looks like a person possessed by some superior spirit. I have been reflecting on him ever since I saw him. He is a man of most universal and surprising genius, but in himself particular beyond expression. — From a letter written in 1750; quoted in Boswell's *Life of Samuel Johnson* (1791).

Hester Lynch Thrale Piozzi

His stature was remarkably high, and his limbs exceedingly large: his strength was more than common I believe, and his activity had been greater I have heard than such a form gave one reason to expect: his features were strongly marked, and his countenance particularly rugged; though the original complexion had certainly been fair, a circumstance somewhat ususual: his sight was near, and otherwise imperfect; yet his eyes, though of a light-grey colour, were so wild, so piercing, and at times so fierce, that fear was I believe the first emotion in the hearts of all his beholders. His mind was so comprehensive, that no language but that he used could have expressed its contents; and so ponderous was his language, that sentiments less lofty and less solid than his were, would have been encumbered, not adorned by it. — *Anecdotes of the late Samuel Johnson, LL.D., during the Last Twenty Years of his Life* (1786).

John Thomas Smith

At this period [1778] I began to think there was something in a prognostication announced to my dear mother by an old *star-gazer* and *tea-grouter*, that, through life, I should be favoured by persons of high rank; for, in this year, Charles Townley, Esq., first noticed me when drawing in Mr. [Joseph] Nollekens' studio, and pouched me half a guinea to purchase paper and chalk. This kindness was followed up by Dr. Samuel Johnson, who was then sitting for his bust. The Doctor, after looking at my drawing, then at the bust I was copying, put his hand heavily upon my head, pronouncing, "Very well, very well." Here I frequently saw him, and recollect his figure and dress with tolerable correctness. He was tall, and must have been, when young, a powerful man: he stooped, with his head inclined to the right shoulder: heavy brows, sleepy eyes, nose very narrow between the eye-brows, but broad at the bottom; lips enormously thick; chin, wide and double. He wore a stock and wrist bands; his wig was what is called a "Busby", but often wanted powder. His hat, a three-cornered one; coats, one a dark mulberry, the other brown, inclining to the colour of Scotch snuff; large brass or gilt buttons, black waistcoat, black stockings, large easy shoes, with buckles; latterly he used a *hooked* walking-stick: his gait was wide and awkwardly sprawling.

I once saw him follow a sturdy thief, who had stolen his hand-kerchief in Grosvenor Square, seize him by the collar by both hands, and shake him violently, after which he quickly let him loose; and then, with his open hand, gave him so powerful a smack on the face, that sent him off the pavement staggering. — *A Book for a Rainy Day* (1845).

Himself

You may observe that I am well-bred to a degree of needless scrupulosity. No man is so cautious not to interrupt another; no man thinks it so necessary to appear attentive when others are speaking; no man so steadily refuses preference to himself, or so willingly bestows it on another, as I do; no body holds so strongly as I do the necessity of ceremony, and the ill effects which follow the breach of it: yet people think me rude. — Quoted by Mrs. Piozzi in *Anecdotes of the late Samuel Johnson, LL.D., during the Last Twenty Years of his Life* (1786).

[Also see Edward Gibbon — George Colman.]

BEN JONSON

William Drummond

He is a great lover and praiser of himself, a contemner and Scorner of others, given rather to losse a friend, than a jest, jealous of every word and action of those about him (especiallie after drink) which is one of the Elements in which he liveth, a dissembler of ill parts which raigne in him, a bragger of some good that he wanteth, thinketh nothing well bot what either he himself, or some of his friends and Countrymen hath said or done. he is passionately kynde and angry, carelesse either to gaine or keep, vindicative, but if he be well answered, at himself. for any religion as being versed in both. Interpreteth best saying and deeds often to the worst: oppressed with fantasie, which hath ever mastered his reason, a generall disease in many poets. his inventions are smooth and easie, but above all he excelleth in a translation. — *Informations be Ben Iohnston to W.D. when he came to Scotland upon foot* (1619).

James Howell

I was invited yesternight to a solemne supper by *B.I.* wher you were deeply remembred, ther was good company excellent chear, choice wines, and joviall welcome; one thing interven'd which almost spoyld the relish of the rest, that *B.* began to engross all the discourse, to vapour extremely of himself, and by villifying others to magnifie his owne *muse*; *T. Ca.* buz'd me in the eare, that though *Ben* had barreld up a great deal of knowledg, yet it seems he had not read the *Ethiques*, which among other precepts of morality forbid self-commendation, declaring it to be an ill favoured solecism in good manners; It made me think upon the Lady (not very young) who having a good while given her guests neat entertainment, a capon being brought upon the table, instead of a spoon she took a mouthfull of claret and spouted it into the poope of the hollow bird; such an accident happened in this entertainment you know — *Proprio laus sordet in ore*; *be a mans breath never so sweet, yet it makes ones prayses stink, if he makes his owne mouth the conduit pipe of it*; But for my part I am content to dispense with this *Roman* infirmity of *B.* now that time hath snowed upon his pericranium. — From a letter to Sir Thomas Hawkins, 5 April 1636.

JAMES JOYCE

Sylvia Beach

I strolled into a little room lined to the ceiling with books. There, drooping in a corner between two bookcases, was Joyce.

Trembling, I asked: "Is this the great James Joyce?"

"James Joyce," he replied.

We shook hands; that is, he put his limp, boneless hand in my tough little paw — if you can call that a handshake.

He was of medium height, thin, slightly stooped, graceful. One noticed his hands. They were very narrow. On the middle and third fingers of the left hand, he wore rings, the stones in heavy settings. His eyes, a deep blue, with the light of genius in them, were extremely beautiful. I noticed, however, that the right eye had a slightly abnormal look and that the right lens of his glasses was thicker than the left. His hair was thick, sandy-colored, wavy, and brushed back from a high, lined forehead over his tall head. He gave an impression of sensitiveness exceeding any I had ever known. His skin was fair, with a few freckles, and rather flushed. On his chin was a sort of goatee. His nose was well-shaped, his lips narrow and fine-cut. I thought he must have been very handsome as a young man.

Joyce's voice, with its sweet tones pitched like a tenor's, charmed me. His enunciation was exceptionally clear. His pronunciation of certain words such as "book" (boo-k) and "look" (loo-k) and those beginning with "th" was Irish, and the voice particularly was Irish. Otherwise there was nothing to distinguish his English from that of the Englishman. He expressed himself quite simply but, as I observed, with a care for the words and the sounds — partly, no doubt, because of his love of language and his musical ear, but also, I believe, because he had spent so many years teaching English....

Suddenly a dog barked, and Joyce turned pale; he actually trembled. The bark came from across the road. I looked out of the window and saw a dog running after a ball. It had a loud bark but, as far as I could tell, no bite.

"Is it coming in? Is it fierce?" Joyce asked me, very uneasy. (He pronounced it "feerrce.") I assured him it wasn't coming in, and didn't look at all fierce, but he was still apprehensive and startled by every bark. He told me he had been afraid of dogs since the age of five, when one of "the animals" had bitten him on the chin. Pointing to his goatee, he said that it was to hide the scar....

Joyce's fear of a great many things was real, though I think it was partly cultivated as a counterbalance to his fearlessness where his art was concerned. He seemed afraid of "catching it" from God Almighty. The Jesuits must have succeeded in putting the fear of God into him. I have seen Joyce, when a thunderstorm was going on, cower in the hall of his apartment till it was over. He was afraid of heights, of the sea, of infection. Then there were his superstitions, which were shared by the family. Seeing two nuns in the street was bad luck (a taxi he was in collided with another vehicle on one of these occasions); numbers and dates were lucky or unlucky. Opening an umbrella in the house, a man's hat on the bed were ill omens. Black cats, on the contrary, were lucky. Arriving one day at the Joyces' hotel, I saw Nora trying to induce a black cat to go into the room where her husband was lying, while through the open door he anxiously observed her efforts. Cats were not only lucky, Joyce liked having them about, and once, when a kitten of his daughter's fell out of the kitchen window, he was as upset about it as she was.

Dogs, on the contrary, he always suspected of being fierce. I used to have to hurry a harmless little white one of mine out of the shop before Joyce would come in. It was useless to remind him of his Odyssean hero, whose faithful dog Argos dropped dead of joy over his master's home-coming. Joyce only exclaimed "*Già!*" with a laugh....

The Joyces were all singers, and Joyce never quite ceased to regret his choice of a writer's instead of a singer's career. "Perhaps I would have done better," he would say to me. "Maybe," I would reply, "but you have done pretty well as a writer." — *Shakespeare and Company* (1959).

Ernest Hemingway

Once in one of those casual conversations you have when you're drinking, Joyce said to me he was afraid his writing was too suburban and that maybe he should get around a bit and see the world. He was afraid of some things — lightning and things, but a wonderful man. He was under great discipline — his wife, his work, and his bad eyes. His wife was there and she said, yes, his work was too suburban — "Jim could do with a spot of that lion-hunting." We would go out to drink and Joyce would fall into a fight. He couldn't even see the man so he'd say: "Deal with him, Hemingway! Deal with him!" — From an article on Hemingway; "An American Storyteller," *Time*, (13 December 1954).

Gertrude Stein

Joyce is *good*. He is a *good* writer. People like him because he is incomprehensible and anybody can understand him. But who came first, Gertrude Stein or James Joyce? Do not forget that my first great book, *Three Lives*, was published in 1908. That was long before *Ulysses*. But Joyce *has* done *something*. His influence, however, is local. Like [John Millington] Synge, another Irish writer, he has had his day. — Quoted by Samuel Putnam in *Paris Was Our Mistress* (1947).

Thomas Wolfe

[Wolfe once rode on the same bus with Joyce and his family but was too shy to introduce himself.] He was with a woman about forty, and a young man, and a girl.... He was wearing a blind over one eye. He was very simply — even shabbily — dressed.... The young man [Joyce's son, George], who wore horn-rim spectacles, and a light sporty looking overcoat, looked very much like an American college boy.... The woman [Joyce's wife, Nora] had the appearance of a thousand middle class French women I've known — a vulgar rather loose mouth; not very intelligent looking.... The girl [Joyce's daughter, Lucia] was rather pretty — I thought at first she was a little American flapper.

Joyce was very simple, very nice. He walked next to the old guide who showed us around, listening with apparent interest to his harangue delivered in broken English, and asking him questions. We came home to Brussels through a magnificent forest, miles in extent — Joyce sat with the driver on the front seat, asked a great many questions. I sat alone on the back seat — it was a huge coach; the woman sat in front of me, the girl in front of her, the young man to one side. Queer arrangement, eh?

Joyce got a bit stagey on the way home, draping his overcoat poetically around his shoulders. But I liked Joyce's looks — not extraordinary at first sight, but growing. His face was highly colored, slightly concave — his mouth thin, not delicate, but extraordinarily humourous. He had a large powerful straight nose — redder than his face, somewhat pitted with scars and boils. — From a letter to Aline Bernstein, 7? September 1928.

JOHN KEATS

Samuel Taylor Coleridge

A loose, slack, not well-dressed youth met Mr. Green and myself in a lane near Highgate. Green knew him, and spoke. It was Keats. He was introduced to me, and stayed a minute or so. After he had left us a little way, he came back, and said, 'Let me carry away the memory, Coleridge, of having pressed your hand!' 'There is death in that hand,' I said to Green, when Keats was gone; yet this was, I believe, before the consumption showed itself distinctly. [See Samuel Taylor Coleridge — John Keats for Keats' version of this meeting.] — *Table Talk* (1835).

Benjamin Robert Haydon

In fireside conversation he was weak and inconsistent, but he was in his glory in the fields. The humming of a bee, the sight of a flower, the glitter of the sun, seemed to make his nature tremble; then his eyes flashed, his cheek glowed, his mouth quivered. He was the most unselfish of human creatures: unadapted to this world, he cared not for himself, and put himself to any inconvenience for the sake of his friends. He was haughty, and had a fierce hatred of rank; but he had a kind gentle heart, and would have shared his fortune with any man who wanted it. His classical knowledge was inconsiderable, but he could feel the beauties of the classical writers. He had an exquisite sense of humour, and too refined a notion of female purity to bear the little sweet arts of love with patience. He had no decision of character, and having no object upon which to direct his great powers was at the mercy of every petty theory ——'s ingenuity might start.

One day he was full of an epic poem; the next day epic poems were splendid impositions on the world. Never for two days did he know his own intentions.

He began life full of hopes, fiery, impetuous and ungovernable, expecting the world to fall at once beneath his powers. Poor fellow! his genius had no sooner begun to bud than hatred and malice spat their poison on its leaves, and sensitive and young it shrivelled beneath their effusions. Unable to bear the sneers of ignorance or the attacks of envy, not having strength of mind enough to buckle himself together like a porcupine and present nothing but his prickles to his enemies, he began to despond, and flew to dissipation as a relief, which after a temporary elevation of spirits plunged him into deeper despondency than ever. For six weeks he was scarcely sober, and — to show what a man does to gratify his appetites when once they get the better of him — once covered his tongue and throat as far as he could reach with cayenne pepper in order to appreciate the "delicious coldness of claret in all its glory" — his own expression.

The death of his brother wounded him deeply, and it appeared to me that he began to droop from that hour. I was much attached to Keats, and he had a fellow-feeling for me. I was angry because he would not bend his great powers to some definite object, and always told him so. Latterly he grew irritated because I would shake my head at his irregularities and tell him that he would destroy himself.

The last time I ever saw him was at Hampstead, lying in a white bed with a book, hectic, and on his back, irritable at his weakness and wounded at the way he had been used. He seemed to be going out of life with a contempt for this world and no hopes of the other. I told him to be calm, but he muttered that if he did not soon get better he would destroy himself. I tried to reason against such violence, but it was no use; he grew angry, and I went away deeply affected.

Poor dear Keats! Had nature but given you firmness as well as fineness of nerve, you would have been glorious in your maturity as great in your promise. May your kind and gentle spirit be now mingling with those of Shakespeare and Milton, before whose minds you have so often bowed! May you be considered worthy of admission to share their musings in heaven, as you were fit to comprehend their imaginations on earth! — *Journals*, 29 March 1821.

Leigh Hunt

Keats, when he died, had just completed his four-and-twentieth year. He was under the middle height; and his lower limbs were small in comparison with the upper, but neat and well turned. His shoulders were very broad for his size: he had a face in which energy and sensibility were remarkably mixed up; an eager power, checked and made patient by ill-health. Every feature was at once strongly cut, and delicately alive. If there was any faulty expression, it was in the mouth, which was not without something of a character of pugnacity. His face was rather long than otherwise; the upper lip projected a little over the under; the chin was bold, the cheeks sunken; the eyes mellow and glowing; large, dark, and sensitive. At the recital of a noble action, or a beautiful thought, they would suffuse with tears, and his mouth trembled. In this, there was ill-health as well as imagination, for he did not like these betrayals of emotion; and he had great personal as well as moral courage. He once chastised a butcher, who had been insolent, by a regular stand-up fight. His hair, of a brown colour, was fine, and hung in natural ringlets. The head was a puzzle for the phrenologists, being remarkably small in the skull; a singularity which he had in common with Byron and Shelley, whose hats I could not get on. Keats was sensible of the disproportion above noticed, between his upper and lower extremities; and he would look at his hand, which was faded, and swollen in the veins, and say it was the hand of a man of fifty. — *Autobiography* (1859).

Joseph Severn

At times during his last days [in Rome] he made me go to see the place where he was to be buried, and he expressed pleasure at my description of the locality of the Pyramid of Caius Cestius, about the grass and the many flowers, particularly the innumerable violets, also about a flock of goats and sheep and a young shepherd — all these intensely interested him. Violets were his favourite flowers, and he enjoyed to hear how they overspread the graves. He assured me 'that he already seemed to feel the flowers growing over him.'

During the last few days of his life he became very calm and resigned. Again and again, while warning me that his death was fast approaching, he besought me to take all care of myself, telling me 'I was not to look at him in his dying gasp nor breathe his passing breath, not even breathe upon him.' From time to time he gave me all his directions as to what he wanted done after his death. It was in the same sad hour when he told me with greater agitation than he had shown on any other subject, to put the letter which had just come from Miss Brawne (which he was unable to bring himself to read, or even to open), with any other that should arrive too late to reach him in life, inside his winding-sheet on his heart — it was then, also, that he asked that I should see cut upon his gravestone as sole inscription, *not his name*, but simply 'Here lies one whose name is writ in water.' — *The Life and Letters of Joseph Severn* by William Sharp (1892).

Percy Bysshe Shelley

The account of Keats is, I fear, too true. Hunt tells me that in the first paroxysms of his disappointment [from adverse criticism of his work by the *Quarterly Review*] he burst a blood-vessel; and thus laid the foundation of a rapid consumption. There can be no doubt but that the irritability which exposed him to this catastrophe was a pledge of future sufferings, had he lived. And yet this argument does not reconcile me to the employment of contemptuous and wounding expressions against a man merely because he has written bad verses; or, as Keats did, some good verses in a bad taste. Some plants, which require delicacy in rearing, might bring forth beautiful flowers if ever they should arrive at maturity. *Your* instance hardly applies. You felt the strength to soar beyond the arrows; the eagle was soon lost in the light in which it was nourished, and the eyes of the aimers were blinded. As to me, I am, perhaps, morbidly indifferent to this sort of praise or blame; and this, perhaps, deprives me of an incitement to do what now I never shall do, i.e., write anything worth calling a poem. Thanks to that happy indifference, I can yet delight in the productions of those who can; nor has ill-success yet turned me into an unfeeling, and malignant critic; that second degree in the descending scale of the Academy of Disappointed Authors. As to Keats' merits as a poet, I principally repose them upon the fragment of a poem entitled "Hyperion," which you may not, perhaps, have seen, and to which I think you would not deny high praise. The energy and beauty of his powers seem to disperse the narrow and wretched taste in which (most unfortunately for the real beauty which they hid) he has clothed his writings. — From a letter to Lord Byron, 4 May 1821.

Himself

Praise or blame has but a momentary effect on the man whose love of beauty in the abstract makes him a severe critic on his own Works. My own domestic criticism has given me pain without comparison beyond what Blackwood or the Quarterly could possibly inflict, and also when I feel I am right, no external praise can give me such a glow as my own solitary reperception & ratification of what is fine. J.S. [a correspondent for *The Morning Chronicle*] is perfectly right in regard to the slip-shod Endymion. That it is so is no fault of mine. — No! — though it may sound a little paradoxical. It is as good as I had power to make it — by myself. Had I been nervous about its being a perfect piece, & with that view asked advice, & trembled over every page, it would not have been written; for it is not in my nature to fumble — I will write independandly. — I have written independently *without Judgment.* — I may write independently, & *with Judgment* hereafter. The Genius of Poetry must work out its own salvation in a man: It cannot be matured by law and precept, but by sensation & watchfulness in itself. That which is creative must create itself — In Endymion, I leaped headlong into the Sea, and thereby have become better acquainted with the Soundings, the quicksands, & the rocks, than if I had stayed upon the green shore, and piped a silly pipe, and took tea & comfortable advice. — I was never afraid of failure; for I would sooner fail than not be among the greatest. — From a letter to James Augustus Hessey, 9 October 1818.

CHARLES LAMB

Thomas Carlyle

Charles Lamb is a ricketty creature in body and mind, sprawls about and walks as if his body consisted of four ill-conditioned flails, and talks as if he were quarter drunk with ale and half with laudanum. — From a letter to Thomas Murray, 24 August 1824.

Charles Lamb I sincerely believe to be in some considerable degree *insane*. A more pitiful, ricketty, gasping, staggering, stammering Tom fool I do not know. He is witty by denying truisms, and abjuring good manners. His speech wriggles hither and thither with an incessant painful fluctuation; not an opinion in it or a fact or even a phrase that you can thank him for: more like a convulsion fit than natural systole and diastole. — Besides he is now a confirmed shameless drunkard; *asks* vehemently for gin-and-water in strangers' houses; tipples till he is utterly mad, and is only not thrown out of doors because he is too much despised for taking such trouble with him. Poor Lamb! Poor England where such a despicable abortion is named genius! — He said: There are just two things I regret in English History; first that Guy Faux's Plot did not take effect (there would have been so glorious an *explosion*); second, that the Royalists did not hang Milton (then we might have laughed at them): &c. &c. *Armer Teufel*! — 2 November 1831; *Two Note Books* (1898).

We saw Charlie Lamb (*Elia*) at tea: a miserable, drink-besotted, spindle-shanked skeleton of a body; whose "humour", as it is called, seemed to me neither more nor less than a fibre of genius shining thro' positive delirium and crackbrainedness (*verrückheit*), and would be to me the most intolerable of all nuisances. — From a letter to his wife, 29 August 1831.

Charles Lamb and his sister came daily once or oftener; a very sorry pair of phenomena. Insuperable proclivity to gin in poor old Lamb. His talk contemptibly small, indicating wondrous ignorance and shallowness, even when it was serious and good-mannered, which it seldom was, usually ill-mannered (to a degree), screwed into frosty artificialities, ghastly make-believe of wit; in fact, more like "diluted insanity" (as I defined it) than anything of real jocosity, humor, or geniality. A most slender fibre of actual worth in that poor Charles, abundantly recognizable to me as to others, in his better times and moods; but he was cockney to the marrow; and cockneydom, shouting, "glorious, marvellous, unparalleled in nature!" all his days had quite bewildered his poor head, and churned nearly all the sense out of the poor man. He was the leanest of mankind, tiny black breeches buttoned to the knee-cap, and no further, surmounting spindle-legs, also in black, face and head fineish, black, bony, lean, and of a Jew type rather; in the eyes a kind of smoky brightness or confused sharpness; spoke with a stutter; in walking tottered and shuffled; emblem of imbecility bodily and spiritual (something of real insanity I have understood), and yet something too of human, ingenuous, pathetic, sportfully much enduring. Poor Lamb! — *Reminiscences* (1881).

Thomas De Quincey

In miscellaneous gatherings Lamb said little unless an opening arose for a pun. And how effectual that sort of small shot was from *him*, I need not say to anybody who remembers his infirmity of stammering, and his dexterous management of it for purposes of light and shade. He was often able to train the roll of stammers into settling upon the words immediately preceding the effective one; by which means the key-note of the jest or sarcasm, benefiting by the sudden liberation of his embargoed voice, was delivered with the force of a pistol shot. That stammer was worth an annuity to him as an ally of his wit. Firing under cover of that advantage he did triple execution; for, in the first place, the distressing sympathy of the hearers with *his* distress of utterance won for him unavoidably the silence of deep attention; and then, whilst he had us all hoaxed into this attitude of mute suspense by an appearance of distress that he perhaps did not really feel, down came a plunging shot into the very thick of us, with ten times the effect it would else have had. — *Biographical and Historical Essays* (1877).

Benjamin Robert Haydon

In the morning of this delightful day [28 December 1817], a gentleman, a perfect stranger, had called on me. He said he knew my friends, had an enthusiasm for Wordsworth, and begged I would procure him the happiness of an introduction. He told me he was a comptroller of stamps, and often had correspondence with the poet. I thought it a liberty; but still, as he seemed a gentleman, I told him he might come.

When we retired to tea we found the comptroller. In introducing him to Wordsworth I forgot to say who he was. After a little time the comptroller looked down, looked up, and said to Wordsworth: 'Don't you think, sir, Milton was a great genius?' Keats looked at me, Wordsworth looked at the comptroller. Lamb who was dozing by the fire turned round and said: 'Pray, sir, did you say Milton was a great genius?' 'No, sir; I asked Mr. Wordsworth if he were not.' 'Oh,' said Lamb, 'then you are a silly fellow.' 'Charles! my dear Charles!' said Wordsworth; but Lamb, perfectly innocent of the confusion he had created, was off again by the fire.

After an awful pause the comptroller said: 'Don't you think Newton a great genius?' I could not stand it any longer. Keats put his head into my books. [Joseph] Ritchie squeezed in a laugh. Wordsworth seemed asking himself: 'Who is this?' Lamb got up, and taking a candle, said: 'Sir, will you allow me to look at your phrenological development?' He then turned his back on the poor man, and at every question of the comptroller he chaunted: 'Diddle diddle dumpling, my son John/ Went to bed with his breeches on.'

The man in office, finding Wordsworth did not know who he was, said in a spasmodic and half-chuckling anticipation of assured victory: 'I have had the honour of some correspondence with you, Mr. Wordsworth.' 'With me, sir?' said Wordsworth, 'not that I remember.' 'Don't you, sir? I am a comptroller of stamps.' There was a dead silence, the comptroller evidently thinking that was enough. While we were waiting for Wordsworth's reply, Lamb sung out: 'Hey diddle diddle/ The cat and the fiddle.'

'My dear Charles!' said Wordsworth. 'Diddle diddle dumpling, my son John,' chaunted Lamb, and then rising, exclaimed: 'Do let me have another look at that gentleman's organs.' Keats and I hurried Lamb into the painting-room, shut the door, and gave way to inextinguishable laughter. [Thomas] Monkhouse followed and tried to get Lamb away. We went back, but the comptroller was irreconcilable. We soothed and smiled, and asked him to supper. He stayed, though his dignity was sorely affected. However, being a good-natured man, we parted all in good humour, and no ill effects followed.

All the while, until Monkhouse succeeded, we could hear Lamb struggling in the painting-room, and calling at intervals: 'Who is that fellow? Allow me to see his organs once more.' — *Autobiography* (1853).

William Hazlitt

There was L—— himself, the most delightful, the most provoking, the most witty and sensible of men. He always made the best pun, and the best remark in the course of the evening. His serious conversation, like his serious writing, is his best. No one ever stammered out such fine, piquant, deep, eloquent things in half a dozen half sentences as he does. His jests scald like tears; and he probes a question with a play upon words. What a keen, laughing, hair-brained vein of home-felt truth! What choice venom! — "On the Conversation of Authors."

Leigh Hunt

Charles Lamb had a head worthy of Aristotle, with as fine a heart as ever beat in human bosom, and limbs very fragile to sustain it.... There never was a true portrait of Lamb. His features were strongly yet delicately cut; he had a fine eye as well as forehead; and no face carried in it greater marks of thought and feeling.... As his frame, so was his genius. It was as fit for thought as could be, and equally as unfit for action; and this rendered him melancholy, apprehensive, humorous, and willing to make the best of every thing as it was, both from tenderness of heart, and abhorrence of alteration. His understanding was too great to admit an absurdity; his frame was not strong enough to deliver it from a fear. His sensibility to strong contrasts was the foundation of his humor, which was that of a wit at once melancholy and willing to be pleased. He would beard a superstition, and shudder at the old phantasm while he did it. One could have imagined him cracking a jest in the teeth of a ghost, and then melting into thin air himself, out of a sympathy with the awful. — *Autobiography* (1859).

Bryan Waller Procter

Persons who had been in the habit of traversing Covent Garden at that time, (seven-and-forty years ago), might by extending their walk a few yards into Russell Street, have noted a small spare man, clothed in black, who went out every morning and returned every afternoon, as regularly as the hands of the clock moved towards certain hours. You could not mistake him. He was somewhat stiff in his manner, and almost clerical in dress; which indicated much wear. He had a long, melancholy face, with keen penetrating eyes; and he walked with a short, resolute step, City-wards. He looked no one in the face for more than a moment, yet contrived to see everything as he went on....

Charles Lamb was about forty years of age when I first saw him; and I knew him intimately for the greater part of twenty years. Small and spare in person, and with small legs, ("immaterial legs," [Thomas] Hood called them), he had a dark complexion, dark, curling hair, almost black, and a grave look, lightening up occasionally, and capable of sudden merriment. His laugh was seldom excited by jokes merely ludicrous; it was never spiteful; and his quiet smile was sometimes inexpressibly sweet: perhaps it had a touch of sadness in it. His mouth was well-shaped; his lip tremulous with expression; his brown eyes were quick, restless, and glittering: and he had a grand head, full of thought. Leigh Hunt said that "he had a head worthy of Aristotle." Hazlitt calls it "a fine Titian head, full of dumb eloquence."...

Although sometimes strange in manner, he was thoroughly unaffected; in serious matters thoroughly sincere. He was, indeed (as he confesses) terribly shy; diffident, not awkward in manner; with occasionally nervous twitching motions that betrayed this infirmity....

Much injustice has been done to Lamb, by accusing him of excess of drinking. The truth is, that a small quantity of any strong liquid (wine, &c.) disturbed his speech, which at best was but an eloquent stammer....

Lamb himself was always dressed in black. "I take it," he says, "to be the proper costume of an author." When this was once objected to, at a wedding, he pleaded the raven's apology in the fable, that "he had no other." His clothes were entirely black; and he wore long black gaiters, up to the knees. His head was bent a little forward, like one who had been reading; and, if not standing or walking, he generally had in his hand an old book, a pinch of snuff, or, later in the evening, a pipe. He stammered a little, pleasantly, just enough to prevent his making speeches; just enough to make you listen eagerly for his words, always full of meaning, or charged with a jest; or referring (but this was rare,) to some line or passage from one of the old Elizabethan writers, which was always ushered in with a smile of tender reverence. When he read aloud it was with a slight tone, which I used to think he had caught from Coleridge; Coleridge's recitation, however, rising to a chant....

It may be convenient, in this place, to specify some of those examples of humour and of jocose speech, for which Charles Lamb in his lifetime was well known....

I once said something in his presence, which I thought possessed smartness. He commended me with a stammer: "Very well, my dear boy, very well; Ben (taking a pinch of snuff), Ben Jonson has said worse things than that — and b — b — better."...

To Coleridge, "Bless you, old sophist, who next to human nature taught me all the corruption I was capable of knowing."...

To Wordsworth (who was superfluously solemn), he writes, "Some d——d people have come in, and I must finish abruptly. By d——d, I only mean deuced."...

"Charles," said Coleridge [once a preacher in Unitarian

Churches] to Lamb, "I think you have heard me preach?" "I n — n — never heard you do anything else," replied Lamb....

Once, whilst waiting in the Highgate stage a woman came to the door and inquired in a stern voice, "Are you quite full inside?" "Yes, ma'am," said Charles, in meek reply, "quite; that plateful of Mrs. Gillman's pudding has quite filled us."

Mrs. K., after expressing her love for her young children, added, tenderly, "And how do *you* like babies, Mr. Lamb?" His answer, immediate, almost precipitate, was "Boi-boi-boiled, ma'am."...

Of a man too prodigal of lampoons and verbal jokes, Lamb said, threateningly, "I'll Lamb-pun him."...

An old lady, fond of her dissenting minister, wearied Lamb by the length of her praises. I speak, because I *know* him well, said she. "Well, I don't;" replied Lamb; "I don't but d——n him, at a 'venture.' " — *Charles Lamb: A Memoir* (1866).

Percy Bysshe Shelley

What a lovely thing is his "Rosamond Gray!" how much knowledge of the sweetest and deepest part of our nature in it! When I think of such a mind as Lamb's, — when I see how unnoticed remain things of such exquisite and complete perfection, what should I hope for myself, if I had not higher objectives in view than fame? — From a letter to Leigh Hunt, 3 September 1819.

Himself

CHARLES LAMB, born in the Inner Temple, 10th of February, 1775; educated in Christ's Hospital; afterwards a clerk in the Accountants' Office, East-India House; pensioned off from that service, 1825, after thirty-three years' service; is now a gentleman at large; can remember few specialties in his life worth noting, except that he once caught a swallow flying (*teste suâ manu*). Below the middle stature; cast of face slightly Jewish, with no Judaic tinge in his complexional religion; stammers abominably, and is therefore more apt to discharge his occasional conversation in a quaint aphorism, or a poor quibble, than in set and edifying speeches; has consequently been libelled as a person always aiming at wit; which, as he told a dull fellow that charged him with it, is at least as good as aiming at dulness. A small eater, but not drinker; confesses a partiality for the production of the juniper-berry; was a fierce smoker of tobacco, but may be resembled to a volcano burnt out, emitting only now and then a casual puff. Has been guilty of obtruding upon the public a tale, in prose, called "Rosamund Gray"; a dramatic sketch, named "John Woodvil"; a "Farewell Ode to Tobacco," with sundry other poems, and light prose matter, collected in two slight crown octavos, and pompously christened his works, though in fact they were his recreations. His true works may be found on the shelves of Leadenhall Street, filling some hundred folios. He is also the true Elia, whose Essays are extant in a little volume, published a year or two since, and rather better known from that name without a meaning than from anything he has done, or can hope to do, in his own name. He was also the first to draw the public attention to the old English dramatists, in a work called "Specimens of English Dramatic Writers who lived about the Time of Shakspeare," published about fifteen years since. In short, all his merits and demerits to set forth would take to the end of Mr. Upcott's book, and then not be told truly.

He died   18 , much lamented. Witness his hand, CHARLES LAMB. — "Charles Lamb's Autobiography," 18 April 1827.

D.H. LAWRENCE

Bertrand Russell

My acquaintance with Lawrence was brief and hectic, lasting altogether about a year. We were brought together by Lady Ottoline Morrell who admired us both and made us think that we ought to admire each other. Pacifism had produced in me a mood of bitter rebellion and I found Lawrence equally full of rebellion. This made us think, at first, that there was a considerable measure of agreement between us, and it was only gradually that we discovered that we differed from each other more than either differed from the Kaiser....

I liked the energy and passion of his feelings, I liked his belief that something very fundamental was needed to put the world right. I agreed with him in thinking that politics could not be divorced from individual psychology. I felt him to be a man of a certain imaginative genius and, at first, when I felt inclined to disagree with him, I thought that perhaps his insight into human nature was deeper than mine. It was only gradually that I came to feel him a positive force for evil and that he came to have the same feeling about me....

Gradually I discovered that he had no real wish to make the world better, but only to indulge in eloquent soliloquy about how bad it was. If anybody overheard the soliloquies so much the better, but they were designed at most to produce a little faithful band of disciples who could sit in the deserts of New Mexico and feel holy. All this was conveyed to me in the language of a fascist dictator as what I *must* preach, the "must" having thirteen underlinings.

His letters grew gradually more hostile. He wrote: "What's the good of living as you do anyway? I don't believe your lectures *are* good. They are nearly over, aren't they? What's the good of sticking in the damned ship and haranguing the merchant pilgrims in their own language? Why don't you drop overboard? Why don't you clear out of the whole show? One must be an outlaw these days, not a teacher or preacher." This seemed to me mere rhetoric. I was becoming more of an outlaw than he ever was and I could not quite see his ground of complaint against me. He phrased his complaint in different ways at different times. On another occasion he wrote: "Do stop working and writing altogether and become a creature instead of a mechanical instrument. Do clear out of the whole social ship. So for your very pride's sake become a mere nothing, a mole, a creature that feels its way and doesn't think. Do for heaven's sake be a baby, and not a savant any more. Don't *do* anything more—but for heaven's sake begin to *be*. Start at the very beginning and be a perfect baby: in the name of courage.

"Oh, and I want to ask you, when you make your will, do leave me enough to live on. I want you to live forever. But I want you to make me in some part your heir." The only difficulty with this program was that if I adopted it I should have nothing to leave.

He had a mystical philosophy of "blood" which I disliked. "There is," he said, "another seat of consciousness than the brain—the nerves. There is a blood consciousness which exists in us independently of the ordinary mental consciousness. One lives, knows and has one's being in the blood, without any reference to nerves and brain. This is one half of life belonging to the darkness. When I take a woman, then the blood percept is supreme. My blood knowing is overwhelming. We should realize that we have a blood being, a blood consciousness, a blood soul complete and apart from a mental and nerve consciousness." This seemed to me frankly rubbish, and I rejected it vehemently, though I did not then know that it led straight to Auschwitz.

He always got into a fury if one suggested that anybody could possibly have kindly feelings toward anybody else, and when I objected to war because of the suffering that it causes, he accused me of hypocrisy. "It isn't in the least true that you, your basic self, want ultimate peace. You are satisfying in an indirect, false way your lust to jab and strike. Either satisfy it in a direct and honorable way, saying, 'I hate you all, liars and swine, and I am out to set upon you,' or stick to mathematics, where you can be true. But to come as the angel of peace — no, I prefer Tirpitz a thousand times in that role."

I find it difficult now to understand the devastating effect that this letter had upon me. I was inclined to believe that he had some insight denied to me, and when he said that my pacifism was rooted in blood lust I supposed he must be right. For twenty-four hours I thought that I was not fit to live and contemplated committing suicide. But at the end of that time, a healthier reaction set in, and I decided to have done with such morbidness. When he said that I *must* preach his doctrines and not mine I rebelled and told him to remember that he was no longer a schoolmaster and I was not his pupil. He had written, "The enemy of all mankind you are, full of the lust of enmity. It is not a hatred of falsehood which inspires you, it is the hatred of people of flesh and blood, it is a perverted mental blood lust. Why don't you own it? Let us become strangers again. I think it is better." I thought so too. But he found a pleasure in denouncing me and continued for some months to write letters containing sufficient friendliness to keep the correspondence alive. In the end, it faded away without any dramatic termination. — *Portraits From Memory* (1956).

Sir Osbert Sitwell

I only met Lawrence once, when he and his wife were living in Tuscany. I was staying nearby and they asked my sister and myself to have tea with them; so we drove through the blossoming countryside — for it was high May — to his farmhouse.... Lawrence opened the door to us, and it was the first time I had ever realised what a fragile and goatish little saint he was: a Pan and a Messiah: for in his flattish face, with its hollow, wan cheeks, and rather red beard, was to be discerned a curious but happy mingling of satyr and ascetic: qualities, too, which must really have belonged to him, since they are continually to be found in his work. It was, certainly, a remarkable appearance. Unlike the faces of most geniuses, it was the face of a genius. — *Penny Foolish: a Book of Tirades and Panegyrics* (1935).

HENRY WADSWORTH LONGFELLOW

William Dean Howells

I can see him now, as he looked up from the proof-sheets on the round table before him, and over at me, growing consciously smaller and smaller, like something through a reversed opera-glass. He had a shaded drop-light in front of him, and in its glow his beautiful and benignly noble head had a dignity peculiar to him.

All the portraits of Longfellow are likenesses more or less bad and good, for there was something as simple in the physiognomy as in the nature of the man. His head, after he allowed his beard to grow and wore his hair long in the manner of elderly men, was leonine, but mildly leonine, as the old painters conceived the lion of St. Mark....

When Longfellow read verse, it was with a hollow, with a mellow resonant murmur, like the note of some deep-throated horn. His voice was very lulling in quality, and at the Dante Club it used to have early effect with an old scholar who sat in a cavernous armchair at the corner of the fire, and who drowsed audibly in the soft tone and the gentle heat. The poet had a fat terrier who wished always to be present at the meetings of the Club, and he commonly fell asleep at the same moment with that dear old scholar, so that when they began to make themselves heard in concert, one could not tell which it was that most took our thoughts from the text of the *Paradiso*. When the duet opened, Longfellow would look up with an arch recognition of the fact, and then go gravely on to the end of the canto. At the close he would speak to his friend and lead him out to supper as if he had not seen or heard anything amiss.

In that elect company I was silent, partly because I was conscious of my youthful inadequacy, and partly because I preferred to listen. But Longfellow always behaved as if I were saying a succession of edifying and delightful things, and from time to time he addressed himself to me, so that I should not feel left out. He did not talk much himself, and I recall nothing that he said. But he always spoke both wisely and simply, without the least touch of pose, and with no intention of effect, but with something that I must call quality for want of a better word; so that at a table where [Oliver Wendell] Holmes sparkled, and [James Russell] Lowell glowed, and [Jean Louis Rodolphe] Agassiz beamed, he cast the light of a gentle gayety, which seemed to dim all those vivider luminaries. — *Literary Friends and Acquaintance* (1900).

THOMAS BABINGTON MACAULAY

Lord Henry Cockburn

He is not intellectual in his outward appearance. In manner his defect is that he is heavy and lumbering, though not big, and has an air of vulgarity. His conversation, of which however I have yet heard very little, is good, but, with the usual defects of professed talkers, it is a great deal too abundant and is not easy. He utters with great rapidity, and with a panting anxiety. Though the matter of his conversation, therefore, is always admirable, the style is not pleasing. Sydney Smith, an enormous talker, complains of Macaulay never letting him get in a word. Smith once said to him, 'Now, Macaulay, when I am gone you'll be sorry you never heard me speak.' On another occasion Smith said that he had found Macaulay in bed from illness, and that he was therefore more agreeable than he had ever seen him: 'There were some glorious flashes of silence.' — *Journal*, 6 June 1839.

Charles C.F. Greville

Macaulay is a most extraordinary man, and his astonishing knowledge is every moment exhibited, but (as far as I have yet seen of him, which is not sufficient to judge) he is not *agreeable*. His propositions and his allusions are rather too abrupt; he starts topics not altogether naturally; then he has none of the graces of conversation, none of that exquisite tact and refinement which are the result of a felicitous intuition or a long acquaintance with good society, or more probably a mixture of both. The mighty mass of his knowledge is not animated by that subtle spirit of taste and discretion which alone can give it the qualities of lightness and elasticity and without which, though he may have the power of instructing and astonishing, he never will attain that of delighting and captivating his hearers. — 12 August 1832, *The Greville Memoirs* (1875).

John Lothrop Motley

His general appearance is singularly commonplace. I cannot describe him better than by saying he has exactly that kind of face and figure which by no possibility would be selected, out of even a very small number of persons, as those of a remarkable personage. He is of middle height, neither above nor below it. The outline of his face in profile is rather good. The nose, very slightly aquiline, is well cut, and the expression of the mouth and chin agreeable. His hair is thick and silvery, and he looks a good deal older than many men of his years.... The face ... seen in front, is blank, and as it were badly lighted. There is nothing luminous in the eye, nothing impressive in the brow. The forehead is spacious, but it is scooped entirely away in the region where benevolence ought to be, while beyond rise reverence, firmness, and self-esteem, like Alps on Alps. The under eyelids are so swollen as almost to close the eyes, and it would be quite impossible to tell the colour of those orbs, and equally so, from the neutral tint of his hair and face, to say of what complexion he had originally been. His voice is agreeable, and its intonations delightful, although that is so common a gift with Englishmen as to be almost a national characteristic. — From a letter to his wife, 30 May 1858.

Leslie Stephen

Macaulay was short, stout, and upright, with homely but expressive features, and a fine brow. He was physically clumsy, and, though he took a simple delight in gorgeous waistcoats, never learnt to tie his neckcloth or wield a razor with moderate skill. He never cared for bodily exercises, and, when offered a horse at Windsor, said that if he rode it must be upon an elephant. He enjoyed pedestrian rambles till his health gave way, but often read as he walked, and preferred to country lanes streets abounding in bookstalls and historical associations. The most obvious of his intellectual qualities was his stupendous memory. He read voraciously, and forgot nothing, from the best classical literature to the most ephemeral rubbish. He learnt by heart 'Paradise Lost' and the 'Cambridge Calendar,' and maintained that every fool could say his archbishops of Canterbury backwards. His memory was the servant, sometimes perhaps the master, of a vivid imagination and vigorous understanding. — *Dictionary of National Biography* (1937).

HERMAN MELVILLE

Nathaniel Hawthorne

A week ago last Monday, Herman Melville came to see me at the Consulate [in Liverpool, England], looking much as he used to do (a little paler, and perhaps, a little sadder), in a rough outside coat, and with his characterisitc gravity and reserve of manner. He had crossed from New York to Glasgow in a screw steamer, about a fortnight before, and had since been seeing Edinburgh, and other interesting places. I felt rather awkward at first, because this is the first time I have met him since my ineffectual attempt to get him a consular appointment from General Pierce. However, I failed only from real lack of power to serve him; so there was no reason to be ashamed, and we soon found ourselves on pretty much our former terms of sociability and confidence. Melville has not been well of late; he has been affected with neuralgic complaints in his head and his limbs, and no doubt has suffered from too constant literary occupation, pursued without much success latterly; and his writings, for a long while past, have indicated a morbid state of mind. So he left his place at Pittsfield, and has established his wife and family, I believe, with his father-in-law in Boston, and is thus far on his way to Constantinople. I do not wonder that he found it necessary to take an airing through the world, after so many years of toilsome pen-labor following after so wild and adventurous a youth as his was. I invited him to come and stay with us at Southport as long as he might remain in this vicinity; and, accordingly, he did come, on the next day, taking with him, by way of luggage, the least little bit of a bundle, which, he told me, contained a nightshirt and a toothbrush. He is a person of very gentlemanly instincts in every respect, save that he is a little heterodox in the matter of clean linen.

He stayed with us from Tuesday till Thursday; and, on the intervening day, we took a pretty long walk together, and sat down in a hollow among the sandhills (sheltering ourselves from the high, cool wind) and smoked a cigar. Melville, as he always does, began to reason of Providence and futurity, and of everything that lies beyond human ken, and informed me that he had 'pretty much made up his mind to be annihilated.'; but still he does not seem to rest in that anticipation, and, I think, will never rest until he gets hold of a definite belief. It is strange how he persists — and has persisted ever since I knew him, and probably long before — in wandering to and fro over these deserts, as dismal and monotonous as the sandhills amid which we were sitting. He can neither believe, nor be comfortable in his unbelief; and he is too honest and courageous not to try to do one or the other. If he were a religious man, he would be one of the most truly religious and reverential; he has a very high and noble nature and is better worth immortality than most of us....

On Saturday, Melville and I went to Chester again.... We left Chester at about four o'clock; and I took the rail for Southport at half-past six, parting from Melville at a street-corner in Liverpool, in the rainy evening. I saw him again on Monday, however. He said that he already felt better than in America; but observed that he did not antici-pate much pleasure in his rambles, for that the spirit of adventure is gone out of him. He certainly is much overshadowed since I saw him last; but I hope he will brighten as he goes onward. He sailed from Liverpool in a steamer on Tuesday, leaving his trunk behind him at my consulate, and taking only a carpet-bag to hold all his travelling-gear. This is the next best thing to going naked; and as he wears his beard and moustache, and so needs no dressing-case — nothing but a toothbrush — I do not know a more independent personage. He learned his travelling-habits by drifting about, all over the South Sea, with no other clothes or equipage than a red flannel shirt and a pair of duck trousers. Yet we seldom see men of less criticizable manners than he. — *Journals*, 20 November 1856.

Sophia Hawthorne

A man with a true, warm heart, and a soul and an intel-lect, — with life to his finger-tips; earnest, sincere, and reverent; very tender and *modest*. And I am not sure that he is not a very great man; but I have not quite decided upon my own opinion. I should say, I am not quite sure that *I do not think him* a very great man; for my opinion is, of course, as far as possible from settling the matter. He has very keen perceptive power; but what astonishes me is, that his eyes are not large and deep. He seems to see everything very accurately; and how he can do so with his small eyes, I cannot tell. They are not keen eyes, either, but quite undistinguished in any way. His nose is straight and rather handsome, his mouth expressive of sensibility and emotion. He is tall and erect, with an air free, brave, and manly. When conversing, he is full of gesture and force, and loses himself in his subject. There is no grace nor polish. Once in a while, his animation gives place to a singu-larly quiet expression, out of these eyes to which I have objected; an indrawn, dim look, but which at the same time makes you feel that he is at that instant taking deepest note of what is before him. It is a strange, lazy glance, but with a power in it quite unique. It does not seem to penetrate through you, but to take you into himself. [Sophia was Nathaniel Hawthorne's wife.] — From a letter to her mother, 4 September 1850.

JOHN STUART MILL

Thomas Carlyle

This young Mill I fancy and hope is "a baying [being] you can love". A slender rather tall and elegant youth, with small clear roman-nosed face, two small earnestly-smiling eyes: modest, remarkably gifted with precision of utterance; enthusiastic, yet lucid, calm; not a great, yet distinctly a gifted and amiable youth. We had almost four hours of the best talk I have mingled in for long. — From a letter to his wife, 4 September 1831.

John Ruskin

An utterly shallow and wretched segment of a human creature, incapable of understanding *Anything* in the ultimate conditions of it, and countenancing with an unhappy fortune, whatever is fatallest in the popular error of English mind. — From a letter to C.E. Norton, 12 September 1869.

JOHN MILTON

John Phillips

Hee was of a moderate Stature, and well proportion'd, of a ruddy Complexion, light brown Hair, & handsom Features; save that his Eyes were none of the quickest. But his blindness, which proceeded from a Gutta Serena, added no further blemish to them. His deport-ment was sweet and affable; and his Gate erect & Manly, bespeaking Courage and undauntedness (or a Nil conscire) On which account hee wore a Sword while hee had his Sight, and was skill'd in using it. Hee had an excellent Ear, and could bear a part both in Vocal & Instrumen-tal Music.... By the great fire in 1666 hee had a house in Bread street burnt: wch was all the Real Estate hee had. Hee rendred his Studies and various Works more easy & pleasant by allotting them thir several portions of the day. Of these the time friendly to the Muses fell to his Poetry; And hee waking early (as is the use of temperate men) had com-monly a good Stock of Verses ready against his Amanuensis came; which if it happend to bee later then ordinary, hee would complain, saying *hee wanted to bee milkd*. The Evenings hee likewise spent in reading some choice Poets, by way of refreshment after the days toyl, and to store his Fancy against Morning. Besides his ordinary lectures out of the Bible and the best Commentators on the week day, That was his sole subject on Sundays. And Davids Psalms were in esteem with him above all Poetry. The Youths that hee instructed from time to time served him often as Amanuenses, & some elderly persons were glad for the benefit of his learned Conversation, to perform that Office. His first Wife dy'd a while after his blindness seizd him, leaving him three Daughters, that liv'd to bee Women. Hee marry'd two more, whereof one surviv'd him. He dy'd in a fitt of the Gout, but, with so little pain or Emotion, that the time of his expiring was not perceiv'd by those in the room. And though hee had bin long troubl'd with that disease, insomuch that his Knuckles were all callous, yet was hee not ever observ'd to bee very impatient. — *The Early Lives of Milton*, ed. Helen Darbishire (1932).

Himself

It is now, I think about ten years since I perceived my vision to grow weak and dull, and, at the same time, I was troubled with pain in my kidneys and bowels, accompanied with flatulency. In the morning, if I began to read, as was my custom, my eyes instantly ached intensely, but were refreshed after a little corporeal exercise. The candle which I looked at seemed as it were encircled with a rainbow. Not long after, the sight in the left part of the left eye (which I lost some years before the other) became quite obscured, and prevented me from discerning any object on that side. The sight in my other eye has now been gradual-ly and sensibly vanishing away for about three years; some months before it had entirely perished, though I stood motionless, every thing I looked at seemed in motion to and fro. A stiff, cloudy vapor seemed to have settled on my forehead and temples, which usually occasions a sort of somnolent pressure upon my eyes, and particularly from dinner till the evening. So that I often recollect what is said of the poet Phineas in the Argonautics: "A stupor deep his cloudy temples bound,/ And when he walked he seemed as whirling round,/ Or in a feeble trance he speechless lay."

I ought not to omit that while I had my sight, as soon as I lay down on my bed and turned on either side, a flood of light used to gush from my eyelids. Then, as my sight became daily more impaired, the colors became more faint, and were emitted with a certain inward crackling sound; but at present, every species of illumination being as it were extinguished, there is diffused around me nothing but darkness, or darkness mingled and streaked with an ashy brown. Yet the darkness in which I am perpetually immersed seems always, both night and day, to approach nearer to white than black; and when the eye is rolling in its socket, it admits a little particle of light, as through a chink. — From a letter to Leonard Philaras, the Athenian, 1654; the original in Latin.

SAMUEL PEPYS

John Evelyn

26th May [1703]. This day died Mr. Samuel Pepys, a very worthy, industrious and curious person, none in England exceeding him in knowledge of the navy, in which he had passed through all the most considerable offices, Clerk of the Acts and Secretary of the Admiralty, all which he performed with great integrity.... He was universally beloved, hospitable, generous, learned in many things, skilled in music, a very great cherisher of learned men whom he had the conversation. His library and collection of other curiosities were of the most considerable, the models of ships especially.... Mr. Pepys had been for near forty years so much my particular friend, that Mr. Jackson sent me complete mourning, desiring me to be one to hold up the pall at his magnificent obsequies; but my indisposition hindered me from doing him this last office. — Diary.

EDGAR ALLAN POE

Thomas Wentworth Higginson

[When Poe read his poem "Al Aaraaf" aloud to a group of Bostonians and came to the words "Ligeia! Ligeia!"] his voice seemed attenuated with such delicacy, and sustained with such sweetness, as I have never heard equalled by other lips.... When the lyric ended, it was like the ceasing of the gypsy's chant in Browning's "Flight of the Duchess"; I remember nothing more, except in walking back to Cambridge my comrades and I felt that we had been under the spell of some wizard. Indeed I feel much the same, in retrospect, to this day....

I distinctly recall his face, with its ample forehead, brilliant eyes, and narrowness of nose and chin; an essentially ideal face, not noble, yet any thing but coarse.... It was a face to rivet one's attention in any crowd, yet a face that no one would feel safe in loving. — Quoted by Edward Wagenknecht in *Edgar Allan Poe: The Man Behind the Legend* (1963).

John H.B. Latrobe

He was, if anything, below the middle size, and yet could not be described as a small man. His figure was remarkably good, and he carried himself erect and well, as one who had been trained to it. He was dressed in black, and his frock-coat was buttoned to the throat, where it met the black stock, then almost universally worn. Not a particle of white was visible. Coat, hat, boots, and gloves had very evidently seen their best days but so far as mending and brushing go, everything had been done, apparently, to make them presentable.... *Gentleman* was written all over him. His manner was easy and quiet, and although he came to return thanks for what he regarded as deserving them, there was nothing obsequious in what he said or did.... His forehead was high, and remarkable for the great development at the temple.... The expression of his face was grave, almost sad, except when he was engaged in conversation, when it became animated and changeable. His voice, I remember, was very pleasing in its tone and well modulated, almost rhythmical, and his words were well chosen and unhesitating. — From an address at the Poe Memorial Exercises in Baltimore, 1877.

Augustine O'Neil

I have seen Poe. His house was near the College of St. John at Fordham. I once went down to the City in the same train and waited a considerable time for the car on the same platform. I had ample opportunity to observe him. I regret that I did not speak to him.... He was entirely alone. He was very neatly dressed in black. He was rather small, slender, pale and had the air of a finished gentleman. I saw him at least once before and possibly oftener. My recollection of him as he appeared at the Fordham Station is at this moment very vivid.... There was much quiet dignity in his manner. In my opinion neither Shakespeare nor Byron could have been handsomer and I am not a woman that I should be impressed by beauty in a man.... I don't know the exact date when I saw him, but it was between sometime in the year 1846 and June 24, 1849. Poe must have been at that time about thirty-six years old, but he looked to be forty. His exterior was very pleasing. There was nothing forbidding in his manner. He simply looked like one who had a decent self-respect. — *Notes and Queries* (18 December 1937), 440.

Richard Henry Stoddard

It was my good — or bad — fortune to come in contact with the unfortunate Edgar Allan Poe in my twenty-first year.... I must relate in as few words as possible my first and last acquaintance with this highly gifted but ill-balanced man of genius.

I began to write at the time that Poe was editing the *Broadway Journal*, which was in 1845. Having met a lady who had had some verses published in the *Journal*, my ambition was fired, and I wrote my first poem, "Ode on a Grecian Flute."

Like all early writing, it was crude; but there was promise in it. I worked over it, made a copy of it, and sent it to the editor of the *Broadway Journal*, — I presume, with a letter addressed to Edgar A. Poe, Esq., — and waited with fear and trembling.

One week, two weeks passed, and it did not appear. Evidently the demand for odes was slack. When I could bear my disappointment no longer I made time to take a long walk, a hot afternoon in June, to the office of the *Broadway Journal*, and asked for Mr. Poe. He was not in.

Might I inquire where he lived? I was directed to a street and a number that I have forgotten, but it was in the eastern part of the city, I think in East Broadway, near Clinton Street — a neighbourhood now given up to sundry of the tribes of Israel. I knocked at the street door, and was presently shown up to Poe's apartments on the second or third floor. He received me with the courtesy habitual with him when he was himself.

I told my errand, and he promised that my ode should be printed next week. I was struck with his polite manner toward me, and with the elegance of his appearance. He was slight and pale, I saw, with large, luminous eyes, and was dressed in black. When I quitted the room I could not but see Mrs. Poe, who was lying on a bed, apparently asleep. She too was dressed in black, and was pale and wasted.

"Poor lady," I thought; "she is dying of consumption." She never stirred, but her mother came out from the back parlour, and was introduced to me by her courtly nephew. Breathing a benediction upon the three, I stole downstairs, and rambled slowly home.

I bought the next issue of the *Broadway Journal*, but the ode was not in it. It was mentioned, however, as follows: —

"To the Author of the Lines on 'Grecian Flute.' We fear that we have mislaid the poem."

And a week later, this: "We doubt the originality of the 'Grecian Flute,' for the reason that it is too good at some points to be so bad at others. Unless the author can reassure us, we decline it."

I was surprised and indignant. Any one in my situation would have been. Not write that immortal production! why, I knew that I had composed it! I thought then, I thought afterward, and I know now, that Poe was no critic. Of course I called within a few days to authenticate my trifle.

It was a forenoon, and a very hot one, in July. I plodded down from the east side of the town, southwardly, westwardly, through Lewis Street, Kivison Street, and Chatham Street, until I reached Clinton Hall, on the southwest corner of Beekman and Nassau streets. It was then past noon, and of course the potent editor of the *Broadway Journal* had gone out to his luncheon, with Briggs, or English, or some other Bohemian with whom he had not yet fallen out.

"Not in, sir," ejaculated the fatuous publisher. I walked away, and cooled myself by wandering in and out of the Park, on that intolerable July afternoon. Returning with my thin blood at fever-heat, I was informed that Poe was in his *sanctum*. He was sitting in a chair asleep, but the publisher awoke him. He was in a morose mood.

"Mr. Poe," I said, "I called to assure you that I did write the 'Ode on a Grecian Flute.'"

Poe started, and glared at me, and shouted, "You lie, d——n you. Get out of here, or I'll throw you out!"

I was more indignant and astounded than before; but I left him, as he desired, and walked slowly home, "chewing the cud of sweet and bitter fancies." I could not understand then why I had been subjected to such an indignity....

I had glimpses of Poe afterward in the streets, but we never spoke. The last time that I remember to have seen him was in the afternoon of a dreary autumn day. A heavy shower had come up suddenly, and he was standing under an awning. I had an umbrella, and my impulse was to share it with him on his way home, but something — certainly not unkindness — withheld me. I went on and left him there in the rain, pale, shivering, miserable, the embodiment of his own "unhappy master,/ Whom unmerciful disaster/ Followed fast, and followed faster." There I still see him, and always shall, — poor, penniless, but proud, reliant, dominant. May the gods forgive me! I can never forgive myself. — *Recollections Personal and Literary* (1903).

Susan Archer Weiss

As I entered the parlour, Poe was seated near an open window, quietly conversing. His attitude was easy and graceful, with one arm lightly resting upon the back of his chair. His dark curling hair was thrown back from his broad forehead — a style in which he habitually wore it. At sight of him, the impression produced upon me was of a refined, high-bred, and chivalrous gentleman. I use this word 'chivalrous' as exactly descriptive of something in his whole *personnel*, distinct from either polish or high-breeding, and which, though instantly apparent, was yet an effect too subtle to be described. He rose on my entrance, and, other visitors being present, stood with one hand resting on the back of his chair, awaiting my greeting. So dignified was his manner, so reserved his expression, that I experienced an involuntary recoil, until I turned to him and saw his eyes suddenly brighten as I offered my hand; a barrier seemed to melt between us, and I felt that we were no longer strangers.

I am thus minute in my account of my first meeting with Poe, because I would illustrate, if possible, the manner peculiar to him, and also the indescribable charm, I might almost say magnetism, which his eyes possessed above any others that I have ever seen....

I can vividly recall him as he appeared on his visits to us. He always carried a cane, and upon entering the shade of the avenue would remove his hat, throw back his hair, and walk lingeringly, as if enjoying the coolness, carrying his hat in his hand, generally behind him. Sometimes he would pause to examine some rare flower, or to pluck a grape from the laden trellises. He met us always with an expression of pleasure illuminating his countenance and lighting his fine eyes.

Poe's eyes, indeed, were his most striking feature, and it was to these that his face owed its peculiar attraction. I have never seen other eyes at all resembling them. They were large, with long, jet-black lashes — the iris dark steel-gray, possessing a crystalline clearness and transparency, through which the jet-black pupil was seen to expand and contract with every shade of thought or emotion. I observed that the lids never contracted, as is so usual in most persons, especially when talking; but his gaze was ever full, open, and unshrinking. His usual expression was dreamy and sad. He had a way of sometimes turning a slightly askance look upon some person who was not observing him, and, with a quiet, steady gaze, appear to be mentally taking the calibre of the unsuspecting subject. 'What *awful* eyes Mr Poe has!' said a lady to me. 'It makes my blood run cold to see him slowly turn and fix them upon me when I am talking.'

Apart from the wonderful beauty of his eyes, I would not have called Poe a very handsome man. He was, in my opinion, rather distinguished-looking than handsome. What he had been when younger I had heard, but at the period of my acquaintance with him he had a pallid and careworn look — somewhat haggard, indeed — very apparent except in his moments of animation. He wore a dark moustache, scrupulously kept, but not entirely concealing a slightly contracted expression of the mouth and an occasional twitching of the upper lip, resembling a sneer. This sneer, indeed, was easily excited — a motion of the lip, scarcely perceptible, and yet intensely expressive. There was in it nothing of ill-nature, but much of sarcasm, as when he remarked of a certain pretentious editor, 'He can make bold plunges in shallow water'; and again, in reference to an editor presenting a costly book to a lady whose poems he had for years published while yet refusing to pay for them, Poe observed, 'He could afford it', with that almost imperceptible curl of the lip, more expressive of contempt than words could have been. — *Scribner's Magazine* (March 1878).

Himself

I can feel for the "constitutional indolence" of which you complain — for it is one of my own besetting sins. I am excessively slothful, and wonderfully industrious — by fits. There are epochs when any kind of mental exercise is torture, and then nothing yields me pleasure but solitary communion with the "mountains & the woods" — the "altars" of Byron. I have thus rambled and dreamed away whole months, and awaken, at last, to a sort of mania for composition. Then I scribble all day, and read all night, so long as the disease endures....

I am *not* ambitious — unless negatively. I, now and then feel stirred up to excel a fool, merely because I hate to let a fool imagine that he may excel me. Beyond this I feel nothing of ambition. I really perceive that vanity about which most men merely prate – the vanity of the human or temporal life. I live continually in a reverie of the future. I have no faith in human perfectibility. I think that human exertion will have no appreciable effect upon humanity. Man is now only more active – not more happy – nor more wise, than he was 6000 years ago....

You speak of "an estimate of my life" – and, from what I have already said, you will see that I have none to give. I have been too deeply conscious of the mutability and evanescence of temporal things, to give any continuous effort to anything – to be consistent in anything. My life has been *whim* – impulse – passion – a longing for solitude – a scorn of all things present, in an earnest desire for the future.

I am profoundly excited by music, and by some poems – those of Tennyson especially – whom, with Keats, Shelley, Coleridge (occasionally) and a few others of like thought and expression, I regard as the *sole* poets. Music is the perfection of the soul, or idea, of Poetry....

I think my best poems, "The Sleeper", "The Conqueror Worm", "The Haunted Palace", "Lenore", "Dreamland" & "The Coliseum" – but all have been hurried & unconsidered. My best tales are "Ligeia"; The "Gold-Bug"; The "Murders in the Rue Morgue", "The Fall of the House of Usher", The "Tell-Tale Heart", The "Black Cat", "William Wilson", & "The Descent into the Maelström." "The Purloined Letter," forthcoming in the "Gift", is, perhaps, the best of my tales of ratiocination. – From a letter to James Russell Lowell, 2 July 1844.

You say – "Can you *hint* to me what was the terrible evil which caused the irregularities so profoundly lamented?" Yes; I can do more than hint. This "evil" was the greatest which can befall a man. Six years ago, a wife, whom I loved as no man ever loved before, ruptured a blood-vessel in singing. Her life was despaired of. I took leave of her forever & underwent all the agonies of her death. She recovered partially and I again hoped. At the end of a year the vessel broke again – I went through precisely the same scene. Again in about a year afterward. Then again – again – again & even once again at varying intervals. Each time I felt all the agonies of her death – and at each accession of the disorder I loved her more dearly & clung to her life with more desperate pertinacity. But I am constitutionally sensitive – nervous in a very unusual degree. I became insane, with long intervals of horrible sanity. During these fits of absolute unconsciousness I drank, God only knows how often or how much. As a matter of course, my enemies referred the insanity to the drink rather than the drink to the insanity. I had indeed, nearly abandoned all hope of a permanent cure when I found one in the *death* of my wife. This I can & do endure as becomes a man — it was the horrible never-ending oscillation between hope & despair which I could *not* longer have endured without the total loss of reason. In the death of what was my life, then, I receive a new but — oh God! how melancholy an existence. — From a letter to George W. Eveleth, 4 January 1848.

ALEXANDER POPE

Lord Chesterfield

Pope in conversation was below himself; he was seldom easy and natural, and seemed afraid that the man should degrade the poet, which made him always attempt wit and humour, often unsuccessfully, and too often unseasonably. I have been with him a week at a time at his house at Twickenham, where I necessarily saw his mind in its undress, when he was both an agreeable and instructive companion.

His moral character has been warmly attacked, and but weakly defended; the natural consequence of his shining turn to satire, of which many felt, and all feared the smart. It must be owned, that he was the most irritable of all the *genus irritabile vatum*, offended with trifles, and never forgetting or forgiving them; but in this I really think, that the poet was more in fault than the man. He was as great an instance as any he quotes of the contrarieties and inconsistencies of human nature; for, notwithstanding the malignancy of his satires, and some blameable passages of his life, he was charitable to his power, active in doing good offices, and piously attentive to an old bed-ridden mother, who died but a little time before him. His poor, crazy, deformed body was a mere Pandora's box, containing all the physical ills that ever afflicted humanity. This, perhaps, whetted the edge of his satire, and may in some degree excuse it. — "Characters," appended to *Miscellaneous Works of the Late Philip Dormer Stanhope, Earl of Chesterfield* (1779).

King George II

"Who is this Pope that I hear so much about?" said George II.; "I cannot discover what is his merit. Why will not my subjects write in prose? I hear a great deal, too, of Shakespeare, but I cannot read him, he is such a *bombast* fellow." — Quoted in Sir James Prior's *Life of Edmond Malone* (1860).

Samuel Johnson

The person of Pope is well known not to have been formed by the nicest model. He has, in his account of the "Little Club," compared himself to a spider, and by another is described as protuberant behind and before. He is said to have been beautiful in his infancy; but he was of a constitution originally feeble and weak; and as bodies of a tender frame are easily distorted, his deformity was probably in part the effect of his application. His stature was so low, that, to bring him to a level with common tables, it was necessary to raise his seat. But his face was not displeasing, and his eyes were animated and vivid.

By natural deformity, or accidental distortion, his vital functions were so much disordered, that his life was a "long disease." His most frequent assailant was the headache, which he used to relieve by inhaling the steam of coffee, which he very frequently required.

Most of what can be told concerning his petty peculiarities was communicated by a female domestic of the Earl of Oxford, who knew him perhaps after the middle of life. He was then so weak as to stand in perpetual need of female attendance; extremely sensible of cold, so that he wore a kind of fur doublet under a shirt of a very coarse warm linen with fine sleeves. When he rose, he was invested in bodice made of stiff canvas, being scarce able to hold himself erect till they were laced, and he then put on a flannel waistcoat. One side was contracted. His legs were so slender, that he enlarged their bulk with three pair of stockings, which were drawn on and off by the maid; for he was not able to dress or undress himself, and neither went to bed nor rose without help. His weakness made it very difficult for him to be clean.

His hair had fallen almost all away; and he used to dine sometimes with Lord Oxford, privately, in a velvet cap. His dress of ceremony was black, with a tye-wig and a little sword.

The indulgence and accommodation which his sickness required had taught him all the unpleasing and unsocial qualities of a valetudinary man. He expected that everything should give way to his ease or humour, as a child whose parents will not hear her cry, has an unresisted dominion in the nursery. "*C'est que l'enfant toujours est homme,/ C'est que l'homme est toujours enfant.*" When he wanted to sleep, he "nodded in company"; and once slumbered at his own table while the Prince of Wales was talking of poetry. — *Lives of the Poets* (1779–81).

Dr. William King

Pope and I, with my Lord Orrery and Sir Harry Bedingfield, dined with the late Earl of Burlington. After the first course Pope grew sick, and went out of the room. When dinner was ended, and the cloth removed, Lord Burlington said he would go out, and see what was become of Pope. And soon after they returned together. But Pope, who had been casting up his dinner, looked very pale, and complained much. My Lord asked him if he would have some mulled wine or a glass of old sack, which Pope refused. I told my Lord Burlington that he wanted a dram. Upon which the little man expressed some resentment against me, and said he would not taste any spirits, and that he abhorred drams as much as I did. However, I persisted, and assured my Lord Burlington that he could not oblige our friend more at that instant than by ordering a large glass of cherry-brandy to be set before him. This was done, and in less than half an hour, while my Lord was acquainting us with an affair which engaged our attention, Pope had sipped up all the brandy. Pope's frame of body did not promise long life; but he certainly hastened his death by feeding much on high-seasoned dishes, and drinking spirits. — *Political and Literary Anecdotes of His Own Times* (1819).

Edmond Malone

Sir Joshua Reynolds once saw Pope. It was about the year 1740, at an auction of books or pictures. He remembers that there was a lane formed to let him pass freely through the assemblage, and he proceeded along bowing to those who were on each side. He was, according to Sir Joshua's account, about four feet six high; very humpbacked and deformed; he wore a black coat; and according to the fashion of that time, had on a little sword. Sir Joshua adds that he had a large and very fine eye, and a long handsome nose; his mouth had those peculiar marks which always are found in the mouths of crooked persons; and the muscles which run across the cheek were so strongly marked as to appear like small cords. — Quoted in Sir James Prior's *Life of Edmond Malone* (1860).

Owen Ruffhead

Mr. Pope was low in stature, and of a diminutive and misshapen figure, which no one ridiculed more pleasantly than himself. His constitution was naturally tender and delicate, and in his temper he was naturally mild and gentle, yet sometimes betrayed that exquisite sensibility which is the concomitant of genius. His lively perception and delicate feeling, irritated by wretched ill health, made him too quickly take fire; but his good sense and humanity soon rendered him placable....

His sickly state of health soon made him sensible of sensual excesses, which, with the uncomeliness of his person, might render him more assiduous to culivate his mental faculties, that he might atone for the defects of an ungraceful figure by the accomplishments of an elegant and polished mind....

His various reading and retentive memory, assisted by a habit of reflection, rendered him intelligent upon most subjects, and his social disposition made him communicative; but he was not formed for a public speaker. He never could speak in public: a story that he could relate with pleasure to any three friends, he could not before a company of twelve. When he was to appear for Atterbury at his trial, though he had but ten words to way, and on a plain, easy point, he made two blunders in them.

He was open, unaffected, and affable in his manners. He never debased himself by an unbecoming levity or servile accommodation: nor did he offend others by an over-weening arrogance and pertinacity. He was free, yet decent; lively, yet discreet. — Quoted in "Characters," appended to *Miscellaneous Works of the Late Philip Dormer Stanhope, Earl of Chesterfield* (1779).

Himself

To reform, and not to chastise, I am afraid, is impossible; and that the best precepts, as well as the best laws, would prove of small use, if there were no example to enforce them. To attack vices in the abstract, without touching persons, may be safe fighting indeed; but it is fighting with shadows. General propositions are obscure, misty, and uncertain, compared with plain, full, and home examples.... The only sign by which I found my writings ever did any good, or had any weight, has been that they raised the anger of bad men; and my greatest comfort and encouragement to proceed has been to see that those who have no shame, and no fear of any thing else, have appeared touched by my satires. — From a letter to Dr. John Arbuthnot, 26 July 1734.

SAMUEL RICHARDSON

Samuel Johnson

You think I love flattery, and so I do; but a little too much always disgusts me: that fellow Richardson, on the contrary, could not be contented to sail quietly down the stream of reputation, without longing to taste the froth from every stroke of the oar. That fellow died merely for want of change among his flatterers; he perished for want of more, like a man obliged to breathe the same air till it is exhausted. — Quoted by Hestern Lynch Piozzi in *Anecdotes of the late Samuel Johnson, LL.D., during the Last Twenty Years of his Life* (1786).

Himself

I go thro' the Park once or twice a week to my little retirement; but I will for a week together be in it every day for three or four hours, at your command, till you tell me you have seen a person who answers to this description, namely, Short; rather plump than emaciated, notwithstanding his complaints: about five foot five inches: fair wig, lightish cloth coat, all black besides: one hand generally in his bosom, the other a cane in it, which he leans upon under the skirts of his coat usually, that it may imperceptibly serve him as a support, when attacked by sudden tremors or startings, and dizziness, which too frequently attack him, but, thank God, not so often as formerly: looking directly fore-right, as passers-by would imagine, but observing all that stirs on either hand of him without moving his short neck; hardly ever turning back: of a light-brown complexion; teeth not yet failing him; smoothish faced, and ruddy cheeked; at sometimes looking to be about sixty-five, at other times much younger: a regular even pace, stealing away ground, rather than seeming to rid it: a gray eye, too often over-clouded by mistinesses from the head: by chance lively; very lively it will be, if he have hope of seeing a lady whom he loves and honours; his eye always on the ladies; if they have very large hoops, he looks down and supercilious, and as if he would be thought wise, but perhaps the sillier for that: as he approaches a lady, his eye is never fixed first upon her face, but upon her feet, and thence he raises it up, pretty quickly for a dull eye; and one would think (if we thought him at all worthy of observation) that from her air and (the last beheld) her face, he sets her down in his mind as *so* or *so*, and then passes on to the next object he meets; only then looking back, if he greatly likes or dislikes, as if he would see if the lady appear to be all of a piece, in the one light or in the other ... from this odd, this grotesque figure, think you, Madam, that you have anything to apprehend? Any thing that will not rather promote than check your mirth? I dare be bold to say (and allow it too) that you would rather see this figure than any other you ever saw, whenever you should find yourself graver than you wish to be. — From a letter to Lady Bradshaigh, 1749.

I recollect that I was early noted for having invention. I was not fond of play, as other boys: my schoolfellows used to call me *Serious* and *Gravity*. And five of them particularly delighted to single me out, either for a walk, or at their fathers' houses or at mine, to tell them stories, as they phrased it. Some I told them from my reading as true; others from my head, as mere invention; of which they would be most fond, and often were affected by them. One of them, particularly, I remember, was for putting me to write a history, as he called it, on the model of Tommy Potts. I now forget what it was; only, that it was of a servant-man preferred by a fine young lady (for his goodness) to a lord who was a libertine. All my stories carried with them, I am bold to say, a useful moral. — From a letter to Johannes Strinstra, 2 June 1753.

EARL OF ROCHESTER

Gilbert Burnet

He came from his Travels in the 18th year of his Age, and appeared at Court with as great Advantages as most ever had. He was a Graceful and well shaped Person, tall and well made, if not a little too slender. He was exactly well bred, and what by a modest behaviour natural to him, what by a Civility become almost as natural, his Conversation was easie and obliging. He had a strange Vivacity of thought, and vigour of expression: His Wit had a subtility and sublimity both, that were scarce imitable. His Style was clear and strong: When he used Figures they were very lively, and yet far enough out of the Common Road: he had made himself Master of the Ancient and Modern Wit, and of the Modern *French* and *Italian* as well as the *English*. He loved to talk and write of Speculative Matters, and did it with so fine a thread, that even those who hated the Subjects that his Fancy ran upon, yet could not but be charmed with his way of treating of them....

He had so entirely laid down the Intemperance that was growing on him before his Travels, that at his Return, he hated nothing more. But falling into Company that loved these Excesses, he was, though not without difficulty, and by many steps, brought back to it again. And the natural heat of his fancy, being inflamed by Wine, made him so extravagantly pleasant, that many to be more diverted by that humour, studied to engage him deeper and deeper in Intemperance: which at length did so entirely subdue him; that, as he told me, for five years together he was continually Drunk; not all the while under the visible effect of it, but his blood was so inflamed, that he was not in all that time cool enough to be perfectly Master of himself. This led him to say and do many wild and unaccountable things.... And though in cold blood he was a generous and good natured man, yet he would go far in his heats after any thing that might turn to a Jest or matter of Diversion: He said to me, He never improved his Interest at Court, to do a premeditate Mischief to other persons. Yet he laid out his Wit very freely in *Libels* and *Satyres*, in which he had a peculiar talent of mixing his Wit and his Malice, and fitting both with such apt words, that Men were tempted to be pleased with them. — *Some Passages of the Life and Death of John Earl of Rochester* (1680).

SAMUEL ROGERS

Thomas Carlyle

Old Rogers with his pale head, white, bare, and cold as snow, will work on you with those large blue eyes, cruel, sorrowful, and that sardonic shelf-chin. — From a letter to Ralph Waldo Emerson, 15 November 1838.

Old Rogers stayed the longest [at the Ashburton residence], indeed as long as ourselves. I do not remember any old man (he is now eighty-three) whose manner of living gave me less satisfaction. A most sorrowful, distressing, distracted old phenomenon, hovering over the ruin of deep eternities with nothing but light babble, fatuity, vanity, and the frostiest London wit in his mouth. Sometimes I felt as I could throttle him, the poor old wretch! but then suddenly I reflected 'it is but for two days more.' — Quoted in James Anthony Froude's *Thomas Carlyle: A History of His Life in London* (1884).

Samuel C. Hall

All who were denizens of London during the twenty years that preceded the last twenty years — no longer ago — met frequently in the aristocratic neighbourhood of St. James's a man evidently aged, yet remarkably active, though with a slight stoop and grizzled hair; not, to my thinking, with a pleasant countenance; certainly not with the frank and free expression of a poet who loved and lived with Nature; but rather that of one whose ever-open book was a ledger, and who counted the day, not by sunrise and sunset, but by Consols and Exchequer bills — things inconceivable to the Order to which Samuel Rogers undoubtedly belonged.

The old man moved rapidly, as if pursuing a vain shadow, always.

He did not often smile, and seldom laughed; anything approaching hilarity, aught akin to enthusiasm, to a genuine flow of heart and soul, was foreign to his nature — or, at all events, seemed to be so. Yet, of a surety, he was a keen observer; he looked "quite through the deeds of men;" and his natural talent had been matured and polished by long and familiar intercourse with all the finer spirits of his age. His conversation to his "set" at home was remarkably brilliant, and his wit often pure and original.

It was curious, interesting, and startling to converse — as I did — in the year of our Lord 1855, with a venerable gentleman whose first book of poems was published in 1786 — just sixty-nine years; who had worn a cocked hat when a boy, as other boys did — recollected seeing the heads of the "rebels" upon poles at Temple Bar — had seen Garrick act — knocked at Dr. Johnson's door in Bolt Court, and chatted there with Boswell — heard Sir Joshua Reynolds lecture, and Haydn play at a concert in a tie wig with a sword at his side — rowed with a boatman who had rowed Alexander Pope — had seen venerable John Wesley lying on his bier "dressed in full canonicals" — had walked with old General Oglethorpe, who had shot snipes where Conduit Street now stands — was the frequent associate of Fox, Burke, Sheridan, Mackintosh, Horne Tooke, and Madame de Staël — and was a man "in years" when Brougham was called to the Bar, John Kemble first played Coriolanus, Walter Scott had not yet issued "Waverley," Byron was writing "Minor Poems," and Ensign Arthur Wellesley was fighting his way to a dukedom and immortality!...

His countenance was the theme of continual jokes. It was "ugly," if not repulsive. The expression was in no way, nor under any circumstances, good; he had a drooping eye and a thick under lip; his forehead was broad, his head large — out of proportion, indeed, to his form; but it was without the organs of benevolence and veneration, although preponderating in that of ideality. His features were "cadaverous." Lord Dudley once asked him why, now that he could afford it, he did not set up his hearse; and it is said that Sydney Smith gave him mortal offence by recommending him, "when he sat for his portrait, to be drawn saying his prayers, with his face hidden by his hands."

It was affirmed by some of his friends that "his purse was ever open to the distressed," and that he was liberal of aid to struggling and suffering genius. That belief, however, is not sustained by evidence.... Rogers was rich, had few claimants on his "much," and his personal wants were limited. He seems, indeed, to have had no great relish for the luxuries that money supplies, and which it is a duty to obtain on the part of those to whom wealth is allotted. He saw little company at his own house; giving breakfasts frequently, the cost of which was small, and seldom entertaining at dinner above two or three at a time. Moreover, they were dinners of no very *recherché* character; at all events, none of his guests ever spoke of them as the feasts of a Sybarite. He never, I believe, kept a carriage — certainly, if he did, he seldom used it. On occasions when he attended meetings of the Royal Society, and other assemblages of that kind, at the close, let the night be ever so severe, if rain or snow were falling, he was invariably seen buttoning up his great-coat in preparation for a walk home. On one occasion I ventured to say to him (it was at an Evening at Lord Northampton's in Connaught Place), "Mr. Rogers, it is a very wet night; I have a fly at the door: may I have the honour to leave you at your house?" but the invitation was declined; the old man faced the weather, from which younger and stronger men would have wisely shrunk. — *A Book of Memories* (1877).

You could not fancy, when you looked upon him, that you saw a good man. It was a repulsive countenance; to say it was ugly would be to pay it a compliment, and I verily believe it was indicative of a naturally shrivelled heart and contracted soul.... With enormous power to do good, how did Rogers use it? If he lent — and it was seldom he did — to a distressed brother of the pen, he required the return of the loan with interest — when it could be had; if he gave, it was grudgingly and with a shrug. He was prudence personified; some one said of him, "I am sure that as a baby he never fell down unless he was pushed, but walked from chair to chair in the drawing-room, steadily and quietly, till he reached a place where the sunbeams fell on the carpet."

He himself records that, when Madame de Staël once said to him, "How very sorry I am for Campbell! his poverty so unsettles his mind that he cannot write," his reply was, "Why does he not take the situation of a clerk? He could then compose verses during his leisure hours." In this cold, unsympathizing fashion the author of "The Pleasures of Memory" continued to look on the troubles of others to the last. — *Retrospect of a Long Life* (1883).

Charles Mackay

It was in the year 1840 that I first made the acquaintance of the venerable Samuel Rogers, banker and poet, whose name had been familiar to me from my boyhood.... I was prepared to find Mr. Rogers hideously ugly, for I remembered many of the epigrams and jokes upon his personal appearance, which had been in circulation ever since I began to read, and which his former friend Lord Byron had taken a malicious pleasure in repeating.... Byron had written some venomous lines which did not see the light till after his death, which I could not help remembering as I turned from St. James's Street at 10 a.m. to breakfast with him at 22, St. James's Place, a house which his long residence had rendered classic ground, —

> Nose and chin would shame a knocker,
> Wrinkles that would puzzle Cocker;
> Mouth which marks the envious scorner,
> With a scorpion in each corner.
> Turns its quick tail to sting you,
> In the place that most may wring you.

There was much more of the same sort, which it was a pity that a poet of such genius as Byron's, should have soiled his pen, his paper, or his mind by writing. The principal jokes against Rogers turned on the supposed fact that his countenance was deathlike. It was said that he was once refused exit from the catacombs at Paris with the observation by one of the custodians of the place, "*on ne laisse pas passer les morts*," and that at Byron's funeral he was warned to keep out of the way of the undertakers lest they should seize *him* also and put him in a coffin. But my first look at the poet, then in his seventy-eighth year, was an agreeable surprise, and a protest in my mind against the malignant injustice which had been done him. As a young man he might have been uncomely if not as ugly as his revilers had painted him, but as an old man there was an intellectual charm in his countenance and a fascination in his manner which more than atoned for any deficiency of personal beauty. No man or woman can be positively good looking if bald and toothless, but even the bald and toothless can be intelligent, benevolent, quick-witted, and agreeable in conversation. And Mr. Rogers was all these and more....

The reputation which Mr. Rogers enjoyed for cynicism was undeserved. He said unkind things, but he did kind ones in the most gracious manner. If he was sometimes severe upon those who were "up," he was always tender to those who were "down." He never closed his purse-strings against a friend, or refused to help the young and the deserving. — *Forty Years' Recollections of Life, Literature, and Public Affairs* (1877).

Bryan Waller Procter

I forget who introduced me to Mr. Rogers in the year 1820. He lived then and until his death in Saint James's Place, in a house that had previously belonged to one of the Dukes of St. Alban's. It was not in a wide street, but it looked southward on to the Green Park. Upon the whole I never saw any residence so tastefully fitted up and decorated. Every thing was good of its kind, and in good order. There was no plethora; no appearance of display, no sign of superfluous wealth. There were good pictures, good drawings, and a few good books. He had choice statuettes, some coins, and vases, and some rare bijouterie. There was not too much of any thing, not even too much welcome; yet no lack of it. His breakfast-table was perfect, in all respects; and the company — where literature mixed with fashion and rank, each having a fair proportion — was always agreeable. And in the midst of all his hospitable glory was the little old pleasant man, not yet infirm, with his many anecdotes, and sub-acid words that gave flavour and pungency to the general talk. He dwelt too much (too much for the taste of some of his hearers) on olden times, on the days of Fox and Pitt and Sheridan, all of whom he knew and mentioned with great respect, never omitting the "Mr." previously to each name. Like most other persons he was, perhaps, too much disposed to overvalue the times and people of his youth. Even the authors of the last century, so manifestly inferior to those of the present, found an advocate with him....

It has been rumoured that he was a sayer of bitter things. I know that he was a *giver* of good things — a kind and amiable patron, where a patron was wanted; never ostentatious or oppressive, and always a friend in need. He was ready with his counsel; ready with his money. I never put his generosity to the test, but I know enough to testify that it existed, and was often exercised in a delicate manner, and on the slightest hint. "I have received the kindest letter in the world from Rogers," said X—— one day, "inclosing a fifty pound note. God knows, it did not come before it was wanted." It appeared that a friend of mine had casually mentioned X——'s great distress, his struggles for bread, and his large family, a few days previously to Rogers, who made no observation beyond a little sympathy, but he took the opportunity of silently giving the money without parade.

He delighted in clever anecdotes, and he told them well. Mr. Wordsworth was breakfasting with him one morning, he said; but he was much beyond the appointed time, and excused himself by stating that he and a friend had been to see Coleridge, who had detained them by one continuous flow of talk. "How was it you called so early upon him?" inquired Rogers. "Oh," replied Wordsworth, "we are going to dine with him this evening, and ——" "And," said Rogers, taking up the sentence, "you wanted to take the sting out of him beforehand." — Recollections of Men of Letters" in *An Autobiographical Fragment* (1877).

DANTE GABRIEL ROSSETTI

Thomas Hall Caine

I should have described Rossetti, at this time, as a man who looked quite ten years older than his actual age, which was fifty-two, of full middle height and inclining to corpulence, with a round face that ought, one thought, to be ruddy but was pale, large grey eyes with a steady introspecting look, surmounted by broad protrusive brows and a clearly-penciled ridge over the nose, which was well cut and had large breathing nostrils. The mouth and chin were hidden beneath a heavy moustache and abundant beard, which grew up to the ears, and had been a mixed black-brown and auburn, and were now streaked with grey. The forehead was large, round, without protuberances, and very gently receding to where thin black curls, that had once been redundant, began to tumble down to the ears. The entire configuration of the head and face seemed to me singularly noble, and from the eyes upwards, full of beauty. He wore a pair of spectacles, and, in reading, a second pair over the first: but these took little from the sense of power conveyed by those steady eyes, and that "bar of Michael Angelo." His

dress was not conspicuous, being however rather negligent than otherwise, and noticeable, if at all, only for a straight sack-coat, buttoned at
the throat, descending at least to the knees, and having large pockets cut
into it perpendicularly at the sides. This garment was, I afterwards
found, one of the articles of various kinds made to the author's own design. When he spoke, even in exchanging the preliminary courtesies of
an opening conversation, I thought his voice the richest I had ever
known any one to possess. It was a full deep barytone, capable of easy
modulation, and with undertones of infinite softness and sweetness, yet,
as I afterwards found, with almost illimitable compass, and with every
gradation of tone at command, for the recitation or reading of
poetry. — *Recollections of Dante Gabriel Rossetti* (1882).

Frederick Locker-Lampson

I have been at Rossetti's house at Cheyne Walk, and he has been
to me in Victoria Street. I liked him on both occasions, but from what I
hear he could hardly have been a comfortable man to abide with. He
collected Oriental china and *bric-à-brac*, and had a congregation of
queer creatures — a raven, and marmots or wombats, &c. — all in the
garden behind his house. I believe he once kept a gorilla. He was much
self-absorbed. I never quite appreciated his pictures. 'Sister Helen' is his
only poem that much impresses me, and it is not far from being repulsive. However, I suppose he draws inspiration from a world of his own.
His pictures and his poems help each other. I like his poems least; but
then I seldom see his pictures. — *My Confidences* (1896).

JOHN RUSKIN

Sydney Carlyle Cockerell

He was fairly tall but his height was already [1887] diminished
by a little hunch in the shoulders. His hair was dark, long and thick, his
beard iron-grey. His head was of the long type. His forehead sloped,
and on each side, between his temples and his ears, there was a noticeable depression. He had heavy eyebrows and the bluest of blue eyes.
Their colour was repeated with a difference in his large blue neckties (I
have one of these and I know nothing that could recall the wearer more
completely). His hands were small and delicate (I have one of his little

gloves). He wore very old-fashioned clothes — trousers and double-breasted waistcoat of home-spun and a long dark coat. Round his neck was a gold chain attached to his watch. His smile was kindness itself, his voice sometimes almost caressing. He could not quite pronounce his r's. — *Friends of a Lifetime* (1940).

Lillie Langtry

An early visitor to this little house of bizarre effects [No. 17, Norfolk Street, Park Lane] was John Ruskin, then Slade Professor of Art at the University of Oxford. He came one afternoon with Oscar Wilde, who assumed an attitude of such extreme reverence and humility toward the "master" that he could scarcely find breath to introduce him to me. This unusually meek demeanour on Oscar's part aggravated my natural shyness and filled me with exaggerated awe. After a few moments, however, Ruskin's winning voice and charm of manner reassured me, and, taking courage to look at him, I noted that his blue-grey eyes were smiling at me under bushy eyebrows, that his forehead was large and intellectual, that his nose was aquiline, and that the side-whiskers, made familiar by his earlier portraits, had become supplementary to a grey leonine beard.

His hair was rather long, and floppy over his ears; indeed, he was a shaggy-looking individual. He held forth on his pet topic — Greek art — in a fervently enthusiastic manner, and as vehemently denounced the Japanese style, then at the beginning of its vogue, describing it as the "glorification of ugliness and artificiality," and contrasting the unbalanced form of Japanese art with the fine composition and colour of Chinese art, of which he declared it to be a caricature. — *The Days I Knew* (1925).

Himself

They've been doing photographs of me again, and I'm an orang outang as usual, and am in despair. I thought with my beard I was beginning to be just the least bit nice to look at. I would give up half my books for a new profile. — *Hortus Inclusus* (1887).

SIR WALTER SCOTT

Lord Byron

There is one part of your observations in the pamphlet which I shall venture to remark upon; — it regards Walter Scott. You say that "his character is little worthy of enthusiasm", at the same time that you mention his productions in the manner they deserve. I have known Walter Scott long and well, and in occasional situations which call forth the *real* character — and I can assure you that his character *is* worthy of admiration — that of all men he is the most *open*, the most *honourable*, the most *amiable*. With his politics I have nothing to do: they differ from mine, which renders it difficult for me to speak of them. But he is perfectly *sincere* in them: and Sincerity may be humble, but she cannot be servile. I pray you, therefore, to correct or soften that passage. You may, perhaps, attribute this officiousness of mine to a false affectation of *candour*, as I happen to be a writer also. Attribute it to what motive you please, but *believe* the *truth*. I say that Walter Scott is as nearly a thorough good man as man can be, because I *know* it by experience to be the case. — From a letter to Henri Beyle, 29 May 1823.

Samuel C. Hall

I can readily recall the robust and hearty frame of the man; his lofty forehead, broad too, but losing its breadth in its remarkable height; his keen yet kindly grey eyes; and his firm yet pleasant mouth, easy to smile, yet evidencing indomitable will. He disappointed no one; his manner was peculiarly gracious; the very humblest of his fellow labourers was at ease with him at once; it was kindness without the weight of condescension, and counsel without the burden of advice. No man better understood that maxim of Lord Shaftsbury, "Politeness is benevolence in trifles." All who had intercourse with him, either personally or by letter, mingled regard with respect, and affection with veneration. It was a poor tailor who hit his character best: — "Sir Walter speaks to every man as if he were his blood relation."—*A Book of Memories* (1877).

Benjamin Robert Haydon

It is singular how success and the want of it operate on two extra-ordinary men — Walter Scott and Wordsworth. Scott enters a room and sits at table with the coolness and self-possession of conscious fame; Wordsworth with a mortified elevation of head, as if fearful he was not estimated as he deserved.

Scott is always cool and very amusing; Wordsworth often ego-tistical and overwhelming. Scott can afford to talk of trifles, because he knows the world will think him a great man who condescends to trifle; Wordsworth must always be eloquent and profound, because he knows that he is considered childish and puerile. Scott seems to wish to appear less than he really is, while Wordsworth struggles to be thought, at the moment, greater than he is suspected to be.

This is natural. Scott's disposition is the effect of success opera-ting on a genial temperament, while Wordsworth's evidently arises from the effect of unjust ridicule wounding an intense self-esteem.

I think that Scott's success would have made Wordsworth in-sufferable, while Wordsworth's failures would not have rendered Scott a whit less delightful.

Scott is the companion of Nature in all her feelings and freaks, while Wordsworth follows her like an apostle, sharing her solemn moods and impressions. — *Journals*, 7 March 1821.

Bryan Waller Procter

I first met Sir Walter Scott at Mr. [Samuel] Rogers', at break-fast. He was tall, stalwart, bluff but courteous, and rather lame. I was at once struck with his bonhomie and easy simplicity of manner. He talked well and good naturedly, and was perfectly self-possessed and very pleasant. Without the slightest appearance of pretension, he spoke like a man well assured of his position. Statesmen, poets, and philoso-phers of all kinds had sought his company, and he was admired by everyone, high and low. I do not think that anyone envied him more than one envies kings. He was placed high beyond competition....

I never observed Sir Walter's self-possession disturbed, except on one occasion, when Rogers told him with a smile that Lady B——'s maid had hid herself amongst the male servants, on the landing at B——house, to watch him as he went downstairs, the preceding evening. He seemed a little ashamed of his admirer. I met him [Scott] afterwards at breakfast, in [Benjamin Robert] Haydon's studio, when a circumstance occurred that threw a different light on his power of self-command. Charles Lamb and Hazlitt and various other people were there, and the conversation turned on the *vraisemblance* of certain dramatis personae in a modern book. Sir Walter's opinion was asked. "Well!" replied he, "they are as true as the personages in 'Waverley' and 'Guy Mannering' are, I think." This was long before he had confessed that he was the author of the Scotch Novels, and when much curiosity was alive on the subject. I looked very steadily into his face as he spoke, but it did not betray any consciousness or suppressed humour. His command of countenance was perfect. — "Recollections of Men of Letters" in *An Autobiographical Fragment* (1877).

WILLIAM SHAKESPEARE

Robert Greene

There is an upstart crow, beautified with our feathers, that with his 'Tiger's heart wrapped in a player's hide', supposes he is as well able to bombast out a blank verse as the best of you; and being an absolute *Johannes fac totum*, is in his own conceit the only Shake-scene in a country. — *Groatsworth of Wit, Bought with a Million of Repentance* (1592).

Ben Jonson

I *remember*, the Players have often mentioned it as an honour to *Shakespeare*, that in his writing, (whatsoever he penn'd) hee never blotted out line. My answer hath beene, would he had blotted a thousand. Which they thought a malevolent speech. I had not told posterity this, but for their ignorance, who choose that circumstance to commend their friend by, wherein he most faulted. And to justifie mine owne candor, (for I lov'd the man, and doe honour his memory (on this side Idolatry) as much as any.) Hee was (indeed) honest, and of an open, and free nature: had an excellent *Phantsie*; brave notions, and gentle expressions: wherein hee flow'd with that facility, that sometime it was necessary he should be stop'd: *Sufflaminandus erat*; as *Augustus* said of *Haterius*. His wit was in his owne power; would the rule of it had been so too. Many times hee fell into those things, could not escape laughter: As when hee said in the person of Caesar, one speaking to him; *Caesar thou dost me wrong*. Hee replyed: *Caesar did never wrong, but with just cause*: and such like, which were ridiculous. But hee redeemed his vices, with his vertues. There was ever more in him to be praysed, then to be pardoned. — *Timber: or Discoveries* (1641).

John Manningham

Upon a time when Burbage played Richard the Third there was a citizen grew so far in liking with him that before she went from the play she appointed him to come that night unto her by the name of Richard the Third. Shakespeare, overhearing their conclusion, went before, was entertained and at his game ere Burbage came. Then message being brought that Richard the Third was at the door, Shakespeare caused return to be made that William the Conqueror was before Richard the Third. Shakespeare's name William. — From Manningham's diary, 13 March 1602.

GEORGE BERNARD SHAW

Bertrand Russell

I heard of him first in 1890, when I, as a freshman, met another freshman who admired his *Quintessence of Ibsenism*, but I did not meet him until 1896 when he took part in an International Socialist Congress in London.... He was at this time still shy. Indeed, I think that his wit, like that of many famous humorists, was developed as a defense against expected hostile ridicule. At this time he was just beginning to write plays, and he came to my flat to read one of them to a small gathering of friends. He was white and trembling with nervousness, and not at all the formidable figure that he became later. Shortly afterward, he and I stayed with the Webbs in Monmouthshire while he was learning the technique of the drama. He would write the names of all his characters on little squares of paper, and, when he was doing a scene, he would put on a chess board in front of him the names of the characters who were on the stage in that scene.

At this time he and I were involved in a bicycle accident, which I feared for a moment might have brought his career to a premature close. He was only just learning to ride a bicycle, and he ran into my machine with such force that he was hurled through the air and landed on his back twenty feet from the place of the collision. However, he got up completely unhurt and continued his ride; whereas my bicycle was smashed, and I had to return by train. It was a very slow train, and at every station Shaw with his bicycle appeared on the platform, put his head into the carriage and jeered. I suspect that he regarded the whole incident as proof of the virtues of vegetarianism....

It used to be the custom among clever people to say that Shaw was not unusually vain, but only unusually candid. I came to think later on that this was a mistake. Two incidents at which I was present convinced me of this. The first was a luncheon in London in honor of [Henri] Bergson, to which Shaw had been invited as an admirer, along with a number of professional philosophers whose attitude to Bergson was more critical. Shaw set to work to expound Bergson's philosophy in the style of the preface to *Methuselah*. In this version, the philosophy was hardly one to recommend itself to professionals, and Bergson mildly interjected, "Ah, no-o! it is not qvite zat!" But Shaw was quite unabashed, and replied, "Oh, my dear fellow, I understand your philosophy much better than you do." Bergson clenched his fists and nearly exploded with rage; but, with a great effort, he controlled himself, and Shaw's expository monologue continued.

The second incident was an encounter with the elder Masaryk, who was in London officially, and intimated through his secretary that there were certain people whom he would like to see at 10:00 A.M. before his official duties began. I was one of them, and when I arrived I discovered that the only others were Shaw and [H.G.] Wells and [Frank] Swinnerton. The rest of us arrived punctually, but Shaw was late. He marched straight up to the Great Man and said: "Masaryk, the foreign policy of Czechoslovakia is all wrong." He expounded this theme for about ten minutes, and left without waiting to hear Masaryk's reply.

Shaw, like many witty men, considered wit an adequate substitute for wisdom. He could defend any idea, however silly, so cleverly as to make those who did not accept it look like fools.... Shaw was at his best as a controversialist. If there was anything silly or anything insincere about his opponent, Shaw would seize on it unerringly to the delight of all those who were on his side in the controversy.... Shaw had many qualities which deserve great admiration. He was completely fearless. He expressed his opinions with equal vigor whether they were popular or unpopular. He was merciless toward those who deserve no mercy — but sometimes, also, to those who did not deserve to be his victims. In sum, one may say that he did much good and some harm. As an iconoclast he was admirable, but as an icon rather less so. — *Portraits from Memory* (1956).

Frank Swinnerton

In 1884 Shaw weighed 142 pounds. His height, without shoes, was six feet one inch. He was lean, pale-faced, bearded, rather ginger, with blue-grey eyes and small hands. Upon a soap box he may well have looked eight feet tall, and of course far above the heads of such men as gathered to listen.... Shaw says he has nothing of a voice; but he knows how to produce it. When he speaks, his Irish accent, and still more his Irish intonation, captivates the English ear. He seems to sing. Moreover, few men think as clearly and adroitly as he does or can express themselves as clearly and adroitly as he can. He is a first-class debater. Whenever I have heard him in debate, he has triumphed because he knew perfectly well what he was saying and doing. This is a terribly rare accomplishment in a public speaker. — *The Georgian Literary Scene* (1938).

Mark Twain

Bernard Shaw has not completed his fifty-second year yet, and therefore is merely a lad. The vague and far-off rumble which he began to make five or six years ago is near-by now, and is recognizable as thunder. The editorial world lightly laughed at him during four or five of those years, but it takes him seriously now; he has become a force, and it is conceded that he must be reckoned with. Shaw is a pleasant man; simple, direct, sincere, animated; but self-possessed, sane, and evenly poised, acute, engaging, companionable, and quite destitute of affectations. I liked him. He shows no disposition to talk about himself or his work, or his high and growing prosperities in reputation and the materialities — but mainly — and affectionately and admiringly — devoted his talk to William Morris, whose close friend he had been and whose memory he deeply reveres. — Quoted in *Mark Twain Himself* by Milton Meltzer (1960).

H.G. Wells

Mr. Shaw objects to my calling him muddleheaded. But I have always considered him muddleheaded. If I have not called him that in public before it is simply because I thought the thing too obvious to need pointing out.

If we see a man making an ass of himself, we indolent English accept him rather than face the boring task of pursuing him into the recesses of his unsoundness. We hump our backs. If we believe a man is systematically propagating some specific error we may take the trouble to study and combat him, but if we perceive that he is flinging himself about in a paroxysm of merely personal activity we leave him alone, or if we notice him, we notice him as we fling a hairbrush at a nocturnal cat, because the irritation has become intolerable.

And that is how things stand between Mr. Shaw and myself. I have been quite exceptionally disposed to take him seriously, and find out what he amounts to, and this is what I find he amounts to. He is an activity, a restless passion for attention. Behind that is a kind of jackdaw's hoard of other people's notions; much from Samuel Butler, scraps of pseudo-philosophical phraseology such as that "Life Force" phrase he got from Dr. Guest, old Hammersmith economics, worn fragments of Herbert Spencer, some Nietzsche, conveyed no doubt from the convenient handbook of Mr. Orage, shreds of theosophy, current superstitions, as for example his idea that fear "poisons" meat, or that wool is a more "natural" and hygenic clothing than cotton, sweepings of all sorts of "advanced" rubbish, but nothing anywhere of which one can say "Here is the thought of a man." And it is just this incoherent emptiness, combined with an amazing knack of fluent inexactitude which gives him his advantage in irresponsible attack, and which from his early repute as the Terror of the Fabian Society has spread his vague and unsubstantial fame about the globe far beyond the range to which even his confusedly entertaining intellectual forces would have taken it.

Mr. Shaw is one of those perpetual children who live in a dream of make-believe, and the make-believe of Mr. Shaw is that he is a person of incredible wisdom and subtlety running the world. He is an elderly adolescent still at play. To understand that is to have the clue to all Shavianism. — *Daily Chronicle* (31 December 1914).

PERCY BYSSHE SHELLEY

Thomas Carlyle

[Robert] Southey and I got to speaking about Shelley.... Southey did not rise into admiration of Shelley either for talent or conduct; spoke of him and his life, without bitterness, but with contemptuous sorrow, and evident aversion mingled with his pity. To me also poor Shelley always was, and is, a kind of ghastly object, colourless, pallid, without health or warmth or vigour; the sound of him shrieky, frosty, as if a ghost were trying to "sing to us;" the temperament of him spasmodic, hysterical, instead of strong or robust; with fine affections and aspirations, gone all such a road: — a man infinitely too weak for that solitary scaling of the Alps which he undertook in spite of the world. — *Reminiscences* (1881).

Thomas Jefferson Hogg

His figure was slight and fragile, and yet his bones and joints were large and strong. He was tall, but he stooped so much, that he seemed of a low stature. His clothes were expensive, and made according to the most approved mode of the day; but they were tumbled, rumpled, unbrushed. His gestures were abrupt and sometimes violent, occasionally even awkward, yet more frequently gentle and graceful. His complexion was delicate, and almost feminine, of the purest red and white; yet he was tanned and freckled by exposure to the sun, having passed the autumn, as he said in shooting. His features, his whole face, and particularly his head, were, in fact, unusually small; yet the last *appeared* of a remarkable bulk, for his hair was long and bushy, and in fits of absence, and in the agonies (if I may use the word) of anxious thought, he often rubbed it fiercely with his hands, or passing his fingers quickly through his locks unconsciously, so that it was singularly wild and rough.... But there was one physical blemish that threatened to neutralize all his excellence. "This is a fine, clever fellow!" I said to myself, "but I can never bear his society; I shall never be able to endure his voice; it would kill me. What a pity it is!" I am very sensible of imperfections, and especially of painful sounds, — and the voice of the stranger was excruciating: it was intolerably shrill, harsh, and discordant: of the most cruel intension, — it was perpetual, and without any remission, — it excoriated the ears....

Bysshe's dietary was frugal and independent; very remarkable and quite peculiar to himself. When he felt hungry he would dash into the first baker's shop, buy a loaf and rush out again, bearing it under his arm; and he strode onwards in his rapid course, breaking off pieces of bread and greedily swallowing them.

But however frugal the fare, the waste was considerable, and his path might be tracked, like that of Hop-O'-my-Thumb through the wood, in Mother Goose her tale, by a long line of crumbs.... He occasionally rolled up little pellets of bread, and, in a sly, mysterious manner, shot them with his thumb, hitting the persons — whom he met in his walks — on the face, commonly on the nose, at which he grew to be very dexterous. — *The Life of Percy Bysshe Shelley* (1858).

Leigh Hunt

Mr. Shelley, when he died, was in his thirtieth year. His figure was tall and slight, and his constitution consumptive. He was subject to violent spasmodic pains, which would sometimes force him to lie on the ground till they were over; but he had always a kind word to give to those about him, when his pangs allowed him to speak. In this organization, as well as in some other respects, he resembled the German poet, Schiller. Though well-turned, his shoulders were bent a little, owing to premature thought and trouble. The same causes had touched his hair with grey: and though his habits of temperance and exercise gave him a remarkable degree of strength, it is not supposed that he could have lived many years. He used to say, that he had lived three times as long as the calendar gave out; which he would prove, between jest and earnest, by some remarks on Time, "That would have puzzled that stout Stagyrite." Like the Stagyrite's, his voice was high and weak. His eyes were large and animated, with a dash of wildness in them; his face small, but well shaped, particularly the mouth and chin, the turn of which was very sensitive and graceful. His complexion was naturally fair and delicate, with a colour in the cheeks. He had brown hair, which, though tinged with grey, surmounted his face well, being in considerable quantity, and tending to a curl. — *Lord Byron and Some of His Contemporaries* (1828).

Charles Lamb

I can no more understand Shelley than you can. His poetry is "thin sown with profit or delight."... For his theories and nostrums, they are oracular enough; but I either comprehend 'em not, or there is "miching malice" and mischief in 'em, but, for the most part, ringing with their own emptiness. Hazlitt said well of 'em — "Many are the wiser and better for reading Shakespeare, but nobody was ever wiser or better for reading Shelley." — From a letter to Bernard Barton, August 1824.

Thomas Love Peacock

About the end of 1813, Shelley was troubled by one of his most extraordinary delusions. He fancied that a fat old woman who sat opposite him in a mail coach was afflicted with elephantiasis, that the disease was infectious and incurable, and that he had caught it from her. He was continually on the watch for its symptoms; his legs were to swell to the size of an elephant's, and his skin was to be crumpled over like goose-skin. He would draw the skin of his own hands, arms, and neck very tight, and if he discovered any deviation from smoothness, he would seize the person next to him, and endeavour by a corresponding pressure to see if any corresponding deviation existed. He often startled young ladies in an evening party by this singular process, which was as instantaneous as a flash of lightning.... When he found that, as the days rolled on, his legs retained their proportion, and his skin its smoothness, the delusion died away. — *Memoirs of Percy Bysshe Shelley* (1858).

Edward John Trelawny

Shelley came of a long-lived race, and, barring accidents, there was no reason why he should not have emulated his forefathers in attaining a ripe age. He had no other complaint than occasional spasms, and these were probably caused by the excessive and almost unremitting strain on his mental powers, the solitude of his life, and his long fasts, which were not intentional, but proceeded from the abstraction and forgetfulness of himself and his wife. If food was near him, he ate it, — if not, he fasted, and it was after long fasts that he suffered from spasms. He was tall, slim, and bent from eternally poring over books; this habit had contracted his chest. His limbs were well proportioned, strong and bony — his head was very small — and his features were expressive of great sensibility, and decidedly feminine. There was nothing about him outwardly to attract notice, except his extraordinarily juvenile appearance. At twenty-nine, he still retained on his tanned and freckled cheeks, the fresh look of a boy — although his long wild locks were coming into blossom, as a polite hairdresser once said to me, whilst cutting mine.

It was not until he spoke that you could discern anything uncommon in him — but the first sentence he uttered, when excited by his subject, riveted your attention. The light from his very soul streamed from his eyes, and every mental emotion of which the human mind is susceptible, was expressed in his pliant and ever-changing features. He left the conviction on the minds of his audience, that however great he was as a Poet, he was greater as an orator. — *Recollections of the Last Days of Shelley and Byron* (1858).

TOBIAS SMOLLETT

Alexander Carlyle

Smollet was a Man of very agreable Conversation, and of much Genuine Humour, and tho' not a profound Scholar, Possess'd a Philosophical Mind, and was capable of making the Soundest Observations on Human Life, and of Discerning the Excellence, or Seeing the Ridicule of Every Character he met with. Fielding only excell'd him in Giving a Dramatick Story to his Novels, but in my Opinion was Inferior to him in the true Comick Vein. He was one of the many very pleasant men with whom it was my Good Fortune to be Intimately Acquainted. — Anecdotes and Characters of the Times (1860).

John Moore

The person of Dr. Smollett was stout and well proportioned, his countenance engaging, his manner reserved, with a certain air of dignity that seemed to indicate that he was not unconscious of his own powers. He was of a disposition so humane and generous, that he was ever ready to serve the unfortunate, and on some occasions to assist them beyond what his circumstances could justify. Though few could penetrate with more acuteness into character, yet none was more apt to overlook misconduct when attended with misfortune....

As nothing was more abhorrent to his nature than pertness or instrusion, few things could render him more indignant than a cold reception; to this however he imagined he had sometimes been exposed on his applications in favour of others; for himself he never made an application to any great man in his life.

Free from vanity, Smollett had a considerable share of pride, and great sensibility; his passions were easily moved, and too impetuous when roused; he could not conceal his contempt of folly, his detestation of fraud, nor refrain from proclaiming his indignation against every instance of oppression.

Though Smollett possessed a versatility of style in writing, which he could accommodate to every character, he had no suppleness in his conduct. His learning, diligence, and natural acuteness would have rendered him eminent in the science of medicine, had he persevered in that profession; other parts of his character were ill-suited for augmenting his practice. He could neither stoop to impose on credulity, nor humour caprice.

He was of an intrepid, independent, imprudent disposition, equally incapable of deceit and adulation, and more disposed to cultivate the acquaintance of those he could serve, than those who could serve him. What wonder that a man of his character was not, what is called, successful in life! — "Memoir of his Life," prefixed to *The Works of Tobias Smollett* (1797).

ROBERT SOUTHEY

Thomas Carlyle

Southey was a man towards well up in the fifties; hair gray, not yet hoary, well setting off his fine clear brown complexion; head and face both smallish, as indeed the figure was while seated; features finely cut; eyes, brow, mouth, good in their kind — expressive all, and even vehemently so, but betokening rather keenness than depth either of intellect or character; a serious, human, honest, but sharp, almost fierce-looking, thin man, with very much of the militant in his aspect — in the eyes especially was visible a mixture of sorrow and of anger, or of angry contempt, as if his indignant fight with the world had not yet ended in victory, but also never should in defeat. A man you were willing to hear speak....

After Southey's bit of recitation [of some verses by Winthrop Mackworth Praed] I think the party must have soon broken up. I recollect nothing more of it, except my astonishment when Southey at last completely rose from his chair to shake hands. He had only half risen and nodded on my coming in; and all along I had counted him a lean little man; but now he shot suddenly aloft into a lean tall one, all legs, in shape and stature like a pair of tongs, which peculiarity my surprise doubtless exaggerated to me, but only made it the more notable and entertaining. Nothing had happened throughout that was other than moderately pleasant; and I returned home (I conclude) well enough satisfied with my evening. Southey's sensitiveness I had noticed on the first occasion as one of his characteristic qualities, but was nothing like aware of the extent of it till our next meeting.

This was a few evenings afterwards, [Henry] Taylor giving some dinner, or party, party in honor of his guest; if dinner, I was not at that, but must have undertaken for the evening sequel, as less incommodious to me, less unwholesome more especially. I remember entering, in the same house, but up-stairs this time, a pleasant little drawing-room, in which, in well-lighted, secure enough condition, sat Southey in full dress, silently reclining, and as yet no other company. We saluted suitably; touched ditto on the vague initiatory points; and were still there, when, by way of coming closer, I asked mildly, with no appearance of special interest, but with more than I really felt, "Do you know De Quincey?" (the opium-eater, whom I knew to have lived in Cumberland as his neighbor). "Yes, sir," said Southey, with extraordinary animosity, "and if you have opportunity, I'll thank you to tell him he is one of the greatest scoundrels living!" I laughed lightly, said I had myself little acquaintance with the man, and could not wish to recommend myself by that message. Southey's face, as I looked at it, was become of slate-color, the eyes glancing, the attitude rigid, the figure altogether a picture of Rhadamanthine rage — that is, rage conscious to itself of being just. He doubtless felt I would expect some explanation from him. "I have told Hartley Coleridge," said he, "that he ought to take a strong cudgel, proceed straight to Edinburgh, and give De Quincey, publicly in the streets there, a sound beating, as a calumniator, cowardly spy, traitor, base betrayer of the hospitable social hearth, for one thing!" It appeared De Quincey was then, and for some time past, writing in "Blackwood's Magazine" something of autobiographic nature, a series of papers on the "Lake" period of his life, merely for the sake of the highly needful trifle of money, poor soul, and with no wish to be untrue (I could believe) or hurt anybody, though not without his own bit of splenetic conviction, and to which latter, in regard of Coleridge in particular, he had given more rein than was agreeable to parties concerned. I believe I had myself read the paper on Coleridge, one paper on him I certainly read, and had been the reverse of tempted by it to look after the others; finding in this, e.g., that Coleridge had the greatest intellect perhaps ever given to man, "but that he wanted, or as good as wanted, common honesty in applying it;" which seemed to me a miserable contradiction in terms, and threw light, if not on Coleridge, yet on De Quincey's faculty of judging him or others. In this paper there were probably withal some domestic details or allusions, to which, as familiar to rumor, I had paid but little heed; but certainly, of general reverence for Coleridge and his gifts and deeds, I had traced, not deficiency in this paper, but glaring exaggeration, coupled with De Quincean drawbacks, which latter had alone struck Southey with such poignancy; or perhaps there had been other more criminal papers, which Southey knew of, and not I? In few minutes we let the topic drop,

I helping what I could, and he seemed to feel as if he had done a little wrong, and was bound to show himself more than usually amicable and social, especially with me, for the rest of the evening, which he did in effect, though I quite forget the details, only that I had a good deal of talk with him, in the circle of the others, and had again more than once to notice the singular readiness of the blushes; amiable red blush, beautiful like a young girl's, when you touched genially the pleasant theme, and serpent-like flash of blue or black blush (this far, very far the rarer kind, though it did recur too) when you struck upon the opposite. All details of the evening, except that primary one, are clean gone; but the effect was interesting, pleasantly stimulating, and surprising. I said to myself, "How has this man contrived, with such a nervous system, to keep alive for near sixty years? Now blushing under his gray hairs, rosy like a maiden of fifteen; now slaty almost, like a rattlesnake or fiery serpent? How has he not been torn to pieces long since, under such furious pulling this way and that? He must have somewhere a great deal of methodic virtue in him; I suppose, too, his heart is throughly honest, which helps considerably." — *Reminiscences* (1881).

Thomas De Quincey

His hair was black, and yet his complexion was fair; his eyes I believe to be hazel and large; but I will not vouch for that fact: his nose aquiline; and he has a remarkable habit of looking up into the air, as if looking at abstractions. The expression of his face was that of a very acute and aspiring man. So far, it was even noble, as it conveyed a feeling of a serene and gentle pride, habitually familiar with elevating subjects of contemplation. And yet it was impossible that this pride could have been offensive to anybody, chastened as it was by the most unaffected modesty; and this modesty made evident and prominent by the constant expression of reverence for the great men of the age, (when he happened to esteem them such,) and for all the great patriarchs of our literature. The point in which Southey's manner failed the most in conciliating regard, was, in all which related to the external expressions of friendliness. No man could be more sincerely hospitable — no man more essentially disposed to give up even his time (the possession which he most valued) to the service of his friends. But there was an air of reserve and distance about him — the reserve of a lofty, self-respecting mind, but, perhaps, a little too freezing — in his treatment of all persons who were not among the *corps* of his ancient fireside friends....

Southey was at that time, (1807,) and has continued ever since, the most industrious of all literary men on record. A certain task he prescribed to himself every morning before breakfast. This could not be a very long one, for he breakfasted at nine, or soon after, and *never* rose before eight, though he went to bed duly at half-past ten; but, as I have many times heard him say, less than nine hours' sleep he found insufficient. From breakfast to a latish dinner (about half after five or six) was his main period of literary toil. After dinner, according to the accident of having or not having visitors in the house, he sate over his wine; or he retired to his library again, from which, about eight, he was summoned to tea. — *Reminiscences of the English Lake Poets* (1907).

Samuel C. Hall

He was the very *beau idéal* of a poet — singularly impressive, tall, somewhat slight, slow in his movements, and very dignified in manner, with the eye of an hawk, and with sharp features, and an aquiline nose, that carried the similitude somewhat further. His forehead was broad and high, his eyebrows dark, his hair profuse and long, rapidly approaching white. I can see vividly, even now, his graceful and winning smile. To the commonest observer he was obviously a man who had lived more with books than men, whose converse had chiefly been with "the mighty minds of old," whose "days," whose "thoughts," whose "hopes," were, as he tells us they were, "with the dead."

In the few and brief conversations I had with him, he impressed me — as, indeed, he did every person who was, even for an hour, in his company — with the conviction that he elevated the profession of letters not only by knowledge acquired and distributed, not alone by the wisdom of his career and the integrity of his life, but by manners unassuming and unexacting, and by a condescending gentleness of demeanour that, if not humility in the common sense of the term, arose out of generous consideration and large charity....

Southey had a great dislike to be "looked at;" and although very regular in his attendance at church, he would stay away when he knew there were many tourists in the neighbourhood. One Sunday, two strangers who had a great desire to see the poet besought the sexton to point him out to them. The sexton, knowing that this must be done secretly, said, "I will take you up the aisle, and, in passing, touch the pew in which he sits." He did so, and no doubt the strangers had "a good stare." A few days after, the sexton met Southey in the street of Keswick. The poet looked somewhat sternly at him, said, "*Don't do it again*," and passed on, leaving the conscience-stricken sexton to ponder over the "crime" in which he had been detected by the poet. — *A Book of Memories* (1877).

William Hazlitt

Mr. Southey's conversation has a little resemblance to a commonplace book; his habitual deportment to a piece of clock-work. He is not remarkable either as a reasoner or an observer: but he is quick, unaffected, replete with anecdote, various and retentive in his reading, and exceedingly happy in his play upon words, as most scholars are who give their minds this sportive turn. We have chiefly seen Mr. Southey in company where few people appear to advantage, we mean in that of Mr. Coleridge. He has not certainly the same range of speculation, nor the same flow of sounding words, but he makes up by the details of knowledge, and by a scrupulous correctness of statement for what he wants in originality of thought, or impetuous declamation. The tones of Mr. Coleridge's voice are eloquence: those of Mr. Southey are meagre, shrill, and dry. Mr. Coleridge's *forte* is conversation, and he is conscious of this: Mr. Southey evidently considers writing as his stronghold, and if gravelled in an argument, or at a loss for an explanation, refers to something he has written on the subject, or brings out his port-folio, doubled down in dog-ears, in confirmation of some fact. He is scholastic and professional in his ideas. He sets more value on what he writes than on what he says: he is perhaps prouder of his library than of his own productions — themselves a library! He is more simple in his manners than his friend Mr. Coleridge; but at the same time less cordial or conciliating. He is less vain, or has less hope of pleasing, and therefore lays himself less out to please. There is an air of condescension in his civility. With a tall, loose figure, a peaked austerity of countenance, and no inclination to *embonpoint*, you would say he has something puritanical, something ascetic in his appearance. He answer's to Mandeville's description of Addison, 'a parson in a tye-wig.' He is not a boon companion, nor does he indulge in the pleasures of the table, nor in any other vice; nor are we aware that Mr. Southey is chargeable with any human frailty but — *want of charity*! Having fewer errors to plead guilty to, he is less lenient to those of others. He was born an age too late. Had he lived a century or two ago, he would have been a happy as well as blameless character.... In all the relations and charities of private life, he is correct, exemplary, generous, just. We never heard a single impropriety laid to his charge; and if he has many enemies, few men can boast more numerous or stauncher friends. — The variety and piquancy of his writings form a striking contrast to the mode in which they are produced. He rises early, and writes or reads till breakfast-time. He writes or reads after breakfast till dinner, after dinner till tea, and from tea till bed-time.... Study serves him for business, exercise, recreation. He passes from verse to prose, from history to poetry, from reading to writing, by a stop-watch. He writes a fair hand, without blots, sitting upright in his chair, leaves off when he comes to the bottom of the page, and changes the subject for another, as opposite as the Antipodes. His mind is after all rather the recipient and transmitter of knowledge, than the originator of it. He has hardly grasp of thought enough to arrive at any great leading truth. His passions do not amount to more than irritability. With some gall in his pen, and coldness in his manner, he has a great deal of kindness in his heart. — *The Spirit of the Age* (1825).

[Also see William Wordsworth — Thomas De Quincey.]

GERTRUDE STEIN

Ernest Hemingway

Miss Stein was very big but not tall and was heavily built like a peasant woman. She had beautiful eyes and a strong German-Jewish face that also could have been Friulano and she reminded me of a northern Italian peasant woman with her clothes, her mobile face and her lovely, thick, alive immigrant hair which she wore put up in the same way she had probably worn it in college....

Writing every day made her happy, but as I got to know her better I found that for her to keep happy it was necessary that this daily output, which varied with her energy, be published and that she receive recognition.

This had not become an acute situation when I first knew her, since she had published three stories that were intelligible to anyone. One of these stories, "Melanctha," was very good and good samples of her experimental writing had been published in book form and had been well praised by critics who had met her or known her. She had such a personality that when she wished to win anyone over to her side she would not be resisted, and critics who met her and saw her pictures took on trust writing of hers that they could not understand because of their enthusiasm for her as a person, and because of their confidence in her judgment. She had also discovered many truths about rhythms and the uses of words in repetition that were valid and valuable and she talked well about them.

But she disliked the drudgery of revision and the obligation to make her writing intelligible, although she needed to have publication and official acceptance, especially for the unbelievably long book called *The Making of Americans.*

This book began magnificently, went on very well for a long way with great stretches of great brilliance and then went on endlessly in repetitions that a more conscientious and less lazy writer would have put in the waste basket. I came to know it very well as I got — forced, perhaps would be the word — Ford Madox Ford to publish it in *The Transatlantic Review* serially, knowing that it would outrun the life of the review. For publication in the review I had to read all of Miss Stein's proof for her as this was a work which gave her no happiness. — *A Moveable Feast* (1964).

Gertrude S. I was very fond of and god knows I was loyal too until she had pushed my face in a dozen times. Last time I saw her she told me she had heard an incident, some fag story, which proved me conclusively to be very queer indeed. I said You knew me for four or five years and you believe that? Oh it was very circumstantial, she said. Very circumstantial indeed. She wouldn't tell me what it was. Just how completely credible and circumstantial it was. Poor old Papa. Well I'll probably read it in her autobiography that you had a piece about in N. Yorker. I never cared a damn about what she did in or out of bed and I liked her very damned much and she got awfully damned patriotic about sex. The first stage was that nobody was any good that wasn't that way. The second was that anybody that was that way was good. The third was that anybody that was any good must be that way. Patriotism is a hell of a vice. — From a letter to Janet Flanner, 8 April 1933.

Samuel Putnam

Gertrude Stein lived in the rue de Fleurus, "about ten jumps from the Dôme," as my friend Wambly Bald put it; but the jumps would have had to be powerful ones. So far as her place of abode was concerned, she was not far removed from the roaring center of Montparnasse life; but for most residents of the Quarter she might as well have lived in Timbuktu.

Her topographical situation was typical of her attitude toward the outside world in general. She was remote and yet not remote. The common impression was that, like Joyce, she was a cloistered being, fearful of any intrusion; she was pictured as one who could be approached only with genuflections and the odor of incense; whereas the truth is that, unlike the creator of *Ulysses*, she was quite accessible to her admirers and to any of the press who chose to look in at her "studio" (there were not many that did in those days)....

I was always afraid of Gertrude. She reminded me a trifle too much of the cigar-smoking Amy Lowell, whom I had known in my younger days. Wambly Bald had named her "the Woman with a Face like Caesar's," and it seemed to fit.

We were at the Dôme one afternoon when Wambly said: "Come on, let's go up and see Gertie."

"What do you mean? She'd throw us out."

Leo Stein, Gertrude's brother, was sitting with us.

"What are you afraid of?" he asked. "My God, Sam, you have no idea how dumb she is! Why, when we were in school, I used to have to do all her home work for her."

Leo and Gertrude definitely did not care for each other; and this remark, I reflected, must be a bit of an exaggeration in view of his sister's record at Johns Hopkins and at Harvard in such abstruse subjects as brain anatomy and abnormal pathology. But it heartened me, nonetheless. I decided to go with Wambly.

"You do the talking," I said to him. "I'll stay in the background."

"And to think," he observed as we came up to the building in which Miss Stein lived, "and to think that it is from here that she has been saving the English language for the last twenty-five years!"

Inside, we found the walls covered with Picassos. Picasso, Picasso, and more Picasso.

"Yes," Miss Stein informed us, "Picasso has done eighty portraits of me. I sat for that one ninety-one times."

Good newspaperman that he is, Wambly lost no time in coming to the point; and the interviewing technique that he chose to adopt, a belligerent one, proved to be admirably suited to the purpose of drawing out the interviewee. But still, I was mildly alarmed at his beginning.

"Your prose, Miss Stein," he blurted out, "strikes me as being obscure, deliberately obscure."

The Woman with the Face Like Caesar's never looked more like him than then, as she drew herself up haughtily and replied:

"My prose is obscure only to the lazy-minded. It is a well, a deep well, well it is like a well and that is well."

"There are some people," persisted Wambly, "who are inclined to believe that it is a bottomless well — or one with a false bottom."

At this, Miss Stein's eyes flashed like Caesar's on the field of battle and her voice rang as she answered:

"Naturally, I have my detractors. What genius does not?"

"You *are* a genius, then?" It was my first question. Miss Stein looked at me as if I were a dot that had suddenly appeared upon the map.

"There are three of us," she enunciated: "Myself, Picasso, and [Alfred North] Whitehead." (She was to repeat this statement in her *Autobiography*.)...

"You feel, then, Miss Stein, that your place in literature is secure?"

"My place in literature? Twentieth-century literature *is* Gertrude Stein. There was Henry James, of course—"

"Yes, there was Henry James—"

"He was my precursor, you might say; but everything really begins with my *Three Lives*."

At this point, Wambly saw fit to remind our hostess of something which Wyndham Lewis had just said about her. Lewis had implied that she was in the same class with Anita Loos.

"That," exclaimed Miss Stein, "is simply British propaganda—against American writers! I am surprised that you pay any attention to it."

"You think that the English are jealous of the Americans?"

"They have a right to be. After all, America made the twentieth century just as England made the nineteenth. America has given Europe everything. America has given Europe Gertrude Stein—"

"What about the other great American writers?"

"There are the big four: Poe, Whitman, James, myself. The line of descent is clear. And James, Whitman, and Poe are dead. I am the last. But I am truly international. My reputation is growing all the time."

"Do you feel that your writing is really American, that is to say, typically American?"

"Certainly. What has been the tendency of American writing?"

Wambly and I exchanged glances, each waiting for the other to speak.

"Toward abstraction, of course. But an abstraction without mysticism. That is the great contribution of Gertrude Stein. Her work is abstract without being mystical. There is no mysticism in my work."

"No mysticism?"

"None whatever," was the emphatic response. "My work is perfectly natural. It is so natural that it is unnatural to those to whom the unnatural is natural. I reproduce things exactly as they are and that is all there is to it. The outer world becomes the inner world and the inner world becomes the outer, and the outward is no longer outward but inward and the inward is no longer inward but outward and it takes genius to do that and Gertrude Stein *is* a genius.... — *Paris Was Our Mistress* (1947).

ROBERT LOUIS STEVENSON

Edmund Gosse

It is nearly a quarter of a century since I first saw Stevenson. In the autumn of 1870, in company with a former schoolfellow, I was in the Hebrides. We had been wandering in the Long Island, as they name the outer archipelago, and our steamer, returning, called at Skye. At the pier of Portree, I think, a company came on board.... At the tail of this chatty, jesting little crowd of invaders came a youth of about my own age, whose appearance, for some mysterious reason, instantly attracted me. He was tall, preternaturally lean, with longish hair, and as restless and questing as a spaniel....

Those who have written about him from later impressions than those of which I speak seem to me to give insufficient prominence to the gaiety of Stevenson. It was his cardinal quality in those early days. A childlike mirth leaped and danced in him; he seemed to skip upon the hills of life. He was simply bubbling with quips and jests; his inherent earnestness or passion about abstract things was incessantly relieved by jocosity; and when he had built one of his intellectual castles in the sand, a wave of humour was certain to sweep in and destroy it. I cannot, for the life of me, recall any of his jokes; and written down in cold blood, they might not be funny if I did. They were not wit so much as humanity, the many-sided outlook upon life. I am anxious that his laughter-loving mood should not be forgotten, because later on it was partly, but I think never wholly, quenched by ill health, responsibility, and the advance of years. He was often, in the old days, excessively and delightfully silly — silly with the silliness of an inspired schoolboy; and I am afraid that our laughter sometimes sounded ill in the ears of age.

A pathos was given to his gaiety by the fragility of his health. He was never well, all the years I knew him; and we looked upon his life as hanging by the frailest tenure. As he never complained or maundered, this, no doubt — though we were not aware of it — added to the charm of his presence. He was so bright and keen and witty, and any week he might die. No one, certainly, conceived it possible that he could reach his forty-fifth year. In 1879 his health visibly began to run lower, and he used to bury himself in lonely Scotch and French places, "tinkering himself with solitude," as he used to say....

Stevenson was not without a good deal of innocent oddity in his dress. When I try to conjure up his figure, I can see only a slight, lean lad, in a suit of blue sea-cloth, a black shirt, and a wisp of yellow carpet that did duty for a necktie. This was long his attire, persevered in to the anguish of his more conventional acquaintances. I have a ludicrous memory of going, in 1878, to buy him a new hat, in company with Mr. [Andrew] Lang, the thing then upon his head having lost the semblance of a human article of dress. Aided by a very civil shopman, we suggested several hats and caps, and Louis at first seemed interested; but having presently hit upon one which appeared to us pleasing and decorous, we turned for a moment to inquire the price. We turned back, and found that Louis had fled, the idea of parting with the shapeless object having proved too painful to be entertained....

In those early days he suffered many indignities on account of his extreme youthfulness of appearance and absence of self-assertion. He was at Inverness — being five or six and twenty at the time — and had taken a room in a hotel. Coming back about dinner-time, he asked the hour of the table d'hôte, whereupon the landlady said, in a motherly way: "Oh, I knew you wouldn't like to sit in there among the grown-up people, so I've had a place put for you in the bar." — "Robert Louis Stevenson, Personal Memories" in *Critical Kit-Kats* (1896).

Mark Twain

It was on a bench in Washington Square that I saw the most of Louis Stevenson. It was an outing that lasted an hour or more and was very pleasant and sociable. I had come with him from his house, where I had been paying my respects to his family. His business in the square was to absorb the sunshine. He was most scantily furnished with flesh, his clothes seemed to fall into hollows as if there might be nothing inside but the frame for a sculptor's statue. His long face and lank hair and dark complexion and musing and melancholy expression seemed to fit these details justly and harmoniously, and the altogether of it seemed especially planned to gather the rags of your observation and focalize them upon Stevenson's special distinction and commanding feature, his splendid eyes. They burned with a smoldering rich fire under the penthouse of his brows and they made him beautiful. — *The Autobiography of Mark Twain*, ed. Charles Neider (1959).

LYTTON STRACHEY

Michael Holroyd

He used two strikingly different types of voice. One, high-pitched and tinny, was employed deliberately to deflate pomposity; to express astonished disagreement with some opinion (when it was often accompanied by a raising of the eyebrow); to introduce either an element of clowning or baiting into the conversation; or to tease someone he liked.... Occasionally, to parody or ridicule some attitude, he would chant whole sentences in a feeble, monotonous falsetto. At other times—in moments of intimacy or when reading out loud—he would employ a rather deep, bass voice, which with a strange inversion of stress might all at once rise to a reedy crescendo in emphatic termination of his sentence. As shown by his letters, he was much affected by the weather, and in rain and cold was apt to fall silent for long stretches. He did not often laugh. But an expression which was not exactly a smile would slip over his face, his eyes gleaming and fixed on whoever was speaking, and the mental climate grew warm and sunny. His two celebrated voices were, then, not entirely natural, but a contrived over-emphasis of a natural idiosyncrasy. In 1909, this dual voice was still something of a novelty, adopted to help establish for himself the *persona* which he wished others to accept and remember. But later in his life these voices, together with other distinctive appendages to his new Bloomsbury image—the beetroot-brown beard, the attenuated fingers, and a variety of runcible hats and cloaks—worked themselves into the recognized fabric of his highly stylized personality. They were no longer put on, but came as it were spontaneously to him, just as lines do to a good actor. In the opinion of Ralph Partridge, who knew Lytton only during the last twelve years of his life, 'these two voices of his were not an affectation but a natural gamut of expression—and the top notes were an echo of Voltaire's "high cackle" from the eighteenth century'.— *Lytton Strachey, A Critical Biography* (1967).

Bertrand Russell

Lady Strachey was a woman of immense vigour, with a great desire that some at least of her children should distinguish themselves. She had an admirable sense of prose and used to read South's sermons aloud to her children, not for the matter (she was a free-thinker), but to give them a sense of rhythm in the writing of English. Lytton, who was too delicate to be sent to a conventional school, was seen by his mother to be brilliant, and was brought up to the career of a writer in an atmosphere of dedication. His writing appeared to me in those days hilariously amusing. I heard him read *Eminent Victorians* before it was published, and I read it again to myself in prison. It caused me to laugh so loud that the officer came round to my cell, saying I must remember that prison is a place of punishment.

Lytton was always eccentric and became gradually more so. When he was growing a beard he gave out that he had measles so as not to be seen by his friends until the hairs had reached a respectable length. He dressed very oddly. I knew a farmer's wife who let lodgings and she told me that Lytton had come to ask her if she could take him in. "At first, Sir," she said, "I thought he was a tramp, and then I looked again and saw he was a gentleman, but a very queer one." He talked always in a squeaky voice which sometimes contrasted ludicrously with the matter of what he was saying. One time when I was talking with him he objected first to one thing and then to another as not being what literature should aim at. At last I said, "Well, Lytton, what should it aim at?" And he replied in one word—"Passion." Nevertheless, he liked to appear lordly in his attitude towards human affairs. I heard someone maintain in his presence that young people are apt to think about Life. He objected, "I can't believe people think about Life. There's nothing in it." Perhaps it was this attitude which made him not a great man.

His style is unduly rhetorical, and sometimes, in malicious moments, I have thought it not unlike Macaulay's. He is indifferent to historical truth and will always touch up the picture to make the lights and shades more glaring and the folly or wickedness of famous people more obvious. These are grave charges, but I make them in all seriousness. —*Autobiography* (1967).

Leonard Woolf

When he arrived at Trinity in 1899 he already had intellectually the equipment which made it possible for him nineteen years later to write *Eminent Victorians* and combined with this intellectual maturity he had the fiery and violent intransigence of youth. With age and success he became extremely mellow and gentle; when a young man, his external demeanour was gentle and almost diffident, but was accompanied by an intellectual prickliness and ruthlessness which was extraordinarily impressive and at times devastating. The effect was increased by his peculiar method of conversation. When he was with those whom he liked, he would talk with animation, dropping every now and then into the general stream of conversation, casually and in his low staccato voice, some maliciously illuminating and extraordinarily witty phrase or comment. But in those days, though his conversation was fascinating and brilliant, it was often difficult, for he required much, including stimulus, from the person to whom he was talking. If the person or persons with whom he found himself in contact happened not to be congenial or their remarks unintelligent, the result would often be a social disaster, painful at the moment to a third party, though extremely amusing in retrospect. His legs inextricably intertwined, he would lie back in his chair, in black gloom and complete silence, and then quite suddenly drop, this time probably into the most uncomfortable moment of silence, a sardonically witty remark which stripped the last shred of self-control and intelligence from his victim.

These combinations of ruthlessness and gentleness, silence and wit, prickliness and affectation only increased the charm of his personality for those whom he liked. It was this charm, when united with his extraordinary intellectual gifts, his highly individual outlook on life, and his very definite opinions, which made him the dominating influence upon three or four generations of Cambridge undergraduates. — *The New Statesman and Nation* (30 January 1932), 118-9.

Virginia Woolf

Friday 24 January [1919] ... There are three words knocking about in my brain to use of Stracheys, — a prosaic race, lacking magnanimity, shorn of atmosphere. As these words have occurred automatically, & will tease me till written down, I daresay there is some truth in them. All the unpleasantness that I wish to introduce into my portrait of Lytton is contained in them, as if in deep wells.... It is an air, a vapour, an indescribable taste of dust in the throat, something tickling & irritating as well as tingling & stimulating. But then one must combine with this a great variety of mental gifts, & gifts of character — honesty, loyalty, intelligence of a spiritual order. One might almost attribute what I mean in Lytton's case at least to lack of physical warmth, lack of creative power, a failure of vitality warning him not to be spendthrift but to eke out his gifts parsimoniously, & tacitly assume his right to a superior share of comfort & opulence. In matters of emotion this has a slightly stingy appearance, nor is he even unthinkingly generous & magnanimous, risking himself. Mentally of course it produces that metallic & conventionally brilliant style which prevents his writing from reaching, to my judgment, the first rate. It lacks originality, & substance; it is brilliant, superbly brilliant journalism, a supremely skilful rendering of the old tune. Written down these words are too emphatic & linear; one should see them tempered & combined with all those charming, subtle & brilliant qualities which compose his being in the flesh. But when I think of a Strachey, I think of someone infinitely cautious, elusive & unadventurous.

Friday 16 May [1919] ... Next day there was Lytton. I need not repeat the stock observations upon his mellow good humour. It is more to the point to chronicle a renewed sense of affection, which has never been seriously in abeyance, & the usual conviction that his wit & what one calls personality are as peculiar to himself as his voice, or his finger nails. And then one thinks that it doesn't much matter if his writing is not profound or original; one begins perhaps to suspect that it may be more original than one thinks.

Sunday 25 May [1919] ... Lytton came to tea on Friday & half maliciously assured me that my industry amazed him. My industry & my competence, for he thinks me the best reviewer alive, & the inventor of a new prose style, & the creator of a new version of the sentence. People's compliments generally manage to reserve the particular praise they wish to have themselves. But we are surprisingly honest; we have a clear perception of the others meaning. He asserted that he was disgusted by his own stereotyped ways: his two semi colons; his method of understatement; & his extreme definiteness. Without agreeing, I conveyed my sense of his dangers, & urged him to write plays — stories — anything to break the mould of the early Victorians. After a volume on Victoria, in the same manner, he is going to attempt it.

Saturday 15 November [1919] ... Lytton — .... Good & simple & tender — a little low in tone; a little invalidish. If I'd married him, I caught myself thinking, I should have found him querulous. He would have laid too many ties on one, & repined a little if one had broken free. He was in his usual health (as they say); but the sense of living so much for health, & assembling so many comforts round him with that object is a little depressing. But I always qualify these strictures, which I'm quick to find I know, with some subconscious idea of justifying myself. I need no justification. And what I feel for Lytton is as true as ever it was. We sit alone over the fire & rattle on, so quick, so agile in our jumps & circumventions. Lytton I suppose if one could disolve all extraneous surroundings has in the centre of him a great passion for the mind. He cares for more than literature only. On his table were the latest editions of Voltaire. His books were as primly ranged & carefully tended as an old maids china. He talked of his own work, not optimistically, but one must discount the effect of my perhaps excessive optimism about my own writing. I was in the vein to feel very highly 'creative', as indeed he said he thought me. But he declares himself entirely without the power.

He can invent nothing, he says; take away his authorities, & he comes to a full stop. Perhaps this is true of all Stracheys, & accounts for the queer feeling — which I will not analyse, since in Lytton's case the rightness, the subtlety, the fineness, of his mind quite overcome my furtive discomfort.

Wednesday 15 September [1920] ... Blessed with fine weather, I could look from my window, through the vine leaves, & see Lytton sitting in the deck chair reading Alfieri from a lovely vellum copy, dutifully looking out words. He wore a white felt hat, & the usual grey clothes; was long, & tapering as usual; looking so mild & so ironical, his beard just cut short. As usual; I got my various impressions: of suavity, a gentle but inflexible honesty; lightning speed; something peevish & exacting; something incessantly living, suffering, reflecting moods. Still he can withdraw in that supercilious way that used to gall me; still show himself superior to me, contemptuous of me — of my morality, that is, not of my mind. — *Diary*.

JONATHAN SWIFT

Samuel Johnson

The person of Swift had not many recommendations. He had a kind of muddy complexion, which, though he washed himself with Oriental scrupulosity, did not look clear. He had a countenance sour and severe, which he seldom softened by an appearance of gaiety. He stubbornly resisted any tendency to laughter.

To his domestics he was naturally rough; and a man of a rigorous temper, with that vigilance of minute attention which his works discover, must have been a master that few could bear. That he was disposed to do his servants good, on important occasions, is no great mitigation; benefaction can be but rare, and tyrannic peevishness is perpetual. He did not spare the servants of others. Once, when he dined alone with the Earl of Orrery, he said of one that waited in the room, "That man has, since we sat to the table, committed fifteen faults." What the faults were, Lord Orrery, from whom I heard the story, had not been attentive enough to discover. My number may perhaps not be exact. — *Lives of the Poets* (1779–81).

Dr. William King

The last time I dined with Dean Swift, which was about three years before he fell into that distemper which totally deprived him of his understanding, I observed, that he was affected by the wine which he drank, about a pint of claret. The next morning, as we were walking together in his garden, he complained much of his head, when I took the liberty to tell him (for I most sincerely loved him) that I was afraid he drank too much wine. He was a little startled, and answered, "that as to his drinking he had always looked on himself as a very temperate man; for he never exceeded the quantity which his physician had allowed and prescribed him." Now his physician never drank less than two bottles of claret after his dinner. — *Political and Literary Anecdotes of His Own Times* (1819).

Earl of Orrery

Let me begin by giving you a short but general view of Swift's character.

He was in the decline of life when I knew him. His friendship was an honour to me, and to say the truth, I have even drawn down advantage from his errors. I have beheld him in all humours and dispositions, and I have formed various speculations from the several weaknesses, to which I observed him liable. His capacity and strength of mind were undoubtedly equal to any task whatever. His pride, his spirit, or his ambition, call it by what name you please, was boundless: but, his views were checked in his younger years, and the anxiety of that disappointment had a visible effect upon all his actions. He was sour and severe, but not absolutely ill-natured. He was sociable only to particular friends, and to them only at particular hours. He knew politeness more than he practised it. He was a mixture of avarice, and generosity: the former was frequently prevalent, the latter, seldom appeared, unless excited by compassion. He was open to adulation, and could not, or would not, distinguish between low flattery, and just applause. His abilities rendered him superiour to envy. He was undisguised and perfectly sincere. I am induced to think, that he entered into orders, more from some private and fixed resolution, than from absolute choice: be that as it may, he performed the duties of the church with great punctuality, and a decent degree of devotion. He read prayers rather in a strong nervous voice, than in a graceful manner: and altho' he has been often accused of irreligion, nothing of that kind appeared in his conversation or behaviour. His cast of mind induced him to think, and speak more of politics than of religion. His perpetual views were directed towards power: and his chief aim was to be removed into *England*: but when he found himself entirely disappointed, he turned his thoughts to opposition, and became the patron of *Ireland*, in which country he was born. — *Remarks on the Life and Writings of Dr. Jonathan Swift* (1752).

Letitia Pilkington

I had ... the much-envied honour of being known to Dr Swift, whose genius, excellent as it was, surpassed not his humanity in the most judicious and useful charities; although often hid under a rough appearance, till he was perfectly convinced both of the honesty and distress of those he bestowed it on. He was a perpetual friend to merit and learning; and utterly incapable of envy. Indeed, why should he not? — who, in true genuine wit, could fear no rival.

Yet as I have frequently observed in life, that where great talents are bestowed, there the strongest passions are likewise given. This truly great man did but too often let them have dominion over him, and that on the most trifling occasions. During meal-times he was evermore in a storm; the meat was always too much or too little done, or the servants had offended in some point, imperceptible to the rest of the company; however, when the cloth was taken away, he made his guests rich amends for the pain he had given them by the former part of his behaviour....

When we came into the parlour, the Dean kindly saluted me, and, without allowing me time to sit down, bade me come and see his study; Mr Pilkington was for following us, but the Dean told him merrily: 'He did not desire his company'; and so he ventured to trust me with him into the library. 'Well', says he, 'I have brought you here to show you all the money I got when I was in the Ministry, but do not steal any of it.' 'I will not indeed, Sir', says I; so he opened a cabinet, and showed me a whole parcel of empty drawers. 'Bless me', says he, 'the money is flown!'...

The Dean amused me in this manner till we were summoned to dinner, where his behaviour was so humorous that I cannot avoid relating some part of it. He placed himself at the head of the table, opposite to a great pier-glass under which was a marble sideboard, so that he could see in the glass whatever the servants did at it. He was served entirely in plate, and with great elegance; but, the beef being over-roasted, put us all in confusion: the Dean called for the cook-maid, and ordered her to take it downstairs, and do it less; the maid answered very innocently: 'That she could not.' 'Why, what sort of a creature are you', says he, 'to commit a fault which cannot be amended?' And, turning to me, he said very gravely: 'That he hoped, as the cook was a woman of genius, he should, by this manner of arguing, be able in about a year's time to convince her she had better send up the meat too little than too much done'; charging the men-servants: 'Whenever they imagined the meat was ready, they should take it, spit and all, and bring it up by force, promising to aid them in case the cook resisted.' The Dean then turning his eye on the looking-glass, espied the butler opening a bottle of ale, helping himself to the first glass and very kindly jumbling the rest together, that his master and guests might all fare alike. 'Ha! friend', says the Dean, 'sharp's the word, I find; you drank my ale, for which I stop two shillings of your board-wages this week, for I scorn to be outdone in anything, even in cheating.' Dinner at last was over, to my great joy; for now I had hope of a more agreeable entertainment than what the squabbling with the servants had afforded us. — *Memoirs* (1928).

Alexander Pope

Dr. Swift has an odd, blunt way that is mistaken by strangers for ill-nature. 'Tis so odd that there's no describing it but by facts. I'll tell you one that first comes into my head.

One evening [John] Gay and I went to see him; you know how intimately we are all acquainted. On our coming in, 'Hey-day, gentlemen,' says the Doctor, 'what's the meaning of this visit? How come you to leave all the great lords that you are so fond of to come hither to see a poor dean?'

Because we would rather see you than any of them.

'Aye, anyone that did not know you so well as I do might believe you. But since you are come I must get some supper for you, I suppose.'

No, Doctor, we have supped already.

'Supped already! That's impossible — why, 'tis not eight o'clock yet.'

Indeed we have.

'That's very strange. But if you had not supped I must have got something for you. Let me see, what should I have had? A couple of lobsters? Aye, that would have done very well — two shillings. Tarts — a shilling. But you will drink a glass of wine with me, though you supped so much before your usual time, only to spare my pocket?'

No, we had rather talk with you than drink with you.

'But if you had supped with me as in all reason you ought to have done, you must then have drank with me: a bottle of wine — two shillings. Two and two is four, and one is five: just two and sixpence a piece. There, Pope, there's half a crown for you, and there's another for you, Sir, for I won't save anything by you. I am determined.'

This was all said and done wtih his usual seriousness on such occasions, and in spite of everything we could say to the contrary, he actually obliged us to take the money. — Spence's *Observations, Anecdotes, and Characters of Books and Men* (1966).

ALGERNON CHARLES SWINBURNE

Georgiana, Lady Burne-Jones

His appearance was very unusual and in some ways beautiful, for his hair was glorious in abundance and colour and his eyes indescribably fine. When repeating poetry he had a perfectly natural way of lifting them in a rapt, unconscious gaze, and their clear green colour softened by thick brown eyelashes was unforgettable: 'Looks commercing with the skies' expresses it without exaggeration. He was restless beyond words, scarcely standing still at all and almost dancing as he walked, while even in sitting he moved continually, seeming to keep time, by a swift movement of the hands at the wrists, and sometimes of the feet also, with some inner rhythm of excitement. He was courteous and affectionate and unsuspicious, and faithful beyond most people to those he really loved. The biting wit which filled his talk so as at times to leave his hearers dumb with amazement always spared one thing, that was an absent friend. — *Memoirs of Edward Burne-Jones* (1904).

Edmund Gosse

Men who to-day have not passed middle age can scarcely form an impression of what the name and fame of Algernon Charles Swinburne meant forty years ago to those who were then young and enthusiastic candidates for apprenticeship in the fine arts....

The world is familiar from portraits, and still better from caricatures, with his unique appearance. He was short, with sloping shoulders, from which rose a long and slender neck, surmounted by a very large head. The cranium seemed to be out of all proportion to the rest of the structure. His spine was rigid, and though he often bowed the heaviness of his head, *lasso papavera collo*, he seemed never to bend his back. Except in consequence of a certain physical weakness, which probably may, in more philosophical days, come to be accounted for and palliated — except when suffering from the external cause, he seemed immune from all the maladies that pursue mankind. He did not know fatigue; his agility and brightness were almost mechanical. I never heard him complain of a headache or a toothache. He required very little sleep, and occasionally when I have parted from him in the evening after saying "Good-night," he has simply sat back in the deep sofa in his sitting-room, his little feet close together, his arms against his side, folded in his frock-coat like a grasshopper in its wing-covers, and fallen asleep, apparently for the night, before I could blow out the candles and steal forth from the door. I am speaking, of course, of early days; it was thus about 1875 that I closely observed him.

He was more a hypertrophied intelligence than a man. His vast brain seemed to weigh down and give solidity to a frame otherwise as light as thistledown, a body almost as immaterial as that of a fairy. In the streets he had the movements of a somnambulist, and often I have seen him passing like a ghost across the traffic of Holborn, or threading the pressure of carts eastward in Gray's Inn Road, without glancing to the left or the right, like something blown before a wind....

No physiologist who studied the corporeal condition of Swinburne could avoid observing the violent elevation of spirits to which he was constantly subject. The slightest emotional excitement, of anger, or pleasure, or admiration, sent him into a state which could scarcely be called anything but convulsive. He was like that little geyser in Iceland which is always simmering, but which, if it is irritated by having pieces of turf thrown into it, instantly boils over and flings its menacing column at the sky. I was never able to persuade myself whether the extraordinary spasmodic action of the arms and legs which accompanied these paroxysms was the result of nature or habit. It was violent and it was long-continued, but I never saw that it produced fatigue. It gradually subsided into a graceful and smiling calm, sometimes even into somnolence, out of which, however, a provocative remark would instantly call up again the surprising spasm of the geyser. The poet's surviving sister, Miss Isabel Swinburne, tells me that this trick of stiffly drawing down his arms from the shoulders and giving a rapid vibratory movement to his hands was voluntary in childhood; she considers that it spoiled his shoulders and made them sloping. In later years I am sure it had become instinctive and unconscious. She describes to me also the extraordinary ecstasy which shook his body and lighted up his face when reading a book which delighted him or when speaking of any intellectual pleasure. Swinburne seemed to me to divide his hours between violent cerebral excitement and sheer immobility, mental and physical. He would sit for a long time together without stirring a limb, his eyes fixed in a sort of trance, and only his lips shifting and shivering a little, without a sound....

Swinburne's conversation had, as was to be expected, some of the characteristics of his poetry. It was rapid, and yet not voluble; it was measured, ornate, and picturesque, and yet it was in a sense homely. It was much less stilted and involved than his prose writing. His extreme natural politeness was always apparent in his talk, unless, of course, some unfortunate *contretemps* should rouse a sudden ebullition, when he could be neither just nor kind. But, as a rule, his courtesy shone out of his blue-grey eyes and was lighted up by the halo of his cloud of orange hair as he waved it, gravely or waggishly, at the company. The ease with which finished and polished sentences flowed from him was a constant amazement to me. I noted (January 1875) that somebody having been so unwise as to speak of the "laborious" versification of Catullus, Swinburne burst forth with a trumpet-note of scorn, and said, "Well, I can only tell you I should have called him the least laborious, and the most spontaneous, in his god-like and bird-like melody, of all the lyrists known to me except Sappho and Shelley; I should as soon call a lark's note 'laboured' as Catullus'." This might have been said of Swinburne's amazing talk; it was a stream of song, no more laboured than a lark's.

Immediately after leaving him I used sometimes, as well as I could, to note down a few of his sentences. It was not easy to retain much where all was so copious and rich, but a whole phrase of even colloquy would linger long in the memory. I think these brief reports may be trusted to give his exact words: nothing could recall his accent and the spontaneous *crescendo* effect of his enthusiasm. I quote from my notebooks almost at random. This is in 1875, about some literary antagonist, but I have neglected to note whom:

"He had better be careful. If I am obliged" [very slowly] "to take the cudgel in my hand" [in rapid exultation] "the rafters of the hovel in which he skulks and sniggers shall ring with the loudest whacks ever administered in discipline or chastisement to a howling churl." All this poured forth, in towering high spirits, without a moment's pause to find a word. — *Portraits and Sketches* (1913).

Guy de Maupassant

M. Swinburne was small and thin, amazingly thin at first sight, a sort of fantastic apparition. When I looked at him for the first time, I thought of Edgar Poe. The forehead was very large under long hair, and the face went narrowing down to a tiny chin, shaded by a thin tuft of beard. A very slight moustache slipped over lips which were extraordinarily delicate and were pressed together, while what seemed an endless neck joined this head, which was alive only in its bright, penetrating, and fixed eyes, to a body without shoulders, since the upper part of Swinburne's chest seemed scarcely broader than his forehead. The whole of this almost supernatural personage was stirred by nervous shudders. He was very cordial, very easy of access; and the extraordinary charm of his intelligence bewitched me from the first moment. — Quoted by Edmund Gosse in *Portraits and Sketches* (1913).

SIR WILLIAM TEMPLE

Lady Giffard

Sir William Temple's Person is best known by his Pictures and Prints: He was rather tall than low; his Shape, when young, very exact; his Hair a dark brown, and curled naturally, and whilst that was esteemed a Beauty no body had it in greater Perfection; his Eyes grey, but lively; and his Body lean, but extream active, so that none acquitted themselves better at all sorts of Exercise.

He had an extraordinary Spirit and Life in his Humour, with so agreeable Turns of Wit and Fancy in his Conversation, that no body was welcomer in all sorts of Company, and some have observed, that he never had a mind to make any body kind to him without compassing his Design.

He was an exact Observer of Truth, thinking none that had fail'd once ought ever to be trusted again; of nice points of Honour; of great Humanity and Good-nature, taking pleasure in making others easy and happy; his Passions naturally warm and quick, but temper'd by Reason and Thought; his Humour gay, but very unequal from cruel Fits of Spleen and Melancholy, being subject to great Damps from sudden Changes of Weather, but chiefly from Crosses and surprising Turns in his Business, and Disappointments he met with so often in his Endeavours to contribute to the Honour and Service of his Country, which he thought himself two or three Times so near Compassing, that he could not think with Patience of what had hinder'd it, or of those that he thought had been the occasion of his Disappointment....

He was not without strong Aversions so as to be uneasy at the first Sight of some he disliked, and impatient of their Conversation; apt to be warm in Disputes and Expostulations, which made him hate the one, and avoid the other, which he used to say, might sometimes do well between Lovers, but never between Friends; He turn'd his Conversation to what was more easy and pleasant, especially at Table, where he said ill Humour ought never to come, and his agreeable Talk at it, if it had been set down, would have been very entertaining to the Reader, as well as to so many that had heard it. He had a very familiar way of conversing with all Sorts of People, from the greatest Princes to the meanest Servants, and even Children, whose imperfect Language, and natural and innocent Talk he was fond of....

He lived healthful 'till Forty Two, then began to be troubled with Rheums upon his Teeth and Eyes, which he attributed to the Air of *Holland*, and which ended, when he was Forty Seven, in the gout, upon which he grew very melancholy, being then Ambassador at the *Hague*; he said, a Man was never good for any thing after it; and though he continued in Business near Three Years longer, 'twas always with Design of winding himself out as fast as he could; making good his own Rules, that no body should make Love after Forty, nor be in Business after Fifty. And though from this Time he had frequent Returns of ill Health, he never cared to consult Physicians; saying, He hoped to die without them, and trusted wholly to the Care and Advice of his Friends, which he often express'd himself so happy in, as to want nothing but Health; which, since Riches could not help him to, he despised them. [Lady Giffard was Sir William Temple's sister.] — *The Life and Character of Sir William Temple, Bart.* (1728).

ALFRED, LORD TENNYSON

Thomas Carlyle

Tennyson is now in Town, and means to come and see me. Of this latter result I shall be very glad: Alfred is one of the new British or Foreign Figures (a not increasing number I think!) who are and remain beautiful to me; — a true human soul, or some authentic approximation thereto, to whom your own soul can say, Brother! — However, I doubt he will not come; he often skips me, in these brief visits to Town; skips everybody indeed; being a man solitary and sad, as certain men are, dwelling in an element of gloom, — carrying a bit of Chaos about him, in short, which he is manufacturing into Cosmos!...

In this way he lives still, now here, now there; the family always within reach of London, never in it; he himself making rare and brief visits, lodging in some old comrade's rooms. I think he must be under forty, not much under it. One of the finest-looking men in the world. A great shock of rough dusty-dark hair; bright-laughing hazel eyes; massive aquiline face, most massive yet most delicate; of sallow-brown complexion, almost Indian-looking; clothes cynically loose, free-and-easy; — smokes infinite tobacco. His voice is musical metallic, — fit for loud laughter and piercing wail, and all that may lie between; speech and speculation free and plenteous: I do not meet, in these late decades, such company over a pipe! — We shall see what he will grow to. He is often unwell; very chaotic, — his way is through Chaos and the Bottomless and Pathless; not handy for making out many miles upon. — From a letter to Ralph Waldo Emerson, 5 August 1844.

Samuel Taylor Coleridge

I have not read through all Mr. Tennyson's poems, which have been sent to me; but I think there are some things of a good deal of beauty in what I have seen. The misfortune is, that he has begun to write verses without very well understanding what metre is. Even if you write in a known and approved metre, the odds are, if you are not a metrist yourself, that you will not write harmonious verses; but to deal in new metres without considering what metre means and requires, is preposterous. What I would, with many wishes for success, prescribe to Tennyson, — indeed without it he can never be a poet in act, — is to write for the next two or three years in none but one or two well known and strictly defined metres, such as the heroic couplet, the octave stanza, or the octo-syllabic measure of the Allegro and Penseroso. He would, probably, thus get imbued with a sensation, if not a sense, of metre without knowing it, just as Eton boys get to write such good Latin verses by conning Ovid and Tibullus. As it is, I can scarcely scan some of his verses. — Table Talk, 24 April 1833.

Ralph Waldo Emerson

I saw Tennyson, first, at the house of Coventry Patmore, where we dined together. His friend Brookfield was also of the party. I was contented with him, at once. He is tall, scholastic-looking, no dandy, but a great deal of plain strength about him, and though cultivated, quite unaffected; quiet, sluggish sense and strength, refined, as all English are, and good-humoured. The print of his head in Horne's book is too rounded and handsome. There is in him an air of general superiority, that is very satisfactory. He lives very much with his college set, — Spedding, Brookfield, Hallam, Rice, and the rest, — and has the air of one who is accustomed to be petted and indulged by those he lives with, like George Bradford. Take away Hawthorne's bashfulness, and let him talk easily and fast, and you would have a pretty good Tennyson....

Tennyson was in plain black suit and wears glasses. Carlyle thinks him the best man in England to smoke a pipe with, and used to see him much; had a place in his little garden, on the wall, where Tennyson's pipe was laid up. — *Journals*, 6 May 1848.

Sir George Leveson-Gower

In his later years his appearance was eccentric. He wore his hair long, flowing over his shoulders. He had a big black sombrero hat with a soft wide brim; a large, loose, soft Byronic collar; a big, floppy tie and a cloak, flung over one shoulder *à la mousquetaire*. He complained to a lady that it was one of the penalties of celebrity that he was stared at and even sometimes followed. Her little girl of eight, hoping to be helpful, suggested: 'Perhaps, sir, if you cut your hair and dressed like other people, they wouldn't stare so much.' He was not pleased. — *Mixed Grill* (1947).

Nathaniel Hawthorne

Tennyson is the most picturesque figure, without affectation, that I ever saw; of middle-size, rather slouching, dressed entirely in black, and with nothing white about him except the collar of his shirt, which methought might have been cleaner the day before. He had on a black, wide-awake hat, with round crown and wide, irregular brim, beneath which came down his long, black hair, looking terribly tangled; he had a long, pointed beard, too, a little browner than the hair, and not so abundant as to encumber any of the expression of his face. His frock coat was buttoned across the breast, though the afternoon was warm. His face was very dark, and not exactly a smooth face, but worn, and expressing great sensitiveness, though not, at that moment, the pain and sorrow which is seen in his bust. His eyes were black; but I know little of them, as they did not rest on me, nor on anything but the pictures [at the Manchester Arts' Exhibit]. He seemed as if he did not see the crowd nor think of them, but as if he defended himself from them by ignoring them altogether; nor did anybody but myself cast a glance at him....

I heard his voice; a bass voice, but not of resounding depth; a voice rather broken as it were, and ragged about the edges, but pleasant to the ear. His manner, while conversing with these people, was not in the least that of an awkward man, unaccustomed to society; but he shook hands with them, evidently as soon as he courteously could, and shuffled away quicker than before. He betrayed his shy and secluded habits more in this, than in anything else that I observed; though, indeed, in his whole presence, I was indescribably sensible of a morbid painfulness in him, a something not to be meddled with. Very soon, he left the saloon, shuffling along the floor with short irregular steps, a very queer gait, as if he were walking in slippers too loose for him. I had observed that he seemed to turn his feet slightly inward, after the fashion of Indians. How strange that in these two or three pages I cannot get one single touch that may call him up hereafter!...

He is exceedingly nervous, and altogether as un–English as possible; indeed an Englishman of genius usually lacks the national characteristics, and is great abnormally. Even the great sailor, Nelson, was unlike his countrymen in the qualities that constituted him a hero; he was not the perfection of an Englishman, but a creature of another kind — sensitive, nervous, excitable, and really more like a Frenchman.

Un-English as he was, and sallow, and unhealthy, Tennyson had not, however, an American look. I cannot well describe the difference; but there was something more mellow in him — softer, sweeter, broader, more simple than we are apt to be. Living apart from men as he does would hurt any one of us more than it does him. I may as well leave him here, for I cannot touch the central point. — *Journals*, 28 July 1857.

WILLIAM MAKEPEACE THACKERAY

Frederick Locker-Lampson

I had a sincere regard for Thackeray. I well remember his striking personality — striking to those who had the ability to recognize it: the look of the man, the latent power, and the occasional keenness of his remarks on men and their actions, as if he saw through and through them. Thackeray drew many unto him, for he had engaging as well as fine qualities. He was open-handed and kind-hearted. He had not an overweening opinion of his literary consequence, and he was generous as regarded the people whom the world chose to call his rivals.

I made Thackeray's acquaintance at the British Embassy, Paris. Events are liable to get confused in the refracting medium of one's memory, but I think it was about 1852 or 1853. From that time to the end of his life we often found ourselves together, and were always good friends....

He was a man of sensibility: he delighted in luxuriously furnished and well-lighted rooms, good music, excellent wines and cookery, exhilarating talk, gay and airy gossip, pretty women and their toilettes, and refined and noble manners, *le bon goût, le ris, l'aimable liberté*. The amenities of life and the traditions stimulated his imagination.

On the other hand, his writings show how he equally enjoyed Bohemianism, and how diverted he could be by those happy-go-lucky fellows of the Foker and Fred Bayham type.

Thackeray expanded in the society of such people, and with them he was excellent company. But, if I am not much mistaken, the man Thackeray was melancholy — he had known tribulation, he had suffered. He was not a light-hearted wag or a gay-natured rover, but a sorrowing man. He could make you a jest, or propound some jovial or outrageous sentiment, and imply, 'Let us be festive,' but the jollity rarely came. However, I ought to say that though Thackeray was not cheerily, he was at times grotesquely, humorous. Indeed, he had a weakness for buffoonery. I have seen him pirouette, wave his arm majestically, and declaim in burlesque — an intentionally awkward imitation of the ridiculous manner that is sometimes met with in French opera.

I remember calling in Palace Gardens, and, while talking with all gravity to Thackeray's daughters, I noticed that they seemed more than necessarily amused. On looking round, I discovered that their father had put on my hat, and, having picked my pocket of my handkerchief, was strutting about, flourishing it in the old Lord Cardigan style. As I was thin-faced, and he, as a hatter once remarked of Thomas Bruce, was 'a gent. as could carry a large body o' 'at,' you may suppose he looked sufficiently funny....

During the last three or four years of Thackeray's life he suffered from bad health, depressing bad health. He lived with his daughters and his intimates, and almost entirely gave up general society — and he was a wise man to do so. My dear reader, whoever you are, think of this illustrious man with tenderness; think of his upright nature, of his affectionate heart, his domestic affliction. These are enough — you need not trouble for his genius. — *My Confidences* (1896).

John Lothrop Motley

He has the appearance of a colossal infant, smooth, white, shiny, ringlety hair, flaxen, alas, with advancing years, a roundish face, with a little dab of a nose upon which it is a perpetual wonder how he keeps his spectacles, a sweet but rather piping voice, with something of the childish treble about it, and a very tall, slightly stooping figure — such are the characteristics of the great 'snob' of England. His manner is like that of everybody else in England, — nothing original, all planed down into perfect uniformity with that of his fellow-creatures. There was not much more distinction in his talk than in his white choker or black coat and waistcoat. — From a letter to his wife, 28 May 1858.

HENRY DAVID THOREAU

William Ellery Channing

In height, he was about the average; in his build, spare, with limbs that were rather longer than usual, or of which he made a longer use. His face, once seen, could not be forgotten. The features were marked: the nose aquiline or very Roman, like one of the portraits of Caesar (more like a beak, as was said); large, overhanging brows above the deepest set blue eyes that could be seen, — blue in certain lights, and in others gray, — eyes expressive of all shades of feeling, but never weak or near-sighted; the forehead not unusually broad or high, full of concentrated energy and purpose; the mouth with prominent lips, pursed up with meaning and thought when silent, and giving out, when open, a stream of the most varied and unusual and instructive sayings. His hair was a dark brown, exceedingly abundant, fine and soft; and for several years he wore a comely beard. His whole figure had an active earnestness, as if he had no moment to waste. The clenched hand betokened purpose. — *Thoreau, The Poet-Naturalist, With Memorial Verses* (1902).

Edward Waldo Emerson

In childhood I had a friend, a free, brave, youthful-seeing man, who wandered in from unknown woods or fields without knocking, "Between the night and day/ When the fairy king has power," passed by the elders' doors, but straightway sought out the children, brightened up the wood-fire forthwith and it seemed as if it were done by a wholesome brave north wind, instead of by the armful of "cat-sticks" which he brought in from the yard. His type was Northern, strong features, light brown hair, an open-air complexion, with suggestion of a seafaring race; the mouth pleasant and flexible when he spoke; aquiline nose, deep-set but wide-open eyes of clear blue-grey, sincere but capable of a twinkle, and again of austerity, but not of softness; those eyes could not be made to rest on what was unworthy, saw much and keenly (but yet in certain worthy directions hardly at all), and did not fear the face of day. A figure short and narrow, but thick; a carriage assuring sturdy strength and endurance. When he walked to get over the ground, one, seeing his long uniform pace, was instinctively reminded of some tireless machine. His body was active, well-balanced, and his step could be light, as of one who could leap, or dance, or skate well at will.

His dress was strong and plain. He was not one of those little men who try to become great by exuvial methods of length of hair or beard, or broad collars, or conspicuous coat.

This youthful, cheery figure was a familiar one in our house, and when he, like the "Pied Piper of Hamelin," sounded his note in the hall, the children must needs come and hug his knees, and he struggled with them, nothing loth, to the fire-place, sat down and told stories, sometimes of the strange adventures of his childhood, or more often of squirrels, muskrats, hawks, he had seen that day, the Monitor-and-Merrimac duel of mud-turtles in the river, or the Homeric battle of the Red and Black Ants. — "Personal Recollections," *Bookman*, LII (June 1917).

Ralph Waldo Emerson

There was somewhat military in his nature, not to be subdued, always manly and able, but rarely tender, as if he did not feel himself except in opposition. He wanted a fallacy to expose, a blunder to pillory, I may say required a little sense of victory, a roll of the drum, to call his powers into full exercise. It cost him nothing to say No; indeed he found it much easier than to say Yes. It seemed as if his first instinct on hearing a proposition was to controvert it, so impatient was he of the limitations of our daily thought. This habit, of course, is a little chilling to the social affectations; and though the companion would in the end acquit him of any malice or untruth, yet it mars conversation. Hence, no equal companion stood in affectionate relations with one so pure and guileless. "I love Henry," said one of his friends, "but I cannot like him; and as for taking his arm, I should as soon think of taking the arm of an elm-tree."

Yet, hermit and stoic as he was, he was really fond of sympathy, and threw himself heartily and childlike into the company of young people whom he loved, and whom he delighted to entertain, as he could only, with the varied and endless anecdotes of his experiences by field and river: he was always ready to lead a huckleberry-party or a search for chestnuts or grapes....

It was said of Plotinus that he was ashamed of his body, and 't is very likely he had good reason for it, — that his body was a bad servant, and he had not skill in dealing with the material world, as happens often to men of abstract intellect. But Mr. Thoreau was equipped with a most adapted and serviceable body. He was of short stature, firmly built, of light complexion, with strong, serious blue eyes, and a grave aspect, — his face covered in the late years with a becoming beard. His senses were acute, his frame well-knit and hardy, his hands strong and skilful in the use of tools. And there was a wonderful fitness of body and mind. He could pace sixteen rods more accurately than another man could measure them with rod and chain. He could find his path in the woods at night, he said, better by his feet than his eyes. He could estimate the measure of a tree very well by his eye; he could estimate the weight of a calf or a pig, like a dealer. From a box containing a bushel or more of loose pencils, he could take up with his hands fast enough just a dozen pencils at every grasp. He was a good swimmer, runner, skater, boatman, and would probably outwalk most countrymen in a day's journey. And the relation of body to mind was still finer than we have indicated. He said he wanted every stride his legs made. The length of his walk uniformly made the length of his writing. If shut up in the house he did not write at all....

It was a pleasure and a privilege to walk with him. He knew the country like a fox or a bird, and passed through it as freely by paths of his own. He knew every track in the snow or on the ground, and what creature had taken this path before him. One must submit abjectly to such a guide, and the reward was great. Under his arm he carried an old music-book to press plants; in his pocket, his diary and pencil, a spyglass for birds, microscope, jack-knife, and twine. He wore a straw hat, stout shoes, strong grey trousers, to brave scrub-oaks and smilax, and to climb a tree for a hawk's or a squirrel's nest. He waded into the pool for the water-plants, and his strong legs were no insignificant part of his armour. On the day I speak of he looked for the Menyanthes, detected it across the wide pool, and, on examination of the florets, decided that it had been in flower five days. He drew out of his breast-pocket his diary, and read the names of all the plants that should bloom on this day, whereof he kept account as a banker when his notes fall due. The Cypripedium not due till tomorrow. He thought that, if waked up from a trance, in this swamp, he could tell by the plants what time of the year it was within two days....

Had his genius been only contemplative, he had been fitted to his life, but with his energy and practical ability he seemed born for great enterprise and for command; and I so much regret the loss of his rare powers of action, that I cannot help counting it a fault in him that he had no ambition. Wanting this, instead of engineering for all America, he was the captain of a huckleberry-party. Pounding beans is good to the end of pounding empires one of these days; but if, at the end of years, it is still only beans! — *Lectures and Biographical Sketches* (1883).

Nathaniel Hawthorne

Mr. Thoreau dined with us yesterday. He is a singular character — a young man with much of wild original nature still remaining in him; and so far as he is sophisticated, it is in a way and method of his own. He is as ugly as sin, long-nosed, queer-mouthed, and with uncouth and rustic, although courteous manners, corresponding very well with such an exterior. But his ugliness is of an honest and agreeable fashion, and becomes him much better than beauty. He was educated, I believe, at Cambridge, and formerly kept school in this town; but for two or three years back, he has repudiated all regular modes of getting a living, and seems inclined to lead a sort of Indian life among civilized men — an Indian life, I mean, as respects the absence of any systematic effort for a livlihood. He has been for some time an inmate of Mr. Emerson's family; and, in requital, he labors in the garden, and performs such other offices as may suit him — being entertained by Mr. Emerson for the sake of what true manhood there is in him. Mr. Thoreau is a keen and delicate observer of nature — a genuine observer — which, I suspect, is almost as rare a character as even an original poet; and Nature, in return for his love, seems to adopt him as her especial child, and shows him secrets which few others are allowed to witness. He is familiar with beast, fish, fowl, and reptile, and has strange stories to tell of adventures and friendly passages with these lower brethren of mortality. Herb and flower, likewise, wherever they grow, whether in garden or wildwood, are his familiar friends. He is also on intimate terms with the clouds, and can tell the portents of storms. It is a characteristic trait, that he has a great regard for the memory of the Indian tribes, whose wild life would have suited him so well; and, strange to say, he seldom walks over a ploughed field without picking up an arrow-point, spear-head, or other relic of the red man, as if their spirits willed him to be the inheritor of their simple wealth.

With all this he has more than a tincture of literature — a deep and true taste for poetry, especially the elder poets, although more exclusive than is desirable, like all other Transcendentalists, so far as I am acquainted with them. He is a good writer — at least he has written one good article, a rambling disquisition on Natural History, in the last Dial, which, he says, was chiefly made up from journals of his own observations. Methinks this article gives a very fair image of his mind and character — so true, innate, and literal in observation, yet giving the spirit as well as the letter of what he sees, even as a lake reflects its wooded banks, showing every leaf, yet giving the wild beauty of the whole scene. Then there are passages in the article of cloudy and dreamy metaphysics, partly affected, and partly the natural exhalations of his intellect; and also passages where his thoughts seem to measure and attune themselves into spontaneous verse, as they rightfully may, since there is real poetry in him. There is a basis of good sense and of moral truth, too, throughout the article, which also in a reflection of his character; for he is not unwise to think and feel, however imperfect is his own mode of action. On the whole, I find him a healthy and wholesome man to know. — *Journals*, 1 September 1842.

William Dean Howells

He came into the room a quaint, stump figure of a man, whose effect of long trunk and short limbs was heightened by his fashionless trousers being let down too low. He had a noble face, with tossed hair, a distraught eye, and a fine aquilinity of profile, which made me think at once of Don Quixote and of Cervantes; but his nose failed to add that foot to his stature which Lamb says a nose of that shape will always give a man. He tried to place me geographically after he had given me a chair not quite so far off as Ohio, though still across the whole room, for he sat against one wall, and I against the other; but apparently he failed to pull himself out of his revery by the effort, for he remained in a dreamy muse, which all my attempts to say something fit about John Brown and Walden Pond seemed only to deepen upon him. — *Literary Friends and Acquaintance* (1900).

Daniel Ricketson

The season was winter, a snow had lately fallen, and I was engaged in shovelling the accumulated mass from the entrance to my house, when I perceived a man walking towards me bearing an umbrella in one hand and a leather travelling-bag in the other. So unlike my ideal Thoreau, whom I had fancied, from the robust nature of his mind and habits of life, to be a man of unusual vigor and size, that I did not suspect, although I had expected him in the morning, that the slight, quaint-looking person before me was the Walden philosopher. There are few Persons who had previously read his works that were not disappointed by his personal appearance....

It was my privilege to know him during the last eight years of his life, when in the full maturity of his powers. The relationship between Thoreau and his most intimate friends was not that of great warmth of affection, but rather of respect for manly virtues....

I do not remember of ever seeing him laugh outright, but he was ever ready to smile at anything that pleased him; and I never knew him to betray any tender emotion except on one occasion, when he was narrating to me the death of his only brother, John Thoreau, from lockjaw, strong symptoms of which, from his sympathy with the sufferer, he himself experienced. At this time his voice was choked, and he shed tears, and went to the door for air. The subject was of course dropped, and never recurred to again.

In person he was rather below the medium stature, though not decidedly short — of rather slender than robust habit of body, and marked for his drooping shoulders. Still he was vigorous and active, and when in good health could perform a good deal of physical labor. His head was of medium size, but well formed according to the rules of phrenology — his brow was full, and his forehead rather broad than prominent; his eyes grayish blue, his nose long and aquiline, and his hair inclined to sandy. When interested in conversation, and standing, he had a decidedly dignified bearing. — "Thoreau," *Daniel Ricketson and His Friends*, ed. Anna and Walton Ricketson (1902).

ANTHONY TROLLOPE

Anonymous

"I remember a man hitting off a very good description of Trollope's manner, by remarking that 'he came in at the door like a frantic windmill.' The bell would peal, the knocker begin thundering, the door be burst open, and the next minute the house be filled by the big resonant voice inquiring who was at home. I should say he had naturally a sweet voice, which through eagerness he had spoilt by holloing. He was a big man, and the most noticeable thing about his dress was a black handkerchief which he wore tied *twice* round his neck. A trick of his was to put the end of a silk pocket-handkerchief in his mouth and to keep gnawing at it — often biting it into holes in the excess of his energy; and a favourite attitude was to stand with his thumbs tucked into the armholes of his waistcoat. He was a full-coloured man, and joking and playful when at his ease. Unless with his intimates, he rarely laughed, but he had a funny way of putting things, and was usually voted good company."

Trollope was five feet ten, but most people would have thought him taller. He was a stout man, large of limb, and always held himself upright without effort. His manner was bluff, hearty, and genial, and he possessed to the full the great charm of giving his undivided attention to the matter in hand. He was always enthusiastic and energetic in whatever he did. He was of an eager disposition, and doing nothing was a pain to him. In early manhood he became bald; in his latter life his full and bushy beard naturally grew to be gray. He had thick eyebrows, and his open nostrils gave a look of determination to his strong capable face. His eyes were grayish-blue, but he was rarely seen without spectacles, though of late years he used to take them off whenever he was reading. From a boy he had always been short-sighted.

Standing with his back to the fire, with his hands clasped behind him and his feet planted somewhat apart, the appearance of Anthony Trollope, as I recall him now, was that of a thorough Englishman in a thoroughly English attitude. He was then, perhaps, nearing sixty, and had far more the look of a country gentleman than of a man of letters. Tall, broad-shouldered, and dressed in a careless though not slovenly fashion, it seemed more fitting that he should break into a vivid description of the latest run with the hounds than launch into book-talk. Either subject, however, and for the matter of that I might add *any* subject, was attacked by him with equal energy. In writing of the man this, indeed, is the chief impression I recall — his energy, his thoroughness. While he talked to me, I and my interests might have been the only things for which he cared; and any passing topic of conversation was, for the moment, the one absorbing topic in the world. Being short-sighted, he had a habit of peering through his glasses which contracted his brows and gave him the appearance of a perpetual frown, and, indeed his expression when in repose was decidedly severe. This, however, vanished when he spoke. He talked well, and had generally a great deal to say; but his talk was disjointed, and he but rarely laughed. In manner he was brusque, and one of his most striking peculiarities was his voice, which was of an extraordinary large compass. — From *Mabel E. Wotton's Word Portraits of Famous Writers* (1887).

Frederick Locker-Lampson

Anthony Trollope, like his ancestor of old, was combative, and he was boisterous, but good naturedly so. He was abrupt in manners and speech; he was ebullient, and therefore he sometimes offended people. I suppose he was a wilful man, and we know that such men are always in the right; but he was a good fellow.

Some of Trollope's acquaintance used to wonder how so commonplace a person could have written such excellent novels; but I maintain that so honourable and interesting a man could not be commonplace.

Hirsute and taurine of aspect, he would glare at you from behind fierce spectacles. His ordinary tones had the penetrative capacity of two people quarrelling, and his voice would ring through and through you, and shake the windows in their frames, while all the time he was most amiably disposed towards you under his waistcoat. To me his *viso sciolto* and bluff geniality were very attractive, and so were his gusty denunciations, but most attractive of all was his unselfish nature. Literary men might make him their exemplar, as I make him my theme; for he may quite well have been the most generous man of letters, of mark, since Walter Scott....

Trollope had a furious hatred of shams and toadyism, and he sometimes recognized and resented these weaknesses where they would hardly have been detected by an ordinary observer. He could not be said to be quarrelsome, but he was crotchety. — *My Confidences* (1896).

MARK TWAIN

Ambrose Bierce

Mark Twain, who, whenever he has been long enough sober to permit an estimate, has been uniformly found to bear a spotless character, has got married. It was not the act of a desperate man — it was not committed while laboring under temporary insanity; his insanity is not of that type, nor does he ever labor—it was the cool, methodical, cumulative culmination of human nature, working in the breast of an orphan hankering for some one with a fortune to love—some one with a bank account to caress. For years he has felt this matrimony coming on. Ever since he left California there has been an undertone of despair running through all his letters like the subdued wail of a pig beneath a washtub. He felt that he was going, that no earthly power could save him, but as a concession to his weeping publishers he tried a change of climate by putting on a linen coat and writing letters from the West Indies. Then he tried rhubarb, and during his latter months he was almost constantly under the influence of this powerful drug. But rhubarb, while it may give a fitful glitter to the eye and a deceitful ruddiness to the gills, cannot long delay the pangs of approaching marriage. Rhubarb was not what Mark wanted. Well, that genial spirit has passed away; that long, bright smile will no more greet the early bar-keeper, nor the old familiar "chalk it down" delight his ear. Poor Mark! he was a good scheme, but he couldn't be made to work. —*News Letter* (19 February 1870).

It is announced that Mark Twain, being above want, will lecture no more. We didn't think that of Mark; we supposed that after marrying a rich girl he would have decency enough to make a show of working for a year or two anyhow. But it seems his native laziness has wrecked his finer feelings, and he has abandoned himself to his natural vice with the stolid indifference of a pig at his ablutions. We have our own private opinion of a man who will do this kind of thing; we regard him as an abandoned wretch. We should like to be abandoned in that way. —*News Letter* (27 August 1870).

Frank Harris

I wonder why it is that I cannot force myself to like Mark Twain? I have never even told of my meetings with him, but I intend to do it now.

I remember when his "Gilded Age" came out, and soon afterwards his "Innocents Abroad." I had hoped great things from him when I read the "Gilded Age," with its exposure of the corruption in the Kansas legislature. A few years later I met him, and thereafter all my interest in him vanished.

It was in Heidelberg. I was a member of the Anglo-American Literary Society when Mark Twain in the eighteen-seventies came to that city. I was chosen, one of two, to call upon him and ask him to address us.

My friend's name was, I think, Waldstein, brother of Sir Charles Waldstein; I am not certain; at any rate, two of us went and saw Twain in his hotel. He met us in a very friendly, human way, and promised to come and speak at one of our meetings if the evening could be settled to suit him. We told him we would make the necessary arrangements. He offered us cigars, and during our talk I told him how I had liked his "Gilded Age," and how I liked Bret Harte. Thereupon, to our astonishment, he began inveighing against Bret Harte. "His talent," if you please, "was infinitely exaggerated, and he was not honest. He was a disgrace to literature, and had no real genius. He had cheated his publishers out of money. Had we never heard the story?"

I shrugged my shoulders. It did not matter to me whom Bret Harte had cheated....

I found exquisite humour in ... Bret Harte's parodies, but Mark Twain would not have it. He became angry at once, declared that he did not care what a man wrote; a writer should pay his debts and be as honest as anybody else....

I ventured something about artists being insufficiently paid and getting anything but good treatment for supreme effort, but that brought no response from Twain. He declared that they did not need to write unless they wanted to; they could make shoes or do manual labour of some sort.

When we, the two envoys, came away we looked at each other. I was hurt to the soul. I said to my friend: "I never want to see that man again; never again do I want to talk with him. Fancy his running down Bret Harte on such paltry grounds!"...

About a year before his death, I saw him at a garden party of King Edward. He walked across the lawn, all in white, with the American Ambassador, who beckoned to me, but I drew out of the way; I did not want to meet Twain....

Like all small men, he wanted success in the day and hour, and was willing to pay the price for it. He wrote for the market, and the million praised and paid him; he had a gorgeous and easy life, and was a friend of millionaires, and went about at the end like a glorified Hall Caine; but he wrote nothing lifeworthy, not a word that has a chance of living except his boys' books, "Tom Sawyer" and "Huckleberry Finn," which may live for a generation, or perhaps even two, with "Treasure Island." It amused me to see, the other day, that Swinburne classed Mark Twain with Martin Tupper; that's about his true place. — *Contemporary Portraits: Fourth Series* (1923).

Bret Harte

His head was striking. He had the curly hair, the aquiline nose, and even the aquiline eye — an eye so eagle-like that a second lid would not have surprised me — of an unusual and dominant nature. His eyebrows were very thick and bushy. His dress was careless, and his general manner one of supreme indifference to surroundings and circumstances....

In the course of conversation he remarked that the unearthly laziness that prevailed in the town he had been visiting was beyond anything in his previous experience. He said the men did nothing all day long but sit around the bar-room stove, spit, and 'swop lies.' He spoke in a slow, rather satirical drawl, which was in itself irresistible. He went on to tell one of those extravagant stories, and half unconsciously dropped into the lazy tone and manner of the original narrator....

The story was 'The Jumping Frog of Calaveras.' It is now known and laughed over, I suppose, wherever the English language is spoken; but it will never be as funny to any one in print as it was to me, told for the first time by the unknown Twain himself on that morning in the San Francisco Mint. — *The Life of Bret Harte* by T. Edgar Pemberton (1903).

William Dean Howells

It was in the little office of James T. Fields, over the book-store of Ticknor & Fields, at 124 Tremont Street, Boston, that I first met my friend of now forty-four years, Samuel L. Clemens....

At the time of our first meeting, which must have been well toward the winter, Clemens (as I must call him instead of Mark Twain, which seemed always somehow to mask him from my personal sense) was wearing a sealskin coat, with the fur out, in the satisfaction of a caprice, or the love of strong effect which he was apt to indulge through life.... With his crest of dense red hair, and the wide sweep of his flaming mustache, Clemens was not discordantly clothed in that sealskin coat, which afterward, in spite of his own warmth in it, sent the cold chills through me when I once accompanied it down Broadway, and shared the immense publicity it won him. He had always a relish for personal effect, which expressed itself in the white suit of complete serge which he wore in his last years, and in the Oxford gown which he put on for every possible occasion, and said he would like to wear all the time. That was not vanity in him, but a keen feeling for costume which the severity of our modern tailoring forbids men, though it flatters women to every excess in it; yet he also enjoyed the shock, the offence, the pang which it gave the sensibilities of others. Then there were times he played these pranks for pure fun, and for the pleasure of the witness. Once I remember seeing him come into his drawing-room at Hartford in a pair of white cowskin slippers, with the hair out, and do a crippled colored uncle to the joy of all beholders. Or, I must not say all, for I remember also the dismay of Mrs. Clemens, and her low, despairing cry of, "Oh, Youth!" That was her name for him among their friends, and it fitted him as no other would, though I fancied with her it was a shrinking from his baptismal Samuel, or the vernacular Sam of his earlier companionships. He was a youth to the end of his days, the heart of a boy with the head of a sage; the heart of a good boy, or a bad boy, but always a wilful boy, and wilfulest to show himself out at every time for just the boy he was....

[Not long ago] I saw him dead, lying in his coffin amid those flowers with which we garland our despair in that pitiless hour. After the voice of his old friend Twichell had been lifted in the prayer which it wailed through in broken-hearted supplication, I looked a moment at the face I knew so well; and it was patient with the patience I had so often seen in it: something of puzzle, a great silent dignity, an assent to what must be from the depths of a nature whose tragical seriousness broke in the laughter which the unwise took for the whole of him. Emerson, Longfellow, Lowell, Holmes — I knew them all and all the rest of sages, poets, seers, critics, humorists; they were like one another and like other literary men; but Clemens was sole, incomparable, the Lincoln of our literature. — *My Mark Twain* (1910).

Rudyard Kipling

You are a contemptible lot over yonder. Some of you are Commissioners and some are Lieutenant-Governors, and some have the V.C., and a few are privileged to walk about the Mall arm in arm with the Viceroy; but I have seen Mark Twain this golden morning, have shaken his hand and smoked a cigar — no, two cigars — with him, and talked with him for more than two hours! Understand clearly that I do not despise you, from the Viceroy downward.

A big, darkened drawing-room, a huge chair; a man with eyes, a mane of grizzled hair, a brown mustache covering a mouth as delicate as a woman's, a strong, square hand shaking mine, and the slowest, calmest, levelest voice in all the world saying:

"Well, you think you owe me something, and you've come to tell me so. That's what I call squaring a debt handsomely."

"Piff!" from a cob-pipe (I always said that a Missouri meerschaum was the best smoking in the world), and behold! Mark

Twain had curled himself up in the big arm-chair, and I was smoking reverently, as befits one in the presence of his superior.

The thing that struck me first was that he was an elderly man; yet, after a minute's thought, I perceived that it was otherwise, and in five minutes, the eyes looking at me, I saw that the gray hair was an accident of the most trivial. He was quite young. I was shaking his hand. I was smoking his cigar, and I was hearing him talk — this man I had learned to love and admire fourteen thousand miles away.

Reading his books, I had striven to get an idea of his personality, and all my preconceived notions were wrong and beneath the reality. Blessed is the man who finds no disillusion when he is brought face to face with a revered writer. — From a letter to the Indian journal, *The Pioneer* (1889); *Mark Twain: A Biography* by Albert Bigelow Paine (1912).

George Bernard Shaw

Mark Twain is by far the greatest American writer. America has two literary assets — Edgar Allan Poe and Mark Twain. The former they sometimes forget, but Mark Twain does not give them much chance of ignoring him. I am speaking of him rather as a sociologist than as a humorist. Of course he is in very much the same position as myself. He has to put things in such a way as to make people who would otherwise hang him believe he is joking. — From an interview; *Mark Twain Himself* by Milton Meltzer (1960).

I am persuaded that the future historian of America will find your works as indispensable to him as a French historian finds the political tracts of Voltaire. I tell you so because I am the author of a play in which a priest says, 'Telling the truth's the funniest joke in the world,' a piece of wisdom which you helped to teach me. — From a note passed from Shaw to Mark Twain at a luncheon in Oxford, June 1907.

Senator William M. Stewart of Nevada

I was seated at my window one morning when a very disreputable looking person slouched into the room. He was arrayed in a seedy suit, which hung upon his loose frame in bunches with no style worth mentioning. A sheaf of scraggy black hair leaked out of a battered old slouch hat, like stuffing from an ancient Colonial sofa, and an evil-smelling cigar butt, very much frazzled, protruded from the corner of his mouth. He had a very sinister appearance. — *Mark Twain: The Man and His Work* by Edward Wagenknecht (1967).

Himself

Meine Beschreibung ist vollenden: Geborn 1835; 5 Fuss 8 1/2 inches hoch; weight doch aber about 145 pfund, sometimes ein wenig unter, sometimes ein wenig ober; dunkel braun Haar und rhotes Moustache, full Gesicht, mit sehr hohe Oren und leicht grau prachtvolles strahlenden Augen und ein Verdammtes gut moral character. Handlungkeit, Author von Bücher. — *Mark Twain: The Man and His Work* by Edward Wagenknecht (1967).

WALT WHITMAN

William Dean Howells

No doubt he was more valued because he was so offensive in some ways than he would have been if he had been in no way offensive, but it remains a fact that they [his young admirers] celebrated him quite as much as was good for them. He was often at Pfaff's with them, and the night of my visit he was the chief fact of my experience. I did not know he was there till I was on my way out, for he did not sit at the table under the pavement, but at the head of one farther into the room. There, as I passed, some friendly fellow stopped me and named me to him, and I remember how he leaned back in his chair, and reached out his great hand to me, as if he were going to give it me for good and all. He had a fine head, with a cloud of Jovian hair upon it, and a branching beard and mustache, and gentle eyes that looked most kindly into mine, and seemed to wish the liking which I instantly gave him, though we hardly passed a word, and our acquaintance was summed up in that glance and the grasp of his mighty fist upon my hand. I doubt if he had any notion who or what I was beyond the fact that I was a young poet of some sort, but he may possibly have remembered seeing my name printed after some very Heinesque verses in the *Press*. I did not meet him again for twenty years, and then I had only a moment with him when he was reading the proofs of his poems in Boston. Some years later I saw him for the last time, one day after his lecture on Lincoln, in that city, when he came down from the platform to speak with some handshaking friends who gathered about him. Then and always he gave me the sense of a sweet and true soul, and I felt in him a spiritual dignity which I will not try to reconcile with his printing in the forefront of his book a passage from a private letter of Emerson's, though I believe he would not have seen such a thing as most other men would, or thought ill of it in another. The spiritual purity which I felt in him no less than the dignity is something that I will no more try to reconcile with what denies it in his page; but such things we may well leave to the adjustment of finer balances than we have at hand. I will make sure only of the greatest benignity in the presence of the man. The apostle of the rough, the uncouth, was the gentlest person; his barbaric yawp, translated into the terms of social encounter, was an address of singular quiet, delivered in a voice of winning and endearing friendliness. — *Literary Friends and Acquaintance* (1900).

Henry David Thoreau

He is apparently the greatest democrat the world has seen. Kings and aristocracy go by the board at once, as they have long deserved to. A remarkably strong though coarse nature, of a sweet disposition, and much prized by his friends. Though peculiar and rough in his exterior, his skin (all over (?)) red, he is essentially a gentleman. I am still somewhat in a quandary about him, — feel that he is essentially strange to me, at any rate; but I am surprised by the sight of him. He is very broad, but, as I have said, not fine. He said that I misapprehended him. I am not quite sure that I do. He told us that he loved to ride up and down Broadway all day on an omnibus, sitting beside the driver, listening to the roar of the carts, and sometimes gesticulating and declaiming Homer at the top of his voice. — Quoted in *A Thoreau Profile* by Milton Meltzer and Walter Harding (1962).

Horace L. Traubel

Walt Whitman is a large man, six feet in height, broad of build, symmetrical, with an ineffable freedom evident even in these days of his broken physical fortunes. In years of health he weighed fully two hundred pounds. His head and face betray power and fortitude in high degree. I have a picture before me as I write, a rare one, taken in Washington in 1863, which reveals phases discoverable in no later portraits. The beard, cropped rather close, and the head, with its elevation and unshadowed energy, express immense virility, mingled with the most delicate evidences of emotion and sympathy. His complexion, while still fine, is nowadays somewhat paled; and yet it has the same marvellous purity and transparency which of old showed its unpolluted origin. The rosy pink tint of the skin, of body as of face, and the skin's peculiar softness and richness of texture, are unlike similar features of any man I have known. His eye is dull — one realizes how dull when he is seen sitting face to face with his friend Dr. Bucke, who has an eagle's orb. Twenty years, with their history of physical disaster, have dimmed and troubled his sight and not infrequently, through painful symptoms, aroused a suspicion of impending eclipse.

His voice has been strong and resonant. Full of music — a rich tenor — it charms ear and heart. It has high tones not so sweet. In ordinary talk it may reflect the faults, with the virtues, of monotone. But for depiction of event or repetition of poetic line or prophetic utterance it is equal to curious and exquisite modulations. Its range is simple, like the simplicity of the language itself.... I have heard him raise his speech in argument till it was as shrill and imperative as a bugle, and talk to babes in tones that cooed like a cradle song. His gestures are few and effective. He has an extraordinarily large ear, set at an unusual line. His hand is the hand of laborer and scribe, large in bone and sinew and shaped for strength and beauty. In all the years of my knowledge of him he has been lamed below the hips, so that I have never seen him in halcyon vigor. His paralysis from the first deprived him of effective locomotive power, and the sad strokes of 1888 almost utterly removed the old certainty of support. The severest loss has been on the left side. Apart from the right arm, which still maintains some actual vigor, his physical energies have declined and departed. — *In re Walt Whitman* (1893).

Himself

An American bard at last! One of the roughs, large, proud, affectionate, eating, drinking, and breeding, his costume manly and free, his face sunburnt and bearded, his postures strong and erect, his voice bringing hope and prophecy to the generous races of young and old....

Self-restraint, with haughty eyes, assuming to himself all the attributes of his country, steps Walt Whitman into literature, talking like a man unaware that there was ever hitherto such a production as a book, or such a being as a writer. Every move of him has the free play of the muscle of one who never knew what it was to feel that he stood in the presence of a superior. Every word that falls from his mouth shows silent disdain and defiance of the old theories and forms....

He leaves houses and their shuttered rooms, for the open air. He drops disguise and ceremony, and walks forth with the confidence and gayety of a child. For the old decorums of writing he substitutes his own decorums. The first glance out of his eyes electrifies him with love and delight. He will have the earth receive and return his affection; he will stay with it as the bridegroom stays with the bride....

No skulker or tea-drinking poet is Walt Whitman. He will bring poems to fill the days and nights — fit for men and women with the attributes of throbbing blood and flesh. The body, he teaches, is beautiful. Sex is also beautiful. Are you to be put down, he seems to ask, to that shallow level of literature and conversation that stops a man's recognizing the delicious pleasure of his sex, or a woman hers? Nature he proclaims inherently clean. Sex will not be put aside; it is a great ordination of the universe. He works the muscle of the male and the teeming fibre of the female throughout his writings, as wholesome realities, impure only by deliberate intention and effort. To men and women he says, You can have healthy and powerful breeds of children on no less terms than these of mine. Follow me, and there shall be taller and richer crops of humanity on the earth....

Who then is that insolent unknown? Who is it, praising himself as if others were not fit to do it, and coming rough and unbidden among writers, to unsettle what was settled, and to revolutionize in fact our modern civilization? Walt Whitman was born on Long Island, on the hills about thirty miles from the greatest American city, on the last day of May, 1819, and has grown up in Brooklyn and New York to be thirty-six years old, to enjoy perfect health, and to understand his country and its spirit. — *In re Walt Whitman* (1893).

JOHN GREENLEAF WHITTIER

Edmund Gosse

Mr. Whittier himself appeared, with all that report had ever told of gentle sweetness and dignified, cordial courtesy. He was then seventy-seven years old, and, although he spoke of age and feebleness, he showed few signs of either; he was, in fact, to live eight years more. Perhaps because the room was low, he seemed surprisingly tall; he must, in fact, have been a little less than six feet high. The peculiarity of his face rested in the extraordinarily large and luminous black eyes, set in black eyebrows, and fringed with thick black eyelashes curiously curved inwards. This bar of vivid black across the countenance was startlingly contrasted with the bushy snow-white beard and hair, offering a sort of contradiction which was surprising and presently pleasing. He was careful to keep on my right side, I noticed, being presumably deaf in the right ear; even if this were the case, which he concealed, his hearing continued to be markedly quick in a man of his years....

He asked me what and whom I had seen. Had I yet visited Concord? I responded that I was immediately about to do so, and then he said quickly, "Ah! thee should have come a little sooner, when we were still united. There were four of us a little while ago, but two are gone, and what is Concord without Emerson?" He spoke with great emotion of Emerson — "the noblest human being I have known" — and of Longfellow — "perhaps the sweetest. But you will see [Oliver Wendell] Holmes," he added. I replied it was my great privilege to be seeing Dr. Holmes every day, and that the night before he had sent all sorts of affectionate messages by me to Mr. Whittier....

If it is not too trifling, I must mention, in connection with his magnificent, lustrous eyes, that, the conversation turning upon the hues of things, Mr. Whittier greatly surprised me by confessing that he was quite colour-blind. He exemplified his condition by saying that if I came to Amesbury I should be scandalised by one of his carpets. It appeared that he was never permitted by the guardian goddesses of his hearth to go "shopping" for himself, but that once, being in Boston, and remembering that he needed a carpet, he had ventured to go to a store and buy what he thought to be a very nice, quiet article, precisely suited to adorn a Quaker home. When it arrived at Amesbury there was a universal shout of horror, for what had struck Mr. Whittier as a particularly soft combination of browns and greys proved to normal eyes to be a loud pattern of bright red roses on a field of the crudest cabbage-green. When he had told me this, it was then easy to observe that the fullness and brillancy of his wonderful eyes had something which was not entirely normal about them.

He struck me as very gay and cheerful, in spite of his occasional references to the passage of time and the vanishing of beloved faces. He even laughed, frequently and with a childlike suddenness, but without a sound. His face had none of the immobility so frequent with very aged persons; on the contrary, waves of mood were always sparkling across his features and leaving nothing stationary there except the narrow, high, and strangely receding forehead. His language, very fluid and easy, had an agreeable touch of the soil, an occasional rustic note in its elegant colloquialism, that seemed very pleasant and appropriate, as if it linked him naturally with the long line of sturdy ancestors of whom he was the final blossoming. In connection with his poetry, I think it would be difficult to form in the imagination a figure more appropriate to

Whittier's writings than Whittier himself proved to be in the flesh. — *Portraits and Sketches* (1913).

OSCAR WILDE

Frank Harris

He looked like a Roman Emperor of the decadence; he was over six feet in height, and both broad and thick-set. He shook hands in a limp way I disliked; his hands were flabby; greasy; his skin looked bilious and dirty. He had a trick which I noticed even then, which grew on him later, of pulling his jowl with his right hand as he spoke, and his jowl was already fat and pouchy. He wore a great green scarab ring on one finger. He was overdressed rather than well dressed; his clothes fitted him too tightly; he was too stout. His appearance filled me with distaste. I lay stress on this physical repulsion because I think most people felt it, and because it is a tribute to the fascination of the man that he should have overcome the first impression so completely and so quickly. I don't remember what we talked about, but I noticed almost immediately that his grey eyes were finely expressive; in turn vivacious, laughing, sympathetic; always beautiful. The carven mouth, too, with its heavy, chiselled, almost colorless lips, had a certain charm in spite of a black front tooth which showed ignobly....

At this time he was a superb talker, more brilliant than any I have ever heard in England, but nothing like what he became later in life. His talk soon made me forget his repellent physical peculiarities; indeed, I soon lost sight of them so completely that I have wondered since how I could have been so disagreeably affected by them. There was an extraordinary physical vivacity and geniality in the man, a winning charm in his gaiety, and lightning quick intelligence. His enthusiasms too were infectious. Every mental question interested him, especially if it had anything to do with art or literature. His whole face lit up as he spoke, and one saw nothing but his soulful eyes, heard nothing but his musical tenor voice; he was indeed what the French call a *charmeur*. — *Contemporary Portraits* (1915).

Coulson Kernahan

From the statement that Wilde's appearance was "repulsive" I entirely dissent. It is true there was a flabby fleshiness of face and neck, a bulkiness of body, an animality about the large and pursy lips — which did not close naturally, but in a hard, indrawn and archless line — that suggested self-indulgence, but did not to me suggest vice. Otherwise, except for this fleshiness and for the animality of the mouth, I saw no evil in Wilde's face. The forehead, what was visible of it — for he disposed brown locks of his thick and carefully parted hair over either temple — was high and finely formed. The nose was well shaped, the nostrils close and narrow — not open and "breathing" as generally seen in highly sensitive men. The eyes were peculiar, the almond-shaped lids being minutely out of alignment. I mean by this that the lids were so cut and the eyes so set in the head that the outer corners of the lids drooped downwards very slightly and towards the ears, as seen sometimes in Orientals. Liquid, soft, large and smiling, Wilde's eyes, if they seemed to see all things — life, death, other mortals and most of all himself — half banteringly, met one's own eyes frankly. His smile seemed to me to come from his eyes, not from his lips, which he tightened rather than relaxed in laughter. His general expression — always excepting the mouth, which, its animality notwithstanding, had none of the cruelty which goes so often with sensuality — was kindly. — *In Good Company: Some Personal Recollections* (1917).

Lillie Langtry

Vividly I recall the first meeting with Oscar Wilde in the studio of Frank Miles, and how astonished I was at his strange appearance. Then he must have been not more than twenty-two. He had a profusion of brown hair, brushed back from his forehead, and worn rather longer than was conventional, though not with the exaggeration which he afterwards affected. His face was large, and so colourless that a few pale freckles of good size were oddly conspicuous. He had a well-shaped mouth, with somewhat coarse lips and greenish-hued teeth. The plainness of his face, however, was redeemed by the splendour of his great, eager eyes.

In height he was about six feet, and broad in proportion. His hands were large and indolent, with pointed fingers and perfectly-shaped filbert nails, indicative of his artistic disposition. The nails, I regretfully record, rarely receiving the attention they deserved. To me he was always grotesque in appearance, although I have seen him described by a French writer as "beautiful" and "Apollo-like." That he possessed a remarkably fascinating and compelling personality, and what in an actor would be termed wonderful "stage presence," is beyond question, and there was about him an enthusiasm singularly captivating. He had one of the most alluring voices that I have ever listened to, round and soft, and full of variety and expression, and the cleverness of his remarks received added value from his manner of delivering them.

His customary apparel consisted of light-coloured trousers, a black frock coat, only the lower button fastened, a brightly flowered waistcoat blossoming underneath, and a white silk cravat, held together by an old intaglio amethyst set as a pin. I do not think I ever met him wearing gloves, but he always carried a pale lavender pair, using them to give point to his gestures, which were many and varied. Apropos of his dress, I recall seeing him (after he had become celebrated and prosperous), at the first night of one of his plays, come before the curtain, in response to the applause of the audience, wearing a black velvet jacket, lavender trousers, and a variegated waistcoat, a white straw hat in one hand and a lighted cigarette in the other.

In the early part of our acquaintance Wilde was *really* ingenuous. His mannerisms and eccentricities were then but the natural outcome of a young fellow bubbling over with temperament, and were not at all assumed. Later, when he began to rise as a figure in the life of London, and his unconscious peculiarities had become a target for the humorous columns of the newspapers, he was quick to realise that they could be turned to advantage, and he proceeded forthwith to develop them so audaciously that it became impossible to ignore them....

When he was writing *The New Helen* [a poem to Lillie Langtry] he became so obsessed with the subject that he would walk round and round the streets in which our little house was situated for hours at a time, probably investing me with every quality I never possessed, and, although Wilde had a keen sense of the ridiculous, he sometimes unconsciously bordered thereon himself. For instance, one night he curled up to sleep on my doorstep, and Mr. Langtry, returning unusually late, put an end to his poetic dreams by tripping over him.

There were times when I found him too persistent in hanging round the house or running about after me elsewhere, and I am afraid that often I said things which hurt his feelings in order to get rid of him. After a frank remark I made on one occasion, I happened to go to the theatre, and, as I sat in my box, I noticed a commotion in the stalls — it was Oscar, who, having perceived me suddenly, was being led away in tears by his friend Frank Miles. — *The Days I Knew* (1925).

Richard Le Gallienne

My acquaintance with Oscar Wilde began in my pre–London days as a member of an audience in Birkenhead, the sister city to Liverpool, assembled to hear him lecture on his 'Impressions of America,' whence he had recently returned....

At that time Wilde had abandoned his knee-breeches and was dressed in a sort of Georgian costume, with tight pantaloon trousers and a huge stock. His amber-coloured hair, naturally straight, was not very long, and was unashamedly curled and massively modelled to his head, somewhat suggesting a wig. His large figure, with his big loose face, grossly jawed, with thick, sensuous lips, and a certain fat effeminacy about him, suggested a sort of caricature Dionysius disguised as a rather heavy dandy of the Regency period. There was something grotesquely excessive about his whole appearance, and while he was in a way handsome, he made one think of an enormous doll, a preposterous, exaggerated puppet such as smile foolishly from floats at the Nice carnival. But his strong, humorous, haughty eyes, his good brow and fine nose must not be forgotten from the general effect, nor his superb and rather insolent *aplomb*, which early dominated his audience. And, of course, his wonderful golden voice, which he modulated with elaborate self-confidence. Exotic as he was, he was at the same time something entirely different from the dilettante, lily-like 'aesthete' we had expected, and the great surprise about him was his impudent humour and sound common sense. That he should talk sense at all was a complete revelation....

I remember that my first feeling at seeing Wilde again was one of boyish disappointment. He didn't seem as 'romantic' as when I had seen him at Birkenhead. His Regency clothes had gone, and he wore a prosaic business suit of some commonplace cloth, tweeds I almost fear. His hair, too, was short and straight, no Dionysiac curls. Also I had a queer feeling of distaste, as my hand seemed literally to sink into his, which were soft and plushy. I never recall those lines in 'The Sphinx' — "Lift up your large black satin eyes,/ Which are like cushions where one sinks," without thinking of Wilde's hands. However, this feeling passed off as soon as he began to talk. One secret of the charm of Wilde's talk, apart from its wit and his beautiful voice, was the evidently sincere interest he took in his listener and what he also had to say. It is seldom that a good talker can listen too, and for this reason even great talkers often end in being bores. Wilde was a better artist in this respect, though I am convinced that it was not merely art. With all his egoism, he had an unselfish sympathetic side to him which was well known to his friends, in whose affairs, particularly their artistic projects, he seemed entirely to forget his own. — *The Romantic '90s* (1926).

George Bernard Shaw

I met Oscar once at one of the at-homes [given by Lady Wilde]; and he came and spoke to me with an evident intention of being specially kind to me. We put each other out frightfully; and this odd difficulty persisted between us to the very last, even when we were no longer mere boyish novices and had become men of the world with plenty of skill in social intercourse. I saw him seldom, as I avoided literary and artistic society like the plague....

In writing about Wilde and Whistler, in the days when they were treated as witty triflers, and called Oscar and Jimmy in print, I always made a point of taking them seriously and with scrupulous good manners. Wilde on his part also made a point of recognizing me as a man of distinction by his manner, and repudiating the current estimate of me as a mere jester. This was not the usual reciprocal-admiration trick. I believe he was sincere, and felt indignant at what he thought was a vulgar underestimate of me; and I had the same feeling about him. My impulse to rally to him in his misfortune, and my disgust at 'the man Wilde' scurrilities of the newspapers, was irresistible: I don't quite know why; for my charity to his perversion, and my recognition of the fact that it does not imply any general depravity or coarseness of character, came to me through reading and observation, not through sympathy.

I have all the normal violent repugnance to homosexuality — if it is really normal, which nowadays one is sometimes provoked to doubt.

Also, I was in no way predisposed to like him. He was my fellow-townsman, and a very prime specimen of the sort of fellow-townsman I most loathed: to wit, the Dublin snob. His Irish charm, potent with Englishmen, did not exist for me; and on the whole it may be claimed for him that he got no regard from me that he did not earn....

Now Oscar was an overgrown man, with something not quite normal about his bigness — something that made Lady Colin Campbell, who hated him, describe him as 'that great white caterpillar.' You yourself describe the disagreeable impression he made on you physically, in spite of his fine eyes and style. Well, I have always maintained that Oscar was a giant in the pathological sense, and that this explains a good deal of his weakness. — From a letter to Frank Harris, printed in Harris' *Oscar Wilde: His Life and Confessions* (1930).

W.B. Yeats

My first meeting with Oscar Wilde was an astonishment. I never before heard a man talking with perfect sentences, as if he had written them all over night with labour and yet all spontaneous.... I noticed, too, that the impression of artificiality that I think all Wilde's listeners have recorded came from the perfect rounding of the sentences and from the deliberation that made it possible. That very impression helped him, as the effect of metre, helped its writers, for he could pass without incongruity from some unforeseen, swift stroke of wit to elaborate reverie....

I saw a good deal of Wilde at that time — was it 1887 or 1888? — I have no way of fixing the date except that I had published my first book *The Wanderings of Usheen* and that Wilde had not yet published his *Decay of Lying*. He had, before our first meeting, reviewed my book and despite its vagueness of intention, and the inexactness of its speech, praised without qualification; and what was worth more than any review he had talked about it; and now he asked me to eat my Christmas dinner with him believing, I imagine, that I was alone in London. He had just renounced his velveteen, and even those cuffs turned backward over the sleeves, and had begun to dress very carefully in the fashion of the moment. He lived in a little house at Chelsea that the architect Godwin had decorated with an elegance that owed something to Whistler. There was nothing mediaeval, nor pre–Raphaelite, no cupboard door with figures upon flat gold, no peacock blue, no dark background. I remember vaguely a white drawing-room with Whistler etchings, "let in" to white panels, and a dining-room all white, chairs, walls, mantel-piece, carpet, except for a diamond-shaped piece of red cloth in the middle of the table under a terra-cotta statuette, and I think a red-shaded lamp hanging from the ceiling to a little above the statuette. It was perhaps too perfect in its unity, his past of a few years before had gone too completely, and I remember thinking that the perfect harmony of his life there, with his beautiful wife and his two young children, suggested some deliberate artistic composition.

He commanded and dispraised himself during dinner by attributing characteristics like his own to his country: "We Irish are too poetical to be poets; we are a nation of brilliant failures, but we are the greatest talkers since the Greeks."... He flattered the intellect of every man he liked; he made me tell him long Irish stories and compared my art of story-telling to Homer's; and once when he had described himself as writing in the census paper "age 19, profession genius, infirmity talent" the other guest, a young journalist fresh from Oxford or Cambridge, said, "What should I have written?" and was told that it should have been "profession talent, infirmity genius". When, however, I called, wearing shoes a little too yellow — unblackened leather had just become fashionable — I realised their extravagance when I saw his eyes fixed upon them; and another day Wilde asked me to tell his little boy a fairy story, and I had but got as far as "Once upon a time there was a giant" when the little boy screamed and ran out of the room. Wilde looked grave and I was plunged into the shame of clumsiness that afflicts the young. And when I asked for some literary gossip for some provincial newspaper, that paid me a few shillings a month, I was told that writing literary gossip was no job for a gentleman....

Wilde lived with no self-mockery at all an imaginary life; perpetually performed a play which was in all things the opposite of all that he had known in childhood and early youth; never put off completely his wonder at opening his eyes every morning on his own beautiful house, and in remembering that he had dined yesterday with a duchess, and that he delighted in Flaubert and Pater, read Homer in the original and not as a schoolmaster reads him for the grammar. I think, too, that because of all that half-civilised blood in his veins he could not endure the sedentary toil of creative art and so remained a man of action, exaggerating, for the sake of immediate effect, every trick learned from his masters, turning their easel painting into painted scenes. He was a parvenu, but a parvenu whose whole bearing proved that if he did dedicate every story in *The House of Pomegranates* to a lady of title, it was to show that he was Jack and the social ladder his pantomine beanstalk.... Such men get their sincerity, if at all, from the contact of events; the dinner table was Wilde's event and made him the greatest talker of his time, and his plays and dialogues have what merit they possess from being now an imitation, now a record, of his talk. — *Autobiographies* (1927).

WILLIAM WORDSWORTH

Thomas Carlyle

I did not expect much; but got mostly what I expected. The old man has a fine shrewdness and naturalness in his expression of face (a long Cumberland figure); one finds also a kind of *sincerity* in his speech:

but for prolixity, thinness, endless dilution it excels all the other speech I had heard from mortal. A genuine man (which is much) but also essentially a *small* genuine man: nothing perhaps is sadder (of the glad kind) than the *unbounded* laudation of such a man; sad proof of the *rarity* of such. I fancy however he has fallen into the garrulity of age, and is not what he was: also that his environment (and rural Prophethood) has hurt him much. He seems impatient that even Shakspear should be admired: "so much out of my own pocket"! The shake of hand he gives you is feckless, egotistical; I rather fancy he *loves* nothing in the world so much as one could wish. When I compare that man with a great man, — alas, he is like dwindling into a contemptibility. Jean Paul (for example), neither was he *great*, could have worn him as a finger-ring. However, when "I go to Cumberland," Wordsworth will still be a glad sight. — From a letter to John A. Carlyle, 23 March 1835.

Of Wordsworth I have little to write that could ever be of use to myself or others. I did not see him much, or till latish in my course see him at all; nor did we deeply admire one another at any time. Of me in my first times he had little knowledge; and any feeling he had towards me, I suspect, was largely blended with abhorrence and perhaps a kind of fear. His works I knew, but never considerably reverenced; could not, on attempting it. A man recognizably of strong intellectual powers, strong character; given to meditation, and much contemptuous of the unmeditative world and its noisy nothingness; had a fine limpid style of writing and delineating, in his small way; a fine limpid vein of melody too in him (as of an honest rustic fiddle, good, and well handled, but wanting two or more of the strings, and not capable of much!). In fact, a rather dull, hard-tempered, unproductive, and almost wearisome, kind of man; not adorable, by any means, as a great poetic genius, much less as the Trismegistus of such; whom only a select few could ever read, instead of misreading, which was the opinion his worshippers confidently entertained of him! Privately I had a real respect for him withal, founded on his early biography (which Wilson of Edinburgh had painted to me as of antique greatness). "Poverty and Peasanthood! Be it so! but we consecrate ourselves to the Muses, all the same, and will proceed on those terms, Heaven aiding!" This, and what of faculty I did recognize in the man, gave me a clear esteem of him, as of one remarkable and fairly beyond common; not to disturb which, I avoided speaking of him to his worshippers; or, if the topic turned up, would listen with an acquiescing air. But to my private self his divine reflections and unfathomabilities seemed stinted, scanty, palish, and uncertain — perhaps in part a feeble reflex (derived at second hand through Coleridge) of the immense German fund of such — and I reckoned his poetic store-house to be far from an opulent or well-furnished apartment....

For the rest, he talked well in his way; with veracity, easy brevity, and force, as a wise tradesman would of his tools and workshop, and as no unwise one could. His voice was good, frank, and sonorous, though practically clear, distinct, and forcible rather than melodious; the tone of him business-like, sedately confident; no discourtesy, yet no anxiety about being courteous. A fine wholesome rusticity, fresh as his mountain breezes, sat well on the stalwart veteran, and on all he said and did. You would have said he was a usually taciturn man; glad to unlock himself to audience sympathetic and intelligent, when such offered itself. His face bore marks of much, not always peaceful meditation; the look of it not bland or benevolent so much as close, impregnable, and hard: a man *multa tacere loquive paratus*, in a world where he had experienced no lack of contradictions as he strode along. The eyes were not very brilliant, but they had a quiet clearness; there was enough of brow, and well shaped; rather too much of cheek ("horse face" I have heard satirists say); face of squarish shape, and decidedly longish, as I think the head itself was (its "length" going horizontal); he was large-boned, lean, but still firm-knit, tall, and strong-looking when he stood, a right good old steel-gray figure, with rustic simplicity and dignity about him, and a vivacious strength looking through him which might have suited one of those old steel-gray markgrafs whom Henry the Fowler set up to ward the "marches," and do battle with the intrusive heathen in a stalwart and judicious manner....

One evening, probably about this time, I got him upon the subject of great poets, who, I thought, might be admirable equally to us both; but was rather mistaken, as I gradually found. Pope's partial failure I was prepared for; less for the narrowish limits visible in Milton and others. I tried him with Burns, of whom he had sung tender recognition; but Burns also turned out to be a limited, inferior creature, any genius he had a theme for one's pathos rather; even Shakespeare himself had his blind sides, his limitations. Gradually it became apparent to me that of transcendent unlimited there was, to this critic, probably but one specimen known—Wordsworth himself! He by no means said so, or hinted so, in words; but on the whole it was all I gathered from him in this considerable *tête-a-tête* of ours; and it was not an agreeable conquest. New notion as to poetry or poet I had not in the smallest degree got; but my insight into the depths of Wordsworth's pride in himself had considerably augmented, and it did not increase my love of him; though I did not in the least hate it either, so quiet was it, so fixed, unappealing, like a dim old lichened crag on the way-side, the private meaning of which, in contrast with any public meaning it had, you recognized with a kind of not wholly melancholy grin. — *Reminiscences* (1881).

Samuel Taylor Coleridge

Of all the men I ever knew, Wordsworth has the least femineity in his mind. He is *all* man. He is a man of whom it might have been said, — "It is good for him to be alone." — *Table Talk* (1835).

Thomas De Quincey

At this period [1807] Southey and Wordsworth entertained a mutual esteem, but did not cordially like each other. Indeed, it would have been odd if they had. Wordsworth lived in the open air; Southey in his library, which Coleridge used to call his wife. Southey had particularly elegant habits (Wordworth called them finical) in the use of books. Wordsworth, on the other hand, was so negligent, and so indulgent in the same case, that, as Southey laughingly expressed it to me some years afterwards, when I was staying at Greta Hall on a visit — "To introduce Wordsworth into one's library, is like letting a bear into a tulip garden." — *Reminiscences of the English Lake Poets* (1907).

Charles Dickens

[Having met Wordsworth on one occasion in 1843, Dickens was asked how he had liked the Poet Laureate.] Like him? Not at all. He is a dreadful Old Ass. — *Life of Dickens* by R. Shelton Mackenzie (1870).

Ralph Waldo Emerson

On the 28th August [1833], I went to Rydal Mount, to pay my respects to Mr. Wordsworth. His daughters called in their father, a plain, elderly, white-haired man, not prepossessing, and disfigured by green goggles. He sat down, and talked with great simplicity. He had just returned from a journey. His health was good, but he had broken a tooth by a fall, when walking with two lawyers, and had said, that he was glad it did not happen forty years ago; whereupon they had praised his philosophy....

Carlyle, he said, wrote most obscurely. He was clever and deep, but he defied the sympathies of everybody. Even Mr. Coleridge wrote more clearly, though he had always wished Coleridge would write more to be understood. He led me out into his garden, and showed me the gravel-walk in which thousands of his lines were composed. His eyes are much inflamed. This is no loss, except for reading, because he never writes prose, and of poetry he carries even hundreds of lines in his head before writing them. He had just returned from a visit to Staffa, and within three days had made three sonnets on Fingal's Cave, and was composing a fourth, when he was called in to see me. He said, "If you are interested in my verses, perhaps you will like to hear these lines." I gladly assented; and he recollected himself for a few moments, and then stood forth and repeated, one after the other, the three entire sonnets with great animation....

This recitation was so unlooked for and surprising, — he the old Wordsworth, standing apart, and reciting to me in a garden-walk, like a schoolboy declaiming, — that I at first was near to laugh; but recollecting myself, that I had come thus far to see a poet, and he was chanting poems to me, I saw that he was right and I was wrong, and gladly gave myself up to hear....

Wordsworth honoured himself by his simple adherence to truth, and was very willing not to shine; but he surprised by the hard limits of his thought. To judge from a single conversation, he made the impression of a narrow and very English mind; of one who paid for his rare elevation by general tameness and conformity. Off his own beat, his opinions were of no value. — *English Traits* (1856).

William Hazlitt

Mr. Wordworth, in his person, is above the middle size, with marked features, and an air somewhat stately and Quixotic. He reminds one of some of Holbein's heads, grave, saturnine, with a slight indication of sly humour, kept under by the manners of the age or by the pretensions of the person. He has a peculiar sweetness in his smile, and great depth and manliness and a rugged harmony, in the tones of his voice. His manner of reading his own poetry is particularly imposing; and in his favourite passages his eye beams with preternatural lustre, and the meaning labours slowly up from his swelling breast. No one who has seen him at these moments could go away with an impression that he was a 'man of no mark or likelihood.' Perhaps the comment of his face and voice is necessary to convey a full idea of his poetry. His language may not be intelligible, but his manner is not to be mistaken. It is clear that he is either mad or inspired. In company, even in a *tête-à-tête*, Mr. Wordsworth is often silent, indolent, and reserved. If he is become verbose and oracular of late years, he was not so in his better days. He threw out a bold or an indifferent remark without either effort or pretension, and relapsed into musing again. He shone most (because he seemed most roused and animated) in reciting his own poetry, or in talking about it. — *The Spirit of the Age* (1825).

James Hogg

It chanced one night, when I was there [at Wordsworth's house], that there was a resplendent arch across the zenith, from the one horizon to the other, of something like the aurora borealis, but much brighter. It was a scene that is well remembered, for it struck the country with admiration, as such a phenomenon had never before been witnessed in such perfection; and, as far as I could learn, it had been more brilliant over the mountains and pure waters of Westmoreland than any where else. Well, when word came into the room of the splendid meteor, we all went out to view it; and, on the beautiful plat-form at Mount Ryedale we were all walking, in twos and threes, arm-in-arm, talking of the phenomenon, and admiring it. Now, be it remembered, that Wordsworth, Professor [John] Wilson, [Charles] Lloyd, De Quincey, and myself, were present, besides several other literary gentlemen, whose names I am not certain that I remember aright. Miss Wordsworth's arm was in mine, and she was expressing some fears that the splendid stranger might prove ominous, when I, by ill luck, blundered out the following remark, thinking that I was saying a good thing: — "Hout, me'm! it is neither mair nor less than joost a treeumphal airch, raised in honour of the meeting of the poets."

"That's not amiss. — Eh? Eh? — that's very good," said the Profes-sor, laughing. But Wordsworth, who had De Quincey's arm, gave a grunt, and turned on his heel, and leading the little opium-chewer aside, he addressed him in these disdainful and venomous words: — "Poets? Poets? — What does the fellow mean? — Where are they?"

Who could forgive this? For my part, I never can, and never will! I admire Wordsworth; as who does not, whatever they may pre-tend? but for that short sentence I have a lingering ill-will at him which I cannot get rid of. It is surely presumption in any man to circumscribe all human excellence within the narrow sphere of his own capacity. The *"Where are they?"* was too bad! I have always some hopes that De Quincey was *leeing*, for I did not myself hear Wordsworth utter the words. — *Memoir of the Author's Life* (1832).

Samuel Rogers

He lives too much alone. He does not associate with his fellow men. He has shut himself up for years among the mountains and the lakes, and worshipped them; he has ended by worshipping himself. He has so continually brooded over his own genius in his darling solitudes, that he has come to consider himself the centre of the universe....

I should not call him a vain man, or even a conceited man, by nature or original disposition, but he has become conceited for want of intercourse with his fellows. He sees nobody at Grasmere who is not inferior to himself, and he comes to the conclusion, unconsciously I have no doubt, that everybody, everywhere else, is inferior to him. If he would spend six months every year in London this idea would be rubbed out of him by the wholesome friction of society. — Quoted by Charles Mackay in *Forty Years' Recollections of Life, Literature, and Public Affairs* (1877).

[Also see Sir Walter Scott — Benjamin Robert Haydon.]

INDEX OF NAMES

*Page numbers in italics contain
significant information on person named*